RENAISSANCE STATE

'A fascinating account of Maharashtra's long and turbulent history, Girish Kuber's *Renaissance State* presents the key facts and faces of some 2,000 years of this great state's existence. Introducing us to mathematicians and warriors, scientific legends and political giants, Kuber's insightful and extensively researched narrative is enriched by compelling detail.'

– SHASHI THAROOR, AUTHOR AND MEMBER OF PARLIAMENT

'One of the unfortunate side effects of rabid nationalism is the loss of regional identities. Maharashtra has a magnificent history, unimpeachable traditions and a unique artistic culture that has always refused to bow before the mighty monarchs of Delhi who believed they owned it all. Freedom came. But Maharashtra is still fighting for its rightful place in Modi's new India. Girish Kuber takes a panoramic view of what makes Maharashtra so special and why its proud people have always refused to bow before Delhi – and still do. For good reason.'

– PRITISH NANDY, SENIOR JOURNALIST AND MEDIA PERSONALITY

'"Though as an individual Shivaji was a practising Hindu, he kept religion at bay when it came to his politics and social life." For me, this is one of the most significant lines in *Renaissance State*, a rigorously clear-eyed study of Maharashtra's past and present.'

– SHANTA GOKHALE, AUTHOR AND TRANSLATOR

'Sweeping through centuries of history, *Renaissance State* is an excellent starting point for anyone trying to understand the dynamics and dynamism of India's richest state. It also offers a window on the paradoxical intellectual currents that have shaped the Marathi Manoos. As Girish Kuber notes, Maharashtra produced both Gandhi's mentor and his murderer.'

– NARESH FERNANDES, EDITOR, *SCROLL*, AND AUTHOR OF *CITY ADRIFT: A SHORT BIOGRAPHY OF BOMBAY*

'This will be the go-to book on Maharashtra and its residents for many decades to come.'

– JERRY PINTO, AUTHOR OF *EM AND THE BIG HOOM* AND *MURDER IN MAHIM*

RENAISSANCE STATE

the UNWRITTEN STORY *of the* MAKING *of* MAHARASHTRA

GIRISH KUBER

HarperCollins *Publishers* India

First published in hardback in India by HarperCollins *Publishers* 2021
4th Floor, Tower A, Building No. 10, Phase II, DLF Cyber City,
Gurugram, Haryana – 122002
www.harpercollins.co.in

This edition published in paperback by HarperCollins India 2022

2 4 6 8 10 9 7 5 3

P-ISBN: 978-93-5629-364-9
E-ISBN: 978-93-9032-740-9

Typeset in 10.5/14.5 Berling LT Std
Manipal Technology Ltd, Manipal

Printed and bound at
Thomson Press (India) Ltd

MIX
Paper
FSC FSC® C010615

This book is produced from independently certified FSC® paper
to ensure responsible forest management.

प्रतिपच्चंद्रलेखेव वर्धिष्णुर्विश्व वंदिता महाराष्ट्रस्य राज्यस्य मुद्रा भद्राय राजते

(The glory of Maharashtra will grow like the new moon.
It will be worshipped by the world
and will shine only for the well-being of its people.)

The motto from the emblem of Maharashtra, based on one found on the rajmudra or the royal seal used by Chhatrapati Shivaji, the difference being that the name of the monarch is replaced by the name of the state.

To the late Professor Narhar Kurundkar,
Maharashtra's pre-eminent scholar, who, like many others from the state, deserved better recognition

Contents

Author's Note

This book is not an academic study of Maharashtra's history. It has not been written from the high perch of a historian, but instead looks at the state's history from the lens of a journalist who is obsessed with finding a story – the story here being what history tells us about the nature of the Marathi Manoos, without taking a chauvinistic view of the matter. History, then, is the medium here, not the mission, to tell that story.

My understanding of the vast annals of history in the pages that follow rests, as the historian Tony Judt put it in his legendary book *Postwar*, 'on the shoulders of other books', a detailed, if not exhaustive, list of which the reader may find at the end. In the absence of published historical material, I have occasionally also referred to online sources that were at hand. Having said that, I hope readers will find the story itself engaging and worth their while.

I am aware that any one book, let alone this one, cannot be comprehensive enough to capture the sheer expanse of Maharashtra's history and that of its people. And in this type of book, the real dilemma an author faces is what to exclude. I faced it too and know that there are many more worthy Maharashtrians whose presence here would have made this book even more valuable.

Muslim reformist Hamid Dalwai, pioneer of the Indian insurance industry Annasaheb Chirmule, and noted economist Dhananjayrao Gadgil, who gave a nascent nation a formula for the devolution of taxes and also conceptualized the cooperative movement along with Vaikunthbhai Mehta, are some of the notable exclusions. My sincere apologies for this.

Though the writing of this book was an absolute pleasure, it was not easy to spare time for it while being entrusted with the responsibilities of the Marathi daily *Loksatta*. I thank Mr Viveck Goenka, Chairman and Managing Director of the Indian Express Group, who was kind enough to allow me to juggle both simultaneously. I am also thankful to Mr George Varghese and Ms Vaidehi Thakar, CEO and Publisher of the Express group respectively, and other colleagues for their encouragement.

I owe special thanks to Prasad Havale, my young teammate in *Loksatta*, for his suggestions and efforts in helping me find the necessary references. Discussions with Prasad, himself a student of Maharashtra's political and social history, were always insightful and were of immense help. A former colleague, Ravi Amle, was also instrumental in procuring the required books for me. I thank him too.

Outside of my workplace, I must mention Siddhesh Inamdar, my editor at HarperCollins, for his painstaking efforts and patient handling of the publication process. His keen interest in the subject helped me stay engaged. I will be failing in my duty if I don't thank Amit Malhotra for the brilliant cover artwork, which perfectly encapsulates the theme of the book.

And, most importantly, thanks to my wife Shami, daughter Mrunmayee and her partner Abhishek for discounting me from family duties, without which it would have been impossible to spare time for the book.

Girish Kuber **Mumbai**
March 2021

Preface

The year was 1991. The V.P. Singh and Chandra Shekhar governments at the Centre had fallen in quick succession. India was grappling with grave political uncertainty. One more general election was on the horizon and, as a political reporter, I was trying to gauge the mood. Travelling from Goa – where I was posted at the time – I landed in Kankavli, a small, sleepy town in the Konkan region of Maharashtra. Madhu Dandavate, the finance minister in the Singh cabinet, was contesting the election from there. It was the constituency that had sent him to Parliament five times in a row.

Nana – as Dandavate was fondly called – was a socialist. I caught up with him late one evening at fellow activist Shashi Taishetye's house. Nana was dressed in a white short-sleeved kurta and old-fashioned striped cotton pyjamas. Since I knew him personally, the conversation was candid and freewheeling. Soon it veered towards the overall decay of values in politics – the topic old-school socialists always like to lament about. Nana unravelled many details about V.P. Singh's style of functioning. And then came the real shocker.

'I was asked to take the lead in dislodging Singh,' Nana said in his usual nonchalant tone.

'What?' I said, caught by surprise, as the implication of what he had said dawned on me.

'A large number of MPs from our party approached me after it became clear that Singh was turning into a burden,' he added. 'They offered to push for his removal and propose my name as they believed I was the most acceptable, non-controversial leader they had. Some of them even assured me support from the Congress party.'

I was eager to know what had happened next. Knowing that Chandra Shekhar was eventually agreed upon for the post, I wanted to understand why and how Dandavate had fallen out of the race.

'Nothing,' he said. 'I simply refused. That's doublecrossing! How could I betray my leader?'

The conversation that followed was a long lecture in political values and the importance of loyalty. I tried to interrupt only once, very meekly, when I asked, 'But, Nana, how could you turn down an opportunity to be the Prime Minister of India? Haven't you done a great injustice to Maharashtra?'

'No!' he said. 'Maharashtra should be proud of the fact that I didn't deceive my leader.'

I realized that he did not see the episode as a wasted opportunity. This was because he was a true-blue 'Marathi Manoos'. In politics, history is replete with examples that show how the Marathi Manoos has been more comfortable serving as an able deputy to another leader than staking claim to ultimate power himself.

Interestingly, only a few months later, another Marathi Manoos, Sharad Pawar, tried to grab the throne but lost out to P.V. Narasimha Rao. Again, it was the same history at play. Barring three distant exceptions – Chhatrapati Shivaji, Peshwa Baji Rao and Bal Gangadhar Tilak – Marathi Manoos is known to have played second fiddle to another master in power politics. At various times these masters were Mughals, Rajputs, Pathans or north Indians. Rarely did the Marathi Manoos think of turning the tables.

'MAHARASHTRA' MEANS A 'GREAT State' and it did live up to its name at one point. Dynasties from this region once ruled more than half of what is India today. In prehistoric times, some of these empires spread right up to Madurai and Rameswaram in the south, Raipur and Jabalpur in the east, Udaipur and Chitrakoot in the north and Girnar in the west. Though its geographical spread is not as vast today, the state remains second only to Uttar Pradesh in terms of political significance and strength in the Lok Sabha. It is geographically larger than all of Great Britain. If it were a separate country, it would rank twelfth in the world by population, leaving behind all European nations except Russia.

But Maharashtra is also a state full of paradoxes and contradictions. A land whose people – Jyotirao Phule, for instance, who worked tirelessly for women's emancipation and the eradication of untouchability – led the nation on the path of social reforms is also home to some of the most socially backward movements. Mohandas Karamchand Gandhi became the foremost leader of India's freedom struggle with the help of a Maharashtrian: Gopal Krishna Gokhale. And it was another Maharashtrian, Nathuram Godse, who shot Gandhi dead. A state that gave the nation its first woman doctor, Anandibai Joshi, has been suffering from rampant female infanticide for decades now. Maharashtra has the largest number of dams of any Indian state – 1,821 to be precise. But it is also a state with a grave ongoing agrarian crisis that has seen thousands and thousands of farmers commit suicide over the past twenty years. A Marathi Manoos, Dadasaheb Phalke, was behind India's first ever motion picture. But the Hindi film industry today hardly has any Maharashtrians. The list of Maharashtra's contradictions can go on…

Maharashtra is one of India's wealthiest, most industrialized states. It is home to Mumbai, India's financial capital, a fast-paced cosmopolitan megalopolis that bustles daily with more than twenty million people. It exemplifies the best of the country even if it also showcases some of its worst. The story of Maharashtra, then, in many ways is also the story of India. It must be told to better understand where we are and how we got here.

1
Maha Rashtra

Rulers rule history. Always. And that is of course true of India too. Historically, rulers of the north have ruled India. No wonder, then, most of the country's history is that of the northern region. It may also be because Aryans first settled in the north. Epics such as the Ramayana and the Mahabharata; emperors such as Nand, Maurya and Shung; historical figures such as Manu, Patanjali, Gautam Buddha and Mahavir were all from the north of the Vindhyas. Caught between the north and the south, Maharashtra has not got its due in the nation's history despite its immense contribution to it.

Aurangzeb spread his reign over nearly all of India, but the region ruled by the Marathas frustrated him the most for over two decades of his life. 'He defeated many Marathas but hardly emerged victorious,' says scholar and historian Narhar Kurundkar, explaining the powerful Mughal emperor's predicament. Maharashtra was where Aurangzeb would eventually die.

Incidentally, this is the region that also kept the British waiting. The East India Company's conquest of India in the nineteenth century was incomplete as Pune had kept the spirit of independence alive. It took a betrayal from among the ruling Peshwas for the Union Jack to be unfurled over the fort of Shaniwar Wada in the city. This was the beginning of the end of Maharashtra's glory days. But more on that later.

Does the name Maharashtra signify the region's geographical strength? Or is it indicative of its people? Perhaps both, though academics are divided on this. A section of them believe that the region got its name because of its size. Some others think that it's because of the people the region produced. In his writings, Dimbha, a fifteenth-century poet of the Mahanubhav sect, has described the region that is 'spread south of the Vindhyas, north of the Krishna (river) and west of the forests. People from this region speak Maharashtri.' Both these sections, however, agree on one point: that it was the language Maharashtri, an offshoot of Sanskrit, that was the genesis of the state of Maharashtra.

In his treatise *Arthashastra*, the legendary teacher of the emperor Chandragupta Maurya, Arya Chanakya (fourth century BCE) – who was also known as Kautilya – has mentioned a region called Ashmak, which is now the district of Nanded in present-day Maharashtra. It was in the third century BCE that the Satavahana empire brought the region under one rule. It was this empire that ruled for around 450 years and gave the region its inimitable cultural, social and geographical identity.

Before the Satavahanas, attempts were made to unify small states to create a big empire. The Magadhs were among the first to succeed. Shaishunag (sixth century BCE) formed his empire and slowly expanded it in the northern region, from Hindukush to today's Assam. Bimbisara was the first well-known emperor from Shaishunag's family. His empire survived for 150 years, after which the Nanda dynasty took over. The Nandas ruled for nearly a hundred years, only to be eliminated by the legendary Chandragupta Maurya after an eleven-year battle.

Studying the reign of the Mauryas is important in understanding the history of India. It was Chandragupta Maurya who defeated Seleucus I, a general from the army of the great Greek warrior Alexander, also known as Sikandar. The size of Chandragupta's empire was mind-boggling: from the Hindukush mountains to the Deccan plateau and even further south to the area known as Mysore today.

After Chandragupta's death, the dynasty was led by his equally capable son Bindusara, followed by Ashoka, who embraced Buddhism. His philosophy of non-violence encouraged attacks by Greek rulers and weakened the empire. The Greeks were followed by the Kushans of Central Asia, a syncretic empire formed by Yuezhi. Eventually, the entire northern region fell to invaders. However, the invaders did not reach the south.

Around the time of Ashoka's death (232 BCE), an equally powerful empire was beginning to rise in the south of the Vindhyas and around the Deccan region – the Satavahana. This was the first dynasty to be formed south of the Vindhyas and was perhaps even stronger than the Mauryas. The history of southern India began with the Satavahanas. They ruled for 460 years, from 235 BCE to AD 225 – possibly the longest continuous rule by a single dynasty in world history.

The founder of the Satavahana dynasty was Simuka. He killed the last Kanva ruler of Magadh and presumably took over that kingdom. The dynasty established its authority from the mouth of the Krishna to encompass the entire Deccan plateau. Satakarni I, a descendant of Simuka, was particularly recognized for his conquests, which took him to the north of the Narmada river into eastern Malwa, which at the time was targeted by the Shakas and the Greeks. He also gained control over the region of Sanchi. Some inscriptions found there describe him as Rajan Shri Satakarni. He then moved southwards to conquer the Godavari valley. The Satavahanas eventually had control over the regions of Kalinga, Andhra, Malwa, Gujrat, Saurashtra and Rajasthan. For a while they also ruled over Magadh and the region south of the Kaveri river.

This was the first Maharashtrian dynasty. Historians widely believe that the Satavahanas originated in the western part of the country and extended their control over the eastern coast, also giving that region its name: Andhra. The earliest inscriptions and epigraphic records of the Satavahanas are found in the western

Deccan – Nashik, Karle (near Pune) and Naneghat – proving their Maharashtrian origins. The Satavahanas had their capital in a town called Pratishthan – Paithan (Marathwada) of today, popular for the style of handloom saree called Paithani.

Compiled by the Satavahana king Hala, *Maha Sattasai* (or *Gatha Sattasai* in Sanskrit) is a collection of poems written by women in Maharashtri – or Prakrut, as the language was called then. The Satavahanas were known to encourage the use of Prakrut over Sanskrit, which was the more common language then. From Prakrut originates Marathi, the present-day language of the state of Maharashtra. That makes *Gatha Sattasai* the first Marathi book.

After the reign of Satakarni I, the Satavahanas were defeated by the Shakas of the Kshaharata clan. The Shakas were driven out by Gautamiputra Satakarni, under whose reign the Satavahanas reached their peak. His twenty-four-year rule is considered one of the most celebrated chapters in the history of the Satavahanas. Gautamiputra Satakarni's empire extended from present-day Rajasthan in the north to the Krishna river in the south, and from Saurashtra in the west to Kalinga in the east. His achievements can only be compared with those of Chhatrapati Shivaji in the seventeenth century AD. He assumed the titles Raja-Raja (King of Kings) and Maharaja (Great King), and was described as the Lord of the Vindhyas.

In the north, where the Shakas were taking over kingdom after kingdom, it was Gautamiputra who not only held his ground but also defeated them. Inscriptions describe him as 'the destroyer of the Shakas, Yavanas and Pahalavas', 'the restorer of the glory of the Satavahana dynasty' and 'the one who crushed the pride of the Kshatrapas'. The followers of almost all religions – and that includes Jains, Buddhists and Vaidiks – have only praise to offer the Satavahanas. Gautamiputra's mother, Gautama Balasri, documented his achievements. These records have been found near Nashik in northern Maharashtra in recent times. Besides being a successful warrior, Gautamiputra was also known for his pro-people administration. He was a father figure to his population. It was this dynasty that is believed to have inaugurated the historical calendar era of Shalivahana Shaka.

The Satavahanas were able rulers with administrative responsibilities clearly defined. The empire was divided into regions, each led by an amatya (minister). The Satavahanas were also connoisseurs of literature and the arts. They built the Karle caves near Pune as well as some of the galleries in the world-famous Ajanta caves.

THE SATAVAHANA DYNASTY SAW a total of thirty-two rulers. After their fall, the region was ruled by the Vakatakas, who originated from present-day Vidarbha; the Chalukyas from Badami, Karnataka; and the Yadavas of Deogiri, Maharashtra. Each of these dynasties made a significant contribution to Maharashtra's identity.

Vindhyashakti founded the Vakataka dynasty. He is believed to have served the last of the Satavahanas. Headquartered near present-day Nagpur, the Vakatakas had spread their rule from Bundelkhand in the north to Hyderabad in the south and from the west coast to the east. However, the real expansion of the Vakatakas began with the rise of the founder's son, Pravarsen. He extended the empire up to the Narmada river in the north. Pravarsen was the first Vakataka ruler who called himself 'Samrat' (emperor). He fought with the Naga kings and was the only one from the dynasty who had sizeable control over northern India along with the whole of the Deccan plateau.

After Pravarsen, it is believed that the Vakataka empire was ruled by his four sons. His eldest son, Gautamiputra, died very early. The next two sons, Rudrasen and Sarvasen, each headed a part of the dynasty in the Vidarbha region. Today, the Vakatakas are remembered for their extraordinary creations at the Ajanta and Ellora caves. The architectural works, cut out of rock, have inscriptions denoting the size of their empire. The Vakatakas had conquered Avanti (Malwa) in the north; Kosala (Chhattisgarh), Kalinga and

Andhra in the east; Lata (central and southern Gujarat) and Trikuta (Nashik district) in the west; and Kuntala (southern Maharashtra) in the south.

The Vakatakas, like the Satavahanas, were noted for their passion for literature along with the arts and architecture. The Prakrut language flourished under their rule. They ruled for over 300 years, up to the year AD 550. Their end was hastened by the incompetence of the next generation.

From the year AD 550 to 753, the region that is Maharashtra today was ruled by the Chalukyas from Badami in Karnataka. Unlike the Satavahanas and the Vakatakas, who were Brahmins, the Chalukyas were Kshatriyas. They came from northern Mysore to Badami, and from there they expanded northward and annexed the former kingdom of the Vakatakas. There were three branches of the Chalukya dynasty. Badami was the first, founded by Pulakesin I – however, his father, Jaisinh, had also tried to set up his kingdom in western Maharashtra.

The Chalukyas are identified with Karnataka but they also had a very strong connection with Maharashtra. Pulakesin I was succeeded by Kirtivarman I, who expanded the kingdom by defeating the Mauryas of northern Konkana, the Nalas of Nalavadi (Bellari) and the Kadambas of Banavasi. Kirtivarman I extended the empire to Bihar and Bengal in the north and the Chola–Pandya regions in the south. After his death, his son Ereya took over the reins of the Chalukya empire.

At his coronation, Ereya assumed the name Pulakesin II. It was during his rule, around the year AD 641, that the Chinese traveller Hiuen Tsang visited the kingdom. He is believed to have met Pulakesin II at Ellora, which was considered the second capital along with Badami. Hiuen Tsang showered praise on Pulakesin II, his well-groomed army and his administration. Pulakesin II was the first king south of the Vindhyas to have issued gold coins as currency. He is also reputed to have defeated two well-known emperors from northern India: Harsha and Vikramaditya II.

The Chalukyas had constant feuds with the Pallavas of Kanchi, in present-day Tamil Nadu. The Pallavas also had a sizeable presence in what is today the state of Andhra Pradesh. Pulakesin II was killed in one of the wars with the Pallavas. His sons – Chandraditya, Adityavarma, Vikramaditya, Jayasimha and Ambera – fought among themselves for succession. Pulakesin II's third son, Vikramaditya I, defeated all his brothers to become the Chalukya king in AD 642. He was also successful in regaining the Chalukyas' lost glory.

Vikramaditya I was the one who ended the Pallavas' thirteen-year occupation of Badami. He was followed by Vikramaditya II, who rebuilt the empire. Some famous temples found in Tamil Nadu were built by Vikramaditya II. Like his father, he too had a grudge against the Pallavas. He was so enraged by the Pallavas that he wanted nothing short of their complete annihilation. This resulted in his too being in constant battle with them. In one such battle, he snatched Kanchipuram. Vikramaditya II is also credited with stopping the Arabs, who invaded from Sindh and wanted to capture the Deccan plateau and the southern regions.

The era of the Rashtrakutas began after Vikramaditya II's death. They ruled the region from AD 750 to 973. Many of their inscriptions have been found in western Maharashtra, especially around Maan in Satara district. Maan was called Manpur during the Rashtrakuta regime and was also its capital for a while. It also appears that there was more than one family bearing the name Rashtrakuta. Historians believe 'Rashtrakuta' is not just a surname. Rather, it denotes a designation in the government hierarchy of the time – much like Kulkarni or Deshmukh or Chitnis among modern names.

Like many other dynasties, Rashtrakutas too can be considered Maharashtrians. They ruled over Maharashtra, parts of Karnataka and Andhra Pradesh. One branch of the Rashtrakutas ruled over Gujarat as well. Some members of the clan parted ways to set up their own empires. One of the well-known Rashtrakutas was Govind III, who took the reins of the empire around the beginning of the ninth century AD. Govind III spread the empire to present-day Uttar

Pradesh, up to the Himalayas. Along with Sindh and Bengal, Benares was also a part of his empire.

After conquering the north, Govind III launched a campaign to take over the south. Small kingdoms such as Chol and Kanchi in present-day Tamil Nadu were smoothly captured. Such was the impact of his campaign that the then king of Ceylon extended a hand of friendship in a bid to enter into a no-war pact, which the Rashtrakuta king happily accepted.

Govind III's phenomenal success can be compared with the Maurya, Satavahana or Gupta empires. He died in the year AD 813. Some historians have likened him to Alexander the Great. It's said that during his regime the 'drums of the Deccan could be heard from the Himalayas to the Malabar coast'. When he passed away, his son Amoghvarsha was only six years old and many of Govind III's rivals dreamt of dethroning him. But the king had anticipated that. To prevent such a takeover he had entrusted the responsibilities of the empire to his nephew, who successfully averted the crisis and held on to the throne till Amoghvarsha grew up.

Amoghvarsha was not a warrior like his father. He preferred friendly relations with neighbouring kings to war. He was also a scholar, having interests in the arts and literature, and wrote several volumes in Kannada and Sanskrit. His peace-loving nature earned him the moniker of 'Ashoka of the South'. Later in life, Amoghvarsha turned to Jainism. The popular Jain temples at Shravanbelagola, Karnataka, were built during the Rashtrakuta regime. But the Rashtrakutas were equally devoted to Hinduism. One of their kings used to worship at the Mahalaxmi temple in Kolhapur. The famous Kailasnatha temple at Ellora was also built during their regime.

The dynasty had a further seven kings after the legendary Amoghvarsha. The last was Khottiga Amoghvarsha, who faced many attacks and was eventually defeated in the year AD 973. That brought about the end of the Rashtrakuta dynasty. The dynasty had an almost unblemished record of rule and, except for the last two kings, all its rulers were known for their valour and large-heartedness.

After the fall of the Rashtrakutas came another spell of the Chalukya empire from Kalyani, from AD 973 to 1150. The connection between the Badami Chalukyas and the Chalukyas from Kalyani is not clear. The latter claimed that the two were related, but historians have contested this.

Initially these Chalukyas ruled from Manyakheta, the capital city of the Rashtrakutas. But subsequently they moved to Kalyani, both cities being in present-day Karnataka. The first king of this branch of the Chalukyas was Tailap, who defeated the Cholas, the Chedis and another branch of the Chalukyas in Gujarat. A better-known king of this dynasty was Someshwar I, who also defeated the Cholas and wrested Kanchi from them. Later, the Cholas would have their revenge by defeating Someshwar I's son Vikramaditya.

But before that defeat, Vikramaditya had come to be known as the most powerful of the Chalukyas. He ruled for about fifty years, from 1076 to 1126, and was widely revered. A notable thing that happened during this regime was the rise of Veerashaivism. Basava, the founder of the sect, was born a Brahmin but challenged the prevailing caste system. Most of the royals were Hindus, and Veerashaivas posed a challenge to the prevailing system. Interestingly, the sect is active even today.

The Kalyani Chalukya era was also known for the literary movement in their native language, Kannada, as well as Sanskrit. It is considered to be the golden age of Kannada literature. Many Jain scholars wrote about the lives of Tirthankars, and Veerashaiva writers – called Vachankars – penned poetry called Vachanas. Among these writers were women poets who wrote on topics such as romance, medicine, mathematics and astrology.

About the time the Kalyani Chalukya regime began floundering, another one was taking baby steps near Halebidu in today's Hassan district of Karnataka: the Yadavas, also known as the Hoysalas. Inscriptions dated 1078 and 1090 indicate that the Hoysalas were descendants of the Yadavas from Mathura in north India. The folklore is that after Lord Krishna left Mathura for Dwarka in

Gujarat, many Yadavas too followed him. Later, they dispersed to various regions in Maharashtra and present-day Karnataka. This is why Yadavas are found in Nashik and also in southern India. All of them describe themselves as Yadukultilak, denoting their connection with the dynasty.

The first official Hoysala family record is dated 950 and mentions that the king Arekalla was succeeded by Maruga and then Nripa Kama I (976). The next ruler, Munda (1006–26), was followed by Nripa Kama II. Initially the Hoysala dynasty was a feudatory of the Kalyani Chalukyas. The Hoysalas started asserting themselves after the Chalukyas weakened. They first defeated the Cholas in 1116 and moved their capital from Belur to Halebidu. Though they always nursed an ambition to set up their own empire, it was Veera Ballala II who freed the Hoysalas from subordination. The Hoysalas, who began as subordinates of the Chalukyas, later went on to set up their own empire in Karnataka.

One of the offshoots of the Hoysalas flourished in Devgiri, in present-day Daulatabad, Maharashtra. It played a major role in shaping what came to be known as Maharashtra and Marathi culture. A stone inscription dated AD 860 found at Anjaneri (near Nashik) suggests that a minor branch of the Yadava family ruled a small district, with Anjaneri as its chief city. They set up a city-state named Chandrapur, which is known as Chandor (in Goa) today. The name came from Sevunchandra, who had first served the Rashtrakutas and, after their decline, worked for the Kalyani Chalukyas. After the Chalukya dynasty faded, this branch of Yadavas set up its own kingdom based around Devgiri.

Bhillam V was the first well-known Yadava king. He shifted the Yadava capital from Sindigram (Sinnar) to Devgiri. From then until the end of this empire, Devgiri was its capital city. Bhillam V ruled from 1147 to 1191. He, and later his son Jaitrapal, spread their kingdom to include the Konkan, Gujarat and Malwa regions. He also fought with the Hoysalas. It was during Jaitrapal's reign that the famous poet-saint Mukundraj published his popular work *Vivek Sindhu*.

The Devgiri Yadavas came to fame with the rise of Singhan, Jaitrapal's son. He is considered the greatest of Yadavas and during his reign the kingdom expanded from the Narmada river in the north to the Tungabhadra river in the south. Singhan brought about the end of the reign of the Hoysalas. Later, he defeated the Shilahars from Kolhapur in western Maharashtra and merged their empire into his own. In fact, nearly all the neighbouring kingdoms surrendered to him and accepted him as their Samrat.

The Yadavas retained the provinces with their principalities such as Shilahar, Kadamba and Sindh. Later, during Ramdevrao Yadava's rule (1271–1309), his son Bheem took over the small kingdom of Mahim (Mumbai) and brought the entire northern Konkan under Yadava control. The Yadavas thus had all of Maharashtra under their rule, which lasted from 1187 to 1318. Ramdevrao was the last of the dynasty to rule over Maharashtra and even expanded the empire to cover a large portion of Indian territory.

MANY HISTORIANS – SUCH as V.K. Rajwade, Dr D.R. Bhandarkar and Dr A.S. Altekar – attribute the rise of Marathi identity to the Yadavas. According to them, the dynasty was the 'first true Marathi empire'. They were also considered to be Maratha Kshatriyas. Jijabai, Chhatrapati Shivaji's mother, belonged to the clan of Jadhavas, who were descendants of the Yadavas. They patronized Marathi and made it their court language. This period is considered very important in the history of the Marathi language. During the period of Sevunchandra's rule, Kannada too enjoyed official status. However, later Marathi became the only official language.

During the Yadava dynasty's rule, the capital Devgiri attracted scholars from all over. They provided a real impetus to the growth of Marathi language and culture. Singhan was a big patron of learning and literature. He established a college of astronomy for the study of the works of the celebrated astronomer Bhaskaracharya. Many inscriptions have been found with details of donations made for charitable and cultural causes.

The Yadavas ruled from the year AD 235 to 1318, and during this time the region produced many home-grown empires. It is important to note that during this period all these empires had their capital cities in present-day Maharashtra. From the Satavahanas to the Yadavas, six out of seven dynasties had capital cities in Paithan, Nandivardhan and Devgiri. The Rashtrakutas too had their base near Ellora of today, which was subsequently shifted to Manyakhet (present-day Malkhed). It is part of Karnataka now but, centuries ago, it was Marathi-speaking. The Chalukyas too had their capital city at Manyakhet. Later, they moved it to Kalyani, which is closer to Kalburgi on the present-day Karnataka–Maharashtra border. This was the era when literature, art and governance flourished in Maharashtra.

However, these dynasties were oblivious to developments in the north. Many of them had marched up to Sindh or Punjab, but none thought of setting up a base there. Thus, they were not prepared for Islamic invasions from the north. This is particularly true of Singhan, who was otherwise the most successful warrior king of the Yadavas. Settled in Maharashtra and content with his empire, he failed to take note of invaders from Delhi marching on to the Malwa and Gujarat regions. The local rulers in those areas, such as the Parmars, were incapable of facing up to the Delhi raiders. Singhan was not only unsuccessful in saving the local satraps in these regions from falling into the invaders' hands, but it also didn't occur to him to organize a united front of all southern and western rulers to take on Delhi.

This lack of vision plunged Maharashtra into an era of darkness, one that lasted for well over 350 years.

2

Darkness at Noon

Maharashtra's political downfall began around the thirteenth century. It was sharp and very steep. Ironically, the region was witnessing an extraordinary spiritual high while it was sinking politically. It was becoming subservient even to small Islamic despots while its Hindu gurus were busy preaching the futility of materialistic life.

It was a little before 1296 – the year the region faced an invasion by Alauddin Khilji, the most powerful emperor of the Khilji dynasty that ruled the Delhi Sultanate – that the legendary saint-point Dnyaneshwar wrote his two magnum opuses, *Dnyaneshwari* and *Amrutanubhav*. The son of a middle-class Sanskrit scholar from Alandi near Pune, who wanted to take sanyas (renounce the world) but couldn't due to family compulsions, Dnyandev – as he is fondly called – was well versed in the Vedas from a very early age, just like his three siblings. He wrote *Dnyaneshwari* when he was only thirteen years old. A commentary on the Gita, it is considered to be one of the finest by Marathi scholars.

On the advice of his guru, Nivrutti, Dnyandev then wrote *Amritanubhava*, a treatise of his spiritual experiences in 800 couplets. Over the years, he went on many pilgrimages with his brothers and sister, including to Rameswaram and Madurai. It was at Pandharpur that he met the saint Namdev and the two became spiritual friends. This meeting inspired Dnyaneshwar to lead the Warkari Sampradaya, of which he became the first apostle. This was the start of the tradition of 'Wari', which sees lakhs of devotees walk a distance of over 250 km from Alandi to Pandharpur during the months of Ashadh (June–July) and/or Kartik (October–November). Many historians believe this was the era that gave birth to the concept of 'Maharashtra Dharma'.

In his book *Rise of Maratha Power*, Mahadev Govind Ranade – scholar, reformer, judge and one of the founding members of the Indian National Congress in the nineteenth century – argued that the political success the legendary king Shivaji achieved in the seventeenth century was a manifestation of religious and social movements that began with Dnyaneshwar. The religious movement led to a steady growth of spiritual virtues within society. The saints associated with the movement represented various sections of society: from Brahmins to Mahars. These saints, as Ranade put it, vindicated 'the eternal verities of the moral law and man's higher spiritual life'.

This phase can be compared to the sixteenth-century Reformation movement in western Europe that challenged the authority of the Church. In Maharashtra, it was Brahmin dominance that came under challenge. This was also the period in Maharashtra's history that witnessed social inclusiveness like never before. According to Ranade, the religion then was 'at once tolerant and catholic, deeply spiritual and yet not iconoclastic'. However, Maharashtra was not the only region that was experiencing such a religious movement. Neighbouring Karnataka too witnessed the rise of a similar campaign led by Veerashaivas, which was later joined by Vaishnavas too.

This religious–spiritual activity apart, the region, during the same period, slowly but surely started losing its political significance.

IN 1296, THE SAME year that Dnyaneshwar took samadhi (a practice of voluntarily accepting death after entering into a deep meditative state), Maharashtra faced its first major invasion, with Alauddin Khilji raiding Devgiri, the power centre of the Yadavas. Alauddin was the nephew of the ruler of the Delhi Sultanate, Jalal-ud-din Khilji. Both were aware of the wealthy rulers of the south and had plans to expand the empire in that direction. Alauddin took the lead with a clear intention in mind: he wanted to capture the wealth of the southern rulers and use it to dethrone Jalal-ud-din and usurp the Delhi Sultanate ultimately. A secret mission initially, on 26 February 1296 Alauddin began his march with an 8,000-man cavalry to capture Devgiri.

The Yadavas by then had become too complacent to anticipate Alauddin's designs. The intelligence gathering system of King Ramachandra was dysfunctional and he was completely in the dark about Alauddin's imminent attack. Alauddin, on the other hand, was marching to Devgiri expecting a long battle ahead. He took a two-day break on his journey at Achalpur, not very far from Devgiri. But even then the Yadavas failed to take note of the impending crisis. Close to Devgiri, however, he faced some resistance, although it wasn't significant enough to make him change his plans. The Yadavas, confined to the comforts of Devgiri, were still unaware of the situation. They realized it only when Alauddin's men were at their doorstep.

Devgiri had not faced an attack or fought a war in a long time. As a result, the city was not fortified the way it should have been. Moreover, Crown Prince Simhana was away on an expedition with a large army. That did not leave enough men behind to protect the city. King Ramachandra, having realized the gravity of the situation so late, couldn't do much except retreat to the fort. Devgiri was then available for Alauddin's men to loot and plunder and ruthlessly murder the locals. Along with jewellery, he captured 1,000 horses and elephants from the royal stable.

In the absence of any other option, King Ramachandra was forced to sign a peace treaty with Alauddin. He offered over 750 kg of gold and large quantities of precious metals and stones in exchange for all the prisoners taken. This was in addition to the loot from Devgiri's people. After collecting it all, Alauddin was in a hurry to leave because he realized that Ramachandra's son Simhana would soon return from his expedition. Sensing the danger of a revival among the Yadava clan, he spread a canard that another 20,000-strong cavalry was on its way from Delhi to join him.

Simhana did return in time and challenged Alauddin just as he was ready to leave. Ramachandra wanted to avoid another conflict and sent a message to his son asking him to honour the treaty. But Simhana was not in the mood to listen. Instead, he asked Alauddin to return the loot. An angry Alauddin left behind a team of 1,000 men from his cavalry to man Devgiri and took on Simhana with the rest. The invaders would have been defeated had Simhana's army stayed on the battlefield since he had a bigger army. In fact, Alauddin was on the verge of losing the battle when his troops in Devgiri heard about his likely defeat and joined him on the front. The Yadavas mistook this contingent for the rumoured cavalry of 20,000 men from Delhi and fled the battlefield in fear. It was all over for the Yadavas.

Alauddin then returned to the fort and laid siege. Devgiri witnessed a dance of death as Alauddin's men killed prisoners and paraded the king's close relatives and nobles in front of the fort. At this juncture, Ramachandra thought of seeking assistance from the neighbouring Hindu kings. But it was too late, and none of them had the vision to understand the gravity of Alauddin's attack. Tired and frustrated, Ramachandra once again pleaded for a peace treaty. Alauddin, who wanted to return quickly, agreed to a truce. Unsurprisingly, he demanded a much larger sum as war indemnity the second time around. Ramachandra had to cough up 8,500 kg of gold, 100 kg of pearls, 30 kg of precious stones, 14,000 kg of silver and over 1,000 bundles of pure silk cloth.

On his part, Alauddin released the surviving prisoners. It had taken him just five days to defeat one of the richest empires of the west. Thus, Alauddin became the first successful Muslim invader of the Deccan who put an end to the 200 years of Yadava reign.

Alauddin never had any intention to stay on in Devgiri. His eyes were set on Delhi. So, he restored Ramachandra in exchange for the large ransom along with the promise of yearly contributions. Once Alauddin went back, Ramachandra showed little interest in paying the agreed sums. Arrears kept mounting. Eventually, Alauddin revisited Devgiri to teach the Yadavas a lesson. In 1307, he sent a force commanded by his general, Malik Kafur, to Devgiri. Assisted by the governors of Malwa and Gujarat, Malik Kafur conquered Devgiri almost without a battle.

This second attack took place eleven years after the first one in 1296. Yet, they were as ill-prepared as before. Ramachandra was arrested and taken to Delhi. Alauddin reinstated him once again after extracting the promise of an even larger sum and the commitment to help him conquer other kingdoms in the south. Ramachandra, now in Alauddin's service, was given the title of Rai Rayan. Ramachandra's successor, Simhana III, attempted to challenge the supremacy of Alauddin, who dispatched Malik Kafur yet again to recapture Devgiri in 1310. In the ensuing battle, Simhana III was killed and Devgiri was captured for good.

The Yadavas were defeated as many as four times in a span of twenty years from 1296. It was curtains for the Yadava empire in 1318. It was not just a military defeat but a complete washout. This goes to show how the Yadavas were totally oblivious to developments in Delhi, which had been witnessing Muslim invasions for well over 300 years.

About ninety years before Alauddin's rise, Qutb-ud-din Aibak, a Turkic, had founded the Mamluk dynasty. He was the first sultan of Delhi. A slave himself, Qutb-ud-din was raised in Persia where a mullah, a local Islamic religious head, bought him. After the mullah's death, his son sold Qutb-ud-din to Muhammad Ghori, who was then the sultan of the Ghurid empire in present-day Afghanistan. Ghori put Qutb-ud-din in charge of the slave department. He went on to command Ghori's army that conquered Delhi in 1193. Ghori returned home, leaving the conquered land in the hands of his slave. Subsequently, Qutb-ud-din became the sultan of Delhi.

By the time the Yadavas faced the complete rout, invaders from West Asia had established a major foothold in India for over a century. With the exception of Nepal, almost the entire northern part of the subcontinent had fallen in their hands. However, none of the kings in the south anticipated the invasions. This lack of preparation in the southern kingdoms – the Kakatiyas of Warangal, the Yadavas of Dwarka and Devgiri, the Pandyas of Madurai – led to their defeat one after the other. In the fourteen years between 1307 and 1321, Malik Kafur single-handedly took over the entire south. This series of defeats reflects the lackadaisical approach to governance of the Deccan kings of the period.

MOREOVER, ALL THIS HAPPENED at a time when the Delhi Sultanate itself was falling into disarray and becoming riddled with factionalism.

Alauddin had killed his uncle to take over the Delhi Sultanate but in his last years was at the mercy of Malik Kafur, who had become all-powerful. Malik killed Alauddin's many wives, blinded his two sons and assassinated several of his lieutenants. Malik himself was later killed in a coup by Mubarak Khilji, Alauddin's elder son, who then proclaimed himself ruler of the Khilji dynasty. Mubarak was killed in yet another coup in 1320 by his army chief Malik Khushru, also known as Khushru Khan.

Like his predecessor, Khushru Khan too killed many of his colleagues who, he believed, held allegiance to the earlier regime. Interestingly, his loyalty to Islam was always in doubt since he was believed to have had a Hindu past. As a result, he was unpopular among the Muslims. Ghiyasuddin Tughluq, governor of Depalpur in present-day Punjab, sensed this unease among his fellow Muslims. Along with the governors of Multan and Sindh, he launched a revolt against Khushru Khan claiming '*Islam khatre mein hai*' (Islam is in danger). Khushru Khan was killed and the Delhi Sultanate had a new king in Ghiyasuddin Tughluq, launching the Tughluq dynasty.

He later sent his son Muhammad bin Tughluq to the south and himself went to conquer regions that are present-day West Bengal and Bihar. In 1325, Ghiyasuddin died under mysterious circumstances: the wooden tent where he was to be felicitated collapsed, crushing him to death. Muhammad, the heir apparent, was suspected to be behind his father's killing.

Muhammad ruled the Delhi Sultanate till 1351. It was he who shifted the capital from Delhi to Devgiri. The decision caused so much disruption that thousands of his men were killed in the transit. In the process, he more or less emptied out the city of Delhi. He can be described as the first Muslim king to have established his rule all over the subcontinent.

Even as the Sultanate dealt with these constant feuds, it continued with some atrocities on its subjects. For instance, Hindus were treated as second-class citizens and forced to pay jizya, a special tax.

Through all this, the Hindu kingdoms in the south remained blissfully unaware of the possible danger and were not prepared to face a northern onslaught. In comparison to the Delhi Sultanate rulers, the southern kings were relatively stable. They were as wealthy – if not more – as their northern counterparts. But they did not think of capturing the Sultanate. Every change of guard in Delhi witnessed bloodshed and uncertainty, but it never faced any challenge from the south. It is no wonder that soon all southern kingdoms fell into the hands of invaders.

Then came the first ever home-grown Muslim empire of the Deccan.

Muhammad bin Tughluq had antagonized many southern rulers. One of them was Hasan Gangu, possibly of Tajik–Persian descent, who was the governor of the region near Ellora. Hasan Gangu revolted against Muhammad bin Tughluq. The revolt was successful, following which, on 3 August 1347, he established an independent state in the Deccan. The Bahmani dynasty comprised regions of present-day Karnataka, Maharashtra and Andhra Pradesh. Hasan Gangu then assumed the name of Alauddin Bahman Shah.

One must note Alauddin's successful revolt against the Sultanate, even as others in the south were failing miserably in their attempts. There is another example to underline the south's inability to come up trumps over the north. Sajjan Singh and Kshetra Singh were two young men who had descended on the south from the royals of Mewar with an aim to create their kingdom around the same time Alauddin Hasan was trying to set up his first southern Muslim empire. Alauddin had been a slave in his early life whereas Sajan Singh and Kshetra Singh were from royal families. However, he was successful in setting up his empire while the two preferred to serve him.

From 1347 to 1425, the Bahmani capital was Ahsanabad (Gulbarga). Later, it was shifted to Muhammadabad (Bidar). The Bahmani Sultanate was at its peak during the vizierate (1466–81) of Mahmud Gawan. Eighteen kings ruled during the nearly 200 years of Bahmani rule. But, of them, only a handful managed to establish eminence. With the exceptions of Alauddin, his son Muhammadshah (1358–75), Firojshah (1397–1422), Ahmedshah Wali (1422–35) and Mahmud (1466–81), the reigns of many others were weak and marred by their personal vices.

The kingdom was later divided into two: Deccanis (old guard) and Afaquis (newcomers). There were serious differences between the two. Many Afaquis found it difficult to win the trust and confidence of the Deccanis. This lack of trust resulted in several executions in the later days. There were divisions also between Shias and Sunnis. Eventually, after 1518, the kingdom got divided further into four smaller ones: Barishahi (of Bidar), Kutbshahi (of Golconda), Adamshahi (of Ahmednagar) and Adilshahi (of Bijapur), known collectively as the Deccan Sultanates.

THE RARE GLORIOUS SPOT in this history of the Deccan was Vijayanagar. Eleven years before the Bahmani empire was set up in Gulbarga in 1347, the kingdom of Vijayanagar had come into being with the sole aim of preventing Muslim invaders. Two brothers, Harihar and Bukka, both ministers in the Kakatiya regime in Warangal, took the lead in setting up the kingdom. They fled from Warangal in 1323 when it witnessed a major Muslim invasion. The invaders, led by Alauddin Khilji, captured the Kakatiya king, Kampili, after which the two brothers crossed the Tungabhadra river and founded a new city in 1336 and named it Vijayanagar. Hampi, now the famous world heritage site in Karnataka, was part of Vijayanagar. The kingdom, named after its capital, survived until 1646.

Harihar and Bukka were warriors. They freed the entire region south of the Tungabhadra of Muslims. In the first two decades after founding the empire, Harihar I successfully took control of most of the area south of the Tungabhadra and earned the title of Purvapaschima Samudradhishavara (master of the eastern and western seas). By 1374, Bukka Raya I, who succeeded Harihara I, went on to capture the small but important kingdom of Arcot, the Reddys of Kondavidu, and Madurai, which was under Muslim rule. He also defeated the Kadambas of Goa in the west and took over the Tungabhadra–Krishna doab. With the Vijayanagar kingdom now settled, Harihar II, the second son of Bukka Raya I, further consolidated the kingdom beyond the Krishna river and brought almost all of southern India under the Vijayanagar umbrella.

The next ruler, Deva Rai, extended the empire right up to present-day Odisha by defeating the Gajapatis in the east. It was during his reign that the Italian traveller Niccolò de' Conti visited India. Conti later described Deva Rai as the 'most powerful ruler of India'. His successor in 1424, Deva Rai II, was one of the most capable rulers of the dynasty, expanding the Vijayanagar empire up to Calicut and Quilon in the south. He even invaded the islands of Lanka and Burma. The empire reached its peak during the rule of Krishnadevaraya, when Vijayanagar armies recorded the highest number of victories. It was during his time that the empire occupied regions under various sultanates in the Deccan right up to the Kalingas' territory in the east. It was Krishnadevaraya's rule that saw the commissioning of many important monuments in the south.

It was also the regime that was known for best administrative practices. The king was assisted by a cabinet of ministers (Pradhana), which was headed by the prime minister (Mahapradhana). The regime also had posts such as those of chief secretary (Karyakartha or Rayaswami) and imperial officer (Adhikari). Military training was mandatory for all high-ranking ministers and officers. A secretariat near the king's palace had employed staff to maintain official records. Rich feudal landlords (Goudas) were authorized to supervise accounts-maintaining staff called Karanikas. Palace administration was decentralized by dividing it into seventy-two departments (Niyogas). The kingdom had several female attendants with minor administrative responsibilities, and some of them functioned as concubines for various nobles. The Vijayanagar kings proclaimed themselves as protectors of Hindus, with titles such as Gobrahamana Pratipalanacharya, but were equally tolerant of all religions and sects.

Interestingly, the Hindu Vijayanagar empire grew alongside the Muslim-dominated Bahmanis. The two kingdoms flourished, side by side, for about 200 years even though they were engaged continuously in some battle or the other, the reasons for which were mainly economic. The Tungabhadra–Krishna doab was extremely fertile and both kingdoms wanted to possess it. It also had many significant ports connecting to other lands like Ceylon, Indonesia, Malaya and Burma. Goa and Dabhol in the Konkan region, which the Bahmanis had been eyeing for long, became part of the Vijayanagar empire after attempts by both powers to prove their supremacy over these areas that had highly profitable routes.

The Bahmanis' opposition ensured that the Vijayanagar empire could not grow in the northern direction. But it kept expanding eastward and westward across the peninsula and southward into the Tamil country. The clashes between the two ensured a change of boundaries between 1336 and 1422. Between 1422 and 1446,

Vijayanagar suffered defeats at the hands of the Bahmanis and that forced it to restructure. From 1465 to 1509, it had to surrender Goa, Chaul and Dabhol ports to the Bahmanis. In the 1490s, Vijayanagar occupied the Tungabhadra region. This was the time when the Bahmani empire was at its weakest and was being split into five different sultanates.

The Vijayanagar rulers and the Bahmani sultans fought at least ten wars from 1336 till the Battle of Talikota in 1565. The strained relationship and frequent wars required Vijayanagar to have a standing army at all times. The belief among Vijayanagar rulers that a lack of good-quality horses was hampering their military prowess forced the empire to buy expensive horses from Arabs and the Portuguese. This strained their resources further. To meet the growing expenses, Vijayanagar had to raise the rate of taxation, which triggered resentment in its farming community. The high taxation caused widespread discontent among the peasantry, leading to a revolt by a number of villages. These conflicts within the Vijayanagar empire played a major role in its defeat at the hands of the Bahmani sultans, since its military forces had to be divided in order to control the rising domestic resentments.

In addition to everything else, the Vijayanagar empire also began facing a power struggle between different ruling families. The divisions helped the Bahmanis to strengthen and assert their control over areas which had originally been under Vijayanagar control. The internal feuds severely weakened the control of the rulers over the Vijayanagar empire by 1542. The Bahmani Sultanate was dealing with its own power struggle. It was so intense that the Bahmani sultan remained just a figurehead while the governors of different regions started exercising real power. They also had frequent skirmishes with each other. But the difference between the two kingdoms was that one of them, the Bahmani dynasty, realized the importance of forming a united front to challenge the other. It made the five sultanates come together to challenge the Vijayanagar empire. Some minor Hindu kingdoms which held grudges against the Vijayanagar empire also helped the sultanates.

It was a watershed battle fought at Talikota, north Karnataka, that ended one of the most glorious empires in Indian history. In 1565, the Deccan Sultanates of Ahmednagar, Berar, Bidar, Bijapur and Golconda formed a grand alliance to defeat the Vijayanagar army. The sultanates had a total infantry of 80,000 and a cavalry of 30,000. Vijayanagar, on the other hand, had 1,40,000 soldiers on foot, with another 10,000 on horseback. The Vijayanagar army also had a large number of war elephants. The decisive battle was sharp and intense. First, the sultanates attacked the primary lines of the Vijayanagar army using cannon fire. That took a heavy toll on Vijayanagar's artillery. This was followed by a frontal attack by the combined armies of the five states that finished the job. The battle ended in a clear victory for the sultanates, with the Vijayanagar king's severed head put on display as a trophy. The looting and plundering of the kingdom followed.

Historians point out many a weakness in the sultanates. And yet they defeated one of the strongest Hindu empires. The land once known for its fighting spirit in the early prehistoric era resigned to its fate during the medieval times. The darkness that enveloped Maharashtra was there to stay for the next seventy-odd years.

3

Islamic Rule

As the fifteenth century was coming to an end, the Deccan had become a theatre for the political drama that was playing out in Delhi. It was not a one-act play. In fact, it had multiple acts and a wide star cast: from the Bahmanis and Vijayanagar to the Nizam, the Adil Shah and the Qutb Shah, along with a cameo of the Mughals, who went on to steal the show later. What is interesting is that all the action was taking place simultaneously. Though separated geographically by a vast distance, it was the Deccan that was shaping the Delhi script. In the beginning, when the power centre in the north was witnessing a rise, the Deccan was a mute spectator to the fading of the Vijayanagar empire. It also witnessed the powerful Bahmani kingdom disintegrate. And even before the Deccan could prepare itself to live with the five different sultanates that were born after the end of the Bahmani empire, the Mughals had entered the arena.

The end of the Bahmani and Vijayanagar empires was nothing short of a spectacular tragedy. The last few of the Bahmani sultans – Ahmad Shah II, Ala-ud-din Shah and Wali-ullah Shah – were mere puppets in the hands of Amir Barid, the prime minister of the empire. Kalim-ullah Shah (1526–38) was the last sultan of the

Bahmani kingdom. By then, the first of the Mughals had entered Delhi, led by Babur, who went on to set up one of the most powerful dynasties in India. After hearing about Babur's conquest of Delhi, Kalim-ullah Shah approached him, offering the regions of Berar and Daulatabad in exchange for a promise to help free him from the clutches of Amir Barid. However, news of this leaked and he had to flee to Bijapur to save his life, and eventually retired in Ahmednagar. After his death, his son Ilham-ullah made his way to Mecca and never returned. And thus came about the inglorious end of the once-powerful Bahmani Sultanate. Before this end, the sultanate had split into five: Ahmednagar, Bijapur, Berar, Golconda and Bidar.

THE AHMEDNAGAR SULTANATE WAS the first of the five offshoots. Set up by Malik Ahmad, the son of Nizam-ul-Mulk Malik Hasan Bahri, who was the prime minister in the Bahmani court, the sultanate was popularly known as the Nizam Shahi. Witness to the wearing off of the Bahmani empire, Malik Ahmad, who was appointed governor of Junnar, dreamt of setting up his own empire. In a bid to fulfil this dream, he fought with the Bahmani army, defeating it on 28 May 1490. He soon claimed independence by transferring his seat of government from Junnar (incidentally, Junnar, near Pune, houses a famous fort that would be named Shivneri after the birth of Shivaji there in 1630) to a small village called Bhingar, somewhat equidistant from Junnar and Daulatabad, the former capital of the Yadavas, which Malik Ahmad was eyeing. He preferred Bhingar to any other place for two reasons: first, it was where he had defeated the Bahmani army led by Jahangir Khan; second, Bhingar was situated on the banks of the Sina river. In 1494, he set up his new capital there and renamed it Ahmednagar.

After his death in 1510, his son Burhan – who was just seven years old at the time of his coronation – went on to rule for nearly forty-three years. It was Burhan who later assumed the title of

Nizam Shah. During his reign, the Nizam Shahi became part of the larger coalition with Bidar, Bijapur, Golconda and Berar to take on Vijayanagar. He also fought against Bijapur. After his death in 1553, Burhan's son Husain Nizam Shah buried differences with the other sultanas and joined forces with them in the Battle of Talikota of 1565.

Husain's death in 1565 brought his son Murtaza Nizam Shah I to power. He tried to defeat the Imad Shahi dynasty of Berar. However, he was of an erratic temperament and started suspecting that his son Miran was plotting against him. Miran countered his father with his own conspiracy and killed him. Murtaza was found dead in his bed. Miran himself couldn't last long and was succeeded by his cousin Ismail, who ruled for two years.

It was during Ismail's regime that for the first time differences between Shias and the Mahdawi sect came to the fore. Ismail was not popular. Sensing the mood, he was replaced by his father, Burhan Nizam Shah II, who took charge of the sultanate. He was challenged by Adil Shah of Bijapur, another splinter of the Bahmani empire. Again, his son Ibrahim replaced him but could rule for just about four months. The Nizam Shahi plunged into chaos since there emerged as many as four claimants to the throne. One of them happened to be the famous Chand Bibi, the daughter of Husain Nizam Shah, who was married to Ali Adil Shah of Bijapur.

Keeping an eye on the developments were the Mughals in Delhi, who were looking to gain a foothold in the Deccan. The Nizam Shahi situation was quite tempting. The Mughals, led by Emperor Akbar, thought conditions were ripe to make a major foray into the south. Akbar's son Murad led the attack on Ahmednagar fort. He was challenged by Chand Bibi, who put up a heroic fight. However, she was ultimately forced to enter into an agreement with the Mughals and had to give up major territories in the bargain. The agreement didn't last long. Soon enough, the Mughals once again laid siege to the capital. It was during this attack that Chand Bibi is believed to have killed herself to avoid falling in the hands of the Mughals.

Surprisingly, the Ahmednagar empire later witnessed a rebirth at the hands of the well-known warrior Malik Ambar. A former Abyssinian slave, he was known as a great statesman and efficient administrator. In a rare act of courage, he raided the Mughal territory by adopting guerrilla tactics (it was this guerrilla warfare that Chhatrapati Shivaji would take to greater heights later). His heroic resistance ended after the Mughal prince Khurram defeated him in 1617 and again in 1621.

Jahangir, who had replaced his father Emperor Akbar in Delhi by then, was impressed with his son Khurram's gallantry and excellent planning. The proud father gave him a new title: Shah Jahan (king of the world) – the one who went on to build the world-famous Taj Mahal at Agra in the memory of his wife, Mumtaz. Interesting to note is the role the Maharashtra region played in making Prince Khurram Shah Jahan.

Five years after the second war, in 1626, Malik Ambar died. It was the beginning of the end of the Nizam Shahi. And the one who performed the last rites was none other than Aurangzeb, who was serving Shah Jahan. Later, the Nizam Shahi was split between the Mughals and the Adil Shahi kingdom of Bijapur.

STRICTLY SPEAKING, IF THE founders of the Nizam Shahi were local Muslims, those of the Adil Shahi were of foreign origin. This was one of the biggest breakaway groups of the Bahmani empire and lasted for around 200 years. The Adil Shahi dynasty ruled well over one-sixth of present-day Maharashtra. Its capital was Bijapur, known as the Agra of the south. Situated in the Deccan plateau of southern India, now part of Karnataka state, it had been a province of the Bahmani sultanate until 1518, when the decline of the sultanate forced its break-up.

It is said that Yusuf Adil Shah, founder of the Adil Shahi, belonged to the Ottoman empire of Constantinople, which is present-day Istanbul, Turkey. His brother Mehmood had wanted to eliminate

Yusuf, who was only seven years old when their father, Murad, died. Their mother saved Yusuf by sending him out of the country with a merchant. Legend has it that a sage came into his dream and asked him to go to Hindustan. He reached Dabhol, a small port in Maharashtra, where he was sold as a slave to Mahmud Gawan, the prime minister of the Bahmani empire then. Internal feuds amongst the Bahmani sultans got Gawan killed, after which Yusuf went on to set up his own sultanate at Bijapur. Yusuf was himself a scholar, an accomplished musician and a great patron of art and literature. He died in 1510.

Yusuf's thirteen-year-old son, Ismail, took over the reins of the sultanate after his death. The young boy soon lost Goa to the Portuguese under their well-known governor Afonso de Albuquerque. Ismail was also unsuccessful in preventing the Vijayanagar army's invasion, led by Krishnadevaraya, their strongest ruler. In the battle, he had to cede Raichur to the Vijayanagar empire. Raichur had been a bone of contention between Vijayanagar and the Bahmani Sultanate for long.

Ismail's son Mallu, who succeeded his father after his death in 1534, was an incapable ruler and was dethroned by Ibrahim, his younger brother, in a matter of a few months. It was Ibrahim who assumed the title of 'Shah'. A staunch Hindustani supporter, he replaced Bijapur's official language Persian with Dakhini Urdu, popularly known as Hindavi. He is also known to have employed many Hindus in his administration. After his death in 1558, his son Ali Adil ascended to the throne. Ali had a running feud with the Nizam Shahi of Ahmednagar over the issue of Solapur, now a popular textile hub in southern Maharashtra. Such were the differences that he entered into an understanding with Rama Raya of Vijayanagar and Ibrahim Qutb Shah of Golconda to invade Ahmednagar. The joint attack forced Husain Nizam Shah I to flee to Junnar. However, what helped these two Islamic sultanates to bury their differences and forge an alliance against the Vijayanagar empire was the matrimonial alliance Ibrahim Adil Shah had forged with the Nizam Shahi by marrying Husain's daughter, Chand Bibi.

As a result, all Muslim confederates joined hands against the might of the Vijayanagar empire in 1565 at the Battle of Talikota.

Internal feuds in the Adil Shahi took a toll on Ali Adil Shah and he was killed in 1580. Since he died childless, his nephew, Ibrahim II, got an opportunity to lead the Adil Shahi, which he did very successfully for forty-seven years. As he was a man of letters, art and culture flourished under his regime. Fond of literature, Ibrahim Adil Shah II penned the famous book of Hindi songs called *Nawras-Namah*. He also witnessed the completion of the *Tarikh-i-Ferishta*, a text on the history of Hindustan based on earlier Persian historical works. Written by Muhammad Kasim Hindu Shah, during the reigns of Akbar and Jahangir, it is considered one of the finest works of the time.

Many Hindus were appointed in various high posts during his regime, which earned him the monicker 'Jagadguru'. Since his ascendancy came at a very early age, his aunt Chand Bibi initially hand-held him. He witnessed her death in the battle with Akbar in 1600, and it left him shattered. His son Muhammad Adil Shah stepped into his shoes in 1627. He recaptured territories that were with Ahmednagar and Vijayanagar. Muhammad Adil Shah died in 1657 and was buried in the Gol Gumbaz, a magnificent tomb and an architectural marvel. Ali Adil Shah II succeeded Muhammad Adil Shah. Sikandar Adil Shah was the last ruler of the Adil Shahi dynasty, which ended in 1686.

Now, two challenges had emerged for the Adil Shahi. One was Shivaji, who had crowned himself Chhatrapati at Raigad in 1674. And the other was Aurangzeb, who was eyeing Shivaji's Maratha empire. Sikandar was too young to face this double whammy. He succumbed; Bijapur was incorporated into the Mughal empire on 12 September 1686. Sikandar died in 1700 at the age of just thirty-two.

OF THE FIVE SULTANATES that were formed after the disintegration of the Bahmani empire, two were very small: the Imad Shahi of

Berar, now in the Vidarbha region of Maharashtra, and the Barid Shahi of Bidar, now in Karnataka. Both struggled with the Nizam Shahi of Ahmednagar and the Adil Shahi of Bijapur. Interestingly, the Imad Shahis sought refuge in Vijayanagar while taking on the Nizam Shahi.

Fathullah Imad-ul-Mulk founded the Imad Shahi. He was a Kannada-speaking Hindu who was captured as a young boy by the Bahmani forces during a war against the Vijayanagar empire and brought up as a Muslim. Under the leadership of Mahmud Gawan, he rose to the rank of officer in command of the forces (Sarlaskar) of Berar and was honoured with the title Imad-ul-Mulk. Soon after Malik Ahmad Nizam Shah broke away from the Bahmani dynasty and declared independence of the Ahmednagar Sultanate, Fathullah Imad-ul-Mulk too thought of separation. He declared himself the Sultan of Berar and went on to set up his capital in Achalpur. His sultanate comprised Akola, Buldhana, Amravati, Yavatmal, Parbhani and most of Nanded and Aurangabad. He was succeeded by his eldest son, Aladdin Imad Shah. Nothing spectacular happened until 1568, when Murtaza Nizam Shah of Ahmednagar invaded Berar and killed the king and annexed the Berar Sultanate to his own.

Like Berar, the Barid Shahi of Bidar too was formed by an 'outsider'. If the founder of the Berar Shahi was a Hindu, that of the Barid Shahi was a Turkish: Qasim Barid, a former Turkish slave who had served the Bahmani empire under Muhammad Shah III. He started his career in defence but went on to become the prime minister of the Bahmani Sultanate. Such was his clout that during the reign of Mahmud Shah Bahmani, Qasim was considered to be the de facto ruler. After his death in 1504, his son Amir Barid became the prime minister and controlled the administration of the Bahmani Sultanate. In 1542, he was succeeded by his son Ali Barid, who was the first to assume the title of Shah. Ali Barid joined the other Deccan sultans in the Battle of Talikota against the Vijayanagar empire. Much like the Imad Shahi, the Barid Shahi too went down in history without any remarkable achievement. Eventually, Bidar was annexed to the Bijapur Sultanate and Amir Barid III and his sons were made prisoners in Bijapur.

ANOTHER MIGRANT WHO EVENTUALLY established his own sultanate was Quli Qutb Shah. A Turkman from Hamadan, one of the oldest cities of modern Iran, Quli Qutb Shah arrived in Delhi with his uncle and some other relatives in the early sixteenth century. Later, he moved to the south to serve the Bahmani empire. As the Bahmani empire began to fall apart, he decided to break away and set up his own sultanate. He made Golconda his home to set up the first Muslim sultanate of the Telangana region. Once formed, Quli kept expanding his regime by seizing forts at Warangal, Rajahmundry and around. Quli Qutb Shah was in perennial war with Adil Shah of Bijapur.

Like the other sultanates, Qutb Shah too was faced with internal feuds for power. This led to his own son, Jamsheed, killing him while he was offering namaz in 1543. The youngest of his sons, Jamsheed was quite ambitious and later blinded his brother Qutbuddin to assume the throne. Another of his brothers, Ibrahim, fled to Vijayanagar to save his own life. Known for his cruelty, Jamsheed's seven-year reign was marked by his people's resentment. He died of an illness in 1550. His son Subhan Quli, who was just around seven years old at the time, was made sultan of Golconda. Too young to rule, he was assisted by Saif Khan, who was from Ahmednagar. Little is known about Subhan's death the same year.

Then came Ibrahim Quli Qutb Shah, who had been living in exile in Vijayanagar till then, to take charge of the fledgling sultanate. After ascending the throne, he encouraged the learning and writing of Telugu like no other Muslim ruler had ever done. Himself an art and literature lover, he invited poets from all over the Deccan to his court. Also noted for his administrative skills, his regime further strengthened Golconda. He is credited with building the Hussain Sagar lake in Hyderabad.

After his death in 1580, he was succeeded by Muhammad Quli Qutb Shah. The great planner and founder of the city of Hyderabad, Muhammad's rule is known for everything that was great in the Qutb Shahi. The legend goes that a young Muhammad was enamoured by a dancer called Bhagmati, who hailed from the place where the famous Charminar now stands. To immortalize his love, he established Bhagyanagar. Bhagmati later converted to Islam and took on the name Hyder Mahal, after which later the city too was renamed Hyderabad. Not everyone, however, agrees with this tale. That apart, Muhammad Quli, like his predecessor Ibrahim, encouraged the use of Telugu, along with Arabic and Persian. An accomplished poet in Telugu himself, Muhammad compiled what is known as the first collection of Deccani poetry. After a fairly long rule of thirty-two years, Muhammad Quli died in 1612. He was survived by his daughter Hayath Bakshi Begum, who married his nephew and successor Sultan Muhammad Qutb Shah. Sultan Muhammad was a book lover who chronicled the history of the Qutb Shahi. He died early, after which his son Abdullah Qutb Shah ascended the throne at the age of just twelve.

During this period, the Mughals had set their eyes on the Deccan. Golconda faced its first major attack by them in 1656 and was forced to pay a heavy indemnity to the Mughals for survival. It was the beginning of the end of around 170 years of the Qutb Shahi. Relatively benevolent of all the five sultanates, it ended during the reign of Tana Shah, the last sultan of Golconda, when the Mughal emperor Aurangzeb seized the fortress. Tana Shah was taken prisoner and held captive first at Bidar and then at Daulatabad for twelve years. He died in captivity.

With that, the surrender of the Deccan to the Mughals was complete.

THE MOST FORMIDABLE OF all the invaders were the Mughals. Their advent, rise and further rise to greater heights make for an absolutely fascinating history for many reasons. Their roots lie somewhere in today's Uzbekistan but they made Hindustan their home, and their journey along the way has all the drama to make their story worthy of a historical blockbuster. The Mughals represent all facets of human life: the good, the bad and the ugly. It is the only empire whose impact can be felt in India even 500 years later.

The founder of the Mughal empire was Babur, a descendant of the Turco-Mongol conqueror Timur on his father's side and of Genghis Khan, the founder of the Mongol empire, on his mother's side. Babur had a very tumultuous life in Fergana, now in Uzbekistan, due to successive defeats in Samarkand. He later conquered Kabul. However, continuous failures in winning Samarkand forced Babur to scout for new regions.

Then came the opportunity from Daulat Khan Lodi, the governor of Lahore, who wanted to break free from the shackles of the Delhi sultan, Ibrahim Lodi. He sought Babur's help in capturing Delhi. Babur came down and, in the First Battle of Panipat, defeated Ibrahim Lodi to set up his own empire in Delhi. The year was 1526. He could rule only for four years and was succeeded by his son Humayun. In 1533, the new emperor personally laid the foundation stone for a new city in Delhi. He is considered the builder of the Mughal empire, although he himself had to be in exile in Persia for some time. He, however, regained the empire with the help of the Persians. At the time of his death, Humayun left behind two things: the Mughal empire that had an expanse of over 10 lakh square kilometres, and his son Akbar.

Born while his father was in exile, Akbar was only fourteen when Humayun died in 1556. He soon acquired the necessary skills that made him one of the best Mughal administrators and conquerors in history. He is the one who shaped the Mughal empire, spreading it from Afghanistan in the north to Bengal in the east, from Sindh in the west to the Godavari basin in the south. Though illiterate himself, Akbar was a great patron of artists and intellectuals and had a passion for knowledge. Legends of enduring popularity such as the singer Tansen, the minister Birbal, and others were part of his court. Fond of literature, he created an elaborate library of around 25,000 books written in Sanskrit, Urdu, Persian, Greek, Latin and Arabic, along with special facilities for women at Fatehpur Sikri. He ruled till 1605.

Akbar was succeeded by his son Salim, who is popularly known as Jahangir. His son Prince Khurram, who won Ahmednagar, was honoured with the title Shah Jahan. After Jahangir's death in October 1627, Shah Jahan inherited a vast and rich empire: perhaps the greatest empire in the world. Later in life, Shah Jahan had to witness a fierce war of succession between his two sons while on his deathbed. The winner was Aurangzeb, who marginalized his older brother Dara Shikoh.

Aurangzeb was one of the most controversial Mughal rulers. He diluted their pluralistic legacy with his strong dislike for Hindus. He had a very long reign of forty-nine years: from 1658 to 1707. It was during his rule that the Mughal empire spread all over the Indian subcontinent. But Maharashtra proved to be this great warrior's nemesis. The last powerful Mughal emperor had to spend as many as twenty-six years of his life on only one mission: defeating the Marathas. But he was never successful. Tired, exhausted and frustrated, Aurangzeb died in Ahmednagar at the age of eighty-eight on 20 February 1707 – twenty-seven years after the passing of the man who had proved to be his undoing and, even after his death, had kept the flame of freedom burning.

The man who kept the mighty Mughal from fulfilling his dream was diminutive in size but the tallest in stature. He was also the first from the south of the Vindhyas to challenge Delhi's predominance.

Enter Shivaji Raje Bhosale, also known as Chhatrapati Shivaji Maharaj.

4

O King Shivaji…

In what far-off country, upon what obscure day
I know not now,
Seated in the gloom of some Mahratta mountain-wood
O King Shivaji,
Lighting thy brow, like a lightning flash,
This thought descended
Into one virtuous rule, this divided broken distracted India,
I shall bind…

This is what Gurudev Rabindranath Tagore wrote about Shivaji many years ago. But what makes Shivaji relevant even today? What is it about him that keeps resurfacing even 350 years after his death? In the 2,000-year history of India, we have had many rulers and monarchs, but few evoke the kind of reverence Shivaji does, even among the common man. Why?

The answer, perhaps, lies in the fact that in a land that largely bred vassals Shivaji was the first to accomplish setting up his own kingdom. Not for himself but the poor peasant – the farmers who were subjected to constant harassment by rulers. He swam against the current of his time, when rulers from Kashmir to Kanyakumari were happy to share power with foreigners. He was also remarkably progressive for his time, and the rudiments of a welfare state – long before the concept in its modern sense came into being – can be found in his administration. Shivaji was the first Indian king to have understood the importance of a strong and efficient naval force.

Not many rulers have continued to inspire people as Shivaji has. He was, according to celebrated historian Sir Jadunath Sarkar, '... the last great constructive genius and nation builder that the Hindu race has produced'. Shivaji was, clearly, a man of many virtues. But to truly comprehend him, it is essential to understand the region called Maharashtra.

Around four centuries ago, Maharashtra was a stretch of land bounded on the north by the Tapti river, on the south by the Krishna and on the east by the Sina. To its west was the Arabian Sea. The small region was largely dependent on the vagaries of the monsoon. The western front, along the Konkan coast, was blessed by the rain gods but the hilly topography meant that not much could be cultivated. During the torrid summers, the land spewed fire, and it seemed like every blade of grass was roasted to shades of brown and ochre. The rocky terrain also threw up another challenge – that of travelling. Four centuries ago, needless to say, it must have been far more difficult to move from one end of the region to the other. This explains why one or two runs by cavalry units couldn't conquer the region. It also explains why those from the community in the region – the Marathas – are considered natural warriors.

Many confuse the Marathas with Marathi. Marathi is a language; the inhabitants of the region identify with it. Maratha is a community or a caste, which is politically dominant. Every Maratha is a Marathi but the converse may not be true. The popular perception about Marathas is that they are courageous, tough, and at times rough, not bothered with niceties. They were also known for their spartan lifestyle. Perennially caught in the wars and conflicts in the region – between the Bahmani empire and Vijayanagar, between the Bahmanis and the Mughals, and between various Bahmani factions – Maharashtra never found itself at peace. Till Shivaji arrived on the scene, the Marathas were fighting each other as part of the armies of the region's different empires.

LIKE MANY OTHER MARATHAS, Shahaji Bhosale had been in the service of various masters – the Nizam Shahi, the Adil Shahi and the Mughals for a while. There were many such Maratha nobles at the time who kept hopping from one sultanate to the other. Mughal emperor Jahangir died in 1627 and his son Shah Jahan succeeded him. Shah Jahan wanted to expand the empire's boundaries to the west. His armies took the fort of Daulatabad and imprisoned Nizam Shah in 1633. In the Nizam's absence, Shahaji Bhosale began to hold de facto power. He installed a young boy from the Nizam's family as the ruler and served the sultanate on his behalf. At no point does Shahaji seem to have attempted to depose the Nizam's family. Initially, he received support from Adil Shah and Qutb Shah in a bid to prevent the Mughals from entering the Deccan. But the Mughals were too strong. This realization forced Adil Shah into a pact with the Mughals. Shahaji, left in the lurch, eventually joined Adil Shah.

Shivaji, Shahaji's second son, was born in 1630, to Jijabai, the daughter of Lakhuji Jadhav, who was of another prominent Maratha family from Sindkhed. Shahaji was travelling when Jijabai gave birth to a boy in a fort in Shivner. From 1630 to 1636, Shahaji was away as he was involved in various military campaigns, leaving Shivaji and Jijabai in the care of his confidant, Dadoji Konddev.

Some historians have a different take on the family's living arrangements and their relationships. According to Sarkar, Shahaji had separated from Jijabai and had started living with Tukabai Mohite, whose son, Vyankoji, was the sole recipient of all of his father's love and affection. For Shivaji, his father was to be a stranger for many years.

This absence of a relationship with his father perhaps explains Shivaji's adoration for his mother, almost to the point of deifying her. Deprived of paternal care, he also became independent from an early age.

In 1636, the mother and son had to move to Pune as Shahaji handed over the fort at Shivner to the Mughals. Shahaji moved to Bijapur to serve Adil Shah and gave his property in Pune to Dadoji Konddev for Jijabai and the young Shivaji. At the time, Pune was in ruins. Caught between the Nizam Shahi and the Adil Shahi, the place was plundered by both armies. The areas around the city were unliveable and overrun by wild animals. Dadoji cleared the land to make it hospitable. He then appealed to people to settle in Pune, offering them long-term land leases. Slowly, the region was brought under tillage. Dadoji also ensured that the local tax was collected. He established a security system by deploying men at the outposts he had created. Pune gradually became a secure place to live.

The young Shivaji was watching and learning the craft of administration. At home, Jijabai used to read out the Ramayana and Mahabharata to him. His friends were mostly from a local community called Mavle, that is, the people from Maval. Young Shivaji roamed the region extensively with them, toughening up in the process and becoming deeply acquainted with the region and his father's jagir – a type of feudal land grant. Dadoji, worried about Shivaji's future, complained to Shahaji about his son's aimless wanderings. Shahaji reprimanded Dadoji, asking him to be more vigilant and assertive with respect to Shivaji. But Shivaji was raring to go.

By now, Shivaji had a sense of purpose. He had started sending out his men – such as Baji Pasalkar, Tanaji Malusare and Yesaji Kank – to discover weaknesses in Adil Shah-controlled forts. He captured one of Adil Shah's forts when he was just sixteen. The Torna fort in Pune district became the first of many to join what was to become Shivaji's kingdom. This act rattled Dadoji, if not Adil Shah, as Shivaji was seen acting against his father's interests.

Dadoji died in 1646. Incidentally, in the same year Adil Shah fell seriously ill, throwing the Adil Shahi into disarray. This, Shivaji realized, was a moment to be seized. With Dadoji gone, there was no one to hold him back. Shivaji soon started building another fort near Torna from the booty of 2 lakh *hun* he collected while seizing the first. He named the new fort Rajgad.

Dadoji's death presented Shivaji with another opportunity. He took complete charge of Shahaji's jagir. Still in his teens, Shivaji was to face a political challenge. Shambhuji Mohite, Shahaji's brother-in-law, refused to take orders from Shivaji after Dadoji's death. Shivaji tried a conciliatory approach but realized the futility of this path when Shambhuji said he recognized only Shahaji's orders. The king in the making wasted no time. Shivaji arrested Shambhuji, commandeered his properties and sent him to Bijapur to serve Shahaji.

The message was clear – to Adil Shah, Shahaji and other Maratha satraps serving various sultanates. Shivaji was on a mission. He seized the Chakan, Purandar and Kondana forts. Coupled with Rajgad and Torna, this brought sizeable territory under Shivaji's control. Soon, he also gained charge of the crucial Sahyadri range around Pune. Shivaji clearly realized the importance of forts for controlling the region. Next, he set his eyes on another important strategic asset – the coastline.

At the time, the coastal region of Thane was ruled by an Arab, Mulla Ahmed, who was working for Adil Shah. Mulla was away in Bijapur for quite some time as Adil Shah was recuperating. Earlier a part of the Nizam Shahi, Thane was yet to come to terms with the new regime. Shivaji snatched that opportunity from the Adil Shahi.

He sent a cavalry unit to capture Thane along with Bhiwandi. Both the cities were without protective walls. It didn't take much effort for Shivaji's men to gain control over them. The real surprise came when they attacked and seized the nearby fort of Mahuli, which was under Shahaji. With this successful foray into northern Konkan, the gates of many small forts in adjoining Colaba opened for Shivaji. The local chieftains, fed up with their rulers, invited Shivaji and offered to serve him. The most significant of these forts was at Rairi, which would later become Raigad, Shivaji's capital. This part of the Konkan was under the control of Siddis, known as the lords of the seas. Siddi forces gave Shivaji's army a tough time. In fact, it is likely that this encounter led him to set up a naval force.

Thus far, Shivaji's conquests had been largely without hiccups. In 1648, he faced his first major challenge. The news of his annexations had sent ripples across the sultanates. Adil Shah, in whose durbar Shahaji was serving, was particularly perturbed. On 6 August, Shahaji was arrested and his property and forces were commandeered and conscripted by Adil Shah's army chief, Mustafa Khan.

The popular belief is that Shahaji was arrested for his son's deeds. But Sarkar, quoting Persian sources, dismisses this claim. In these accounts, Shahaji was arrested for insubordination. He apparently refused to take orders from Khan, who on that morning had sent Bajirao Ghorpade to arrest him. He was fast asleep when Ghorpade's troops raided his camp. Shahaji tried to run away but was overcome by Ghorpade, who handcuffed him to present him before Adil Shah. Afzal Khan, who transported Shahaji to Bijapur, was later killed by Shivaji.

Whatever the reason behind Shahaji's arrest, it undoubtedly put Shivaji in a fix. It seemed as though the eighteen-year-old warrior had just two options. He could save his father by surrendering – Adil Shah would release Shahaji if his son complied – or he could leave him at the mercy of his captors and pursue his dream of setting up an independent kingdom. Shivaji's greatness shone through in creating a third option. And the tool he employed was diplomacy: he befriended his enemy's enemy.

Shivaji wrote to the Mughals, requesting them to pardon his father, who had once served them. He assured the Mughals that he would join them along with him. Given their animosity towards Adil Shah, the Mughals fell for the trick. In parallel, Shivaji held parleys with Ranadulla Khan, one of the most senior courtiers in Bijapur. He too was instrumental in securing Shahaji's release. All the while, till Shahaji was released, Shivaji kept a low profile. But after that came another major chapter in Shivaji's life – the conquest of Jawali.

Jawali is an important principality and served as a crucial link between western Maharashtra and south Konkan. It was the fiefdom of a rich Maratha family, the Mores, who ruled the area on behalf of the Adil Shahi. Over eight generations, the Mores had filled their coffers as rulers of the hilly, densely forested region. Their over 10,000-strong cavalry and the difficult terrain made it nearly impossible for them to be defeated in war. But Shivaji wanted Jawali for its logistical importance. Diplomacy was not an option since the Mores were headstrong and unlikely to listen to another Maratha who, according to them, did not match up to them. The only path left for Shivaji was that of deception. And this meant killing Chandrarao More.

Shivaji plotted to exploit More's weaknesses. He sent Raghunath Korade, one of his trusted aides, to him with a marriage proposal. Shivaji offered to marry More's daughter as a way to form an alliance. Korade spent a few days with More finalizing the nitty-gritty of the marriage. Meanwhile, he asked Shivaji to camp nearby and be ready to attack. Once he knew Shivaji was in Mahabaleshwar with a small battalion, Korade went to More one night on the pretext of planning the wedding. After conversation – and alcohol – had sufficiently lulled his mark, Korade pulled out his dagger and stabbed More, killing him on the spot. More's younger brother was injured. Korade and his accomplice quickly left the scene. Before the Mores' lethargic army could realize the gravity of the situation, Korade successfully gave Shivaji the all-clear. With his agile and alert band, Shivaji seized the moment and attacked Jawali. Within six hours, he gained control of the town. Most of the More family were taken as prisoners to Pune. The rest were killed. With Jawali, Shivaji now had easy access to south Konkan. But with this conquest he antagonized the senior Adil Shahi general Afzal Khan, who would later draw him back to Jawali.

After the victory at Jawali, Shivaji wasted no time. He entered Ratnagiri and, without having to fight, gained control of the principality. The successes gave Shivaji's kingdom a sizeable sphere of influence over important regions in western Maharashtra, along with the equally important Konkan, barring the ports. Thereafter Shivaji opened up yet another front – this time, with the Mughals.

AFTER ADIL SHAH'S DEATH in November 1656, the Delhi-based governor for the Deccan set his sights on Bijapur. The governor was Prince Aurangzeb. As he was beginning to make major plans to annex the Adil Shahi, Shivaji sensed an opportunity. He realized that since Aurangzeb's forces would be concentrating on the Adil Shahi, they would leave another front exposed. To exploit the situation, Shivaji played a double game. He engaged Aurangzeb with a plea to take him under his protection. At the same time, he started raiding Mughal territories. As an astute strategist and warrior, Shivaji probably sensed that his eventual battle would be with the Mughals and he could not be content with his victories over the Adil Shahi.

Aurangzeb was equally sharp in his assessment of Shivaji. The Mughal was fully aware of the danger Shivaji posed. How right he was became evident soon enough.

While the Mughals were busy planning an assault on the Adil Shahi, Shivaji's men plundered the Nagar region, which the former had annexed. The loot of Ahmednagar, once the capital of the Nizam Shahi and an important centre for the Mughals, was the most daring. Shivaji led his men in plundering Junnar and took away 3 lakh *huns* in cash along with 200 horses and a lot of jewellery. Clearly, Shivaji had caught the Mughals off guard. Enraged, Aurangzeb sent reinforcements to Nagar but Shivaji had fled by then. The move, however, worked as it prevented any further attacks. In one battle in the region, Shivaji had to flee after many of his men were killed by Mughal forces.

It was a case of bad timing for the Mughals. Aurangzeb had to rush to Delhi – Emperor Shah Jahan was critically ill and the struggle for the throne was getting bitter. At this juncture, Shivaji once again sought the Mughals' forgiveness and offered to accept their suzerainty. Aurangzeb could neither accept nor reject Shivaji's proposal. For over two years, 1658 and 1659, he was entangled in one of the most bitter wars of succession in the subcontinent. This provided Shivaji some much-needed breathing space before facing his next challenge.

Afzal Khan, one of Adil Shah's seniormost nobles, had left Bijapur with a pledge to get hold of Shivaji 'alive or dead'. Shivaji faced his first existential crisis. He was aware of Afzal Khan's abilities and strength. Khan was familiar with the terrain as well, having served as the governor of Wai, near Kolhapur. He adopted a two-pronged strategy to defeat Shivaji. First, he wanted to destroy the faith common men and women had in Shivaji, which was the backbone of Maratha rule. The other challenge was on the military front. To meet the first objective, Khan started destroying temples, hoping that people would lose their confidence in Shivaji's ability to protect them. He launched this mission by demolishing the shrine of the goddess Bhavani at Tuljapur, the presiding deity of Shivaji's family. He then uprooted the Lord Vitthal temple at Pandharpur. His idea was simple: provoke Shivaji and force him into an open, face-to-face battle.

Shivaji's strategy was to not let Khan set the terms of engagement. While Afzal Khan was busy in looting Maratha territory, Shivaji moved and confined himself at Pratapgad, the fort he had built after defeating the Mores of Jawali. It was a mind game. Shivaji knew Khan would come all the way to Pratapgad, since it fell in the region once ruled by him. The tactic worked. Khan offered to meet Shivaji with a promise to pardon him. The person mediating between the two was Krishnaji Bhaskar, a confidant of Khan's. Up to that point, Shivaji was in a fix and didn't know how to handle Khan. He was fully aware that taking on his forces would be futile and accepting his proposal to surrender would be fatal. The person who helped Shivaji decide his future course of action was Bhaskar.

Shivaji met Bhaskar secretly and invoked religious solidarity. Bhaskar was a Hindu. Shivaji, in a one-on-one meeting, appealed to him to reveal Khan's intentions. Bhaskar hinted at Khan's malicious intent. This left Shivaji with only one option – Afzal Khan could not leave their meeting alive.

In a display of excellent planning and strategizing, Shivaji caught Khan completely unawares. A prisoner of his own bravado, he was killed by Shivaji in what can be described as one of the most audacious acts in war history. But Shivaji's men didn't stop at killing Khan. The entire army, ready for war, pounded his panic-stricken men caught in the deep forest around Jawali. The two men who led the heroic attack on Khan's army were Moropant Trimbak Pingle and Netaji Palkar – one a Brahmin and the other a Maratha. In three hours, Shivaji's men killed around 3,000 soldiers in the battle. Those who surrendered were spared. The victory over Afzal Khan was important not only strategically but also economically – it won the Marathas sixty-five elephants, 4,000 horses and 1,200 camels along with 10 lakh rupees in cash. As was the tradition, all the captured men were sent back to their homes.

Afzal Khan's defeat triggered a wave of exultation across the Maratha region. Shivaji soon became the subject of folklore and ballads. Many credited him with divine powers. But Shivaji was not one to rest on his laurels. With the death of a senior noble like Afzal Khan, the Adil Shahi was considerably weakened. Shivaji wasted no time. His men stormed the Konkan and Kolhapur regions, further wearing down the Adil Shahi. Soon after Afzal Khan's death, by February 1660, Shivaji captured Panhala fort near Kolhapur and some parts of the Konkan region. Keeping an eye on Shivaji's successes was Aurangzeb, who had won the war of succession in Delhi.

While Shivaji was planning his strategy for dealing with Afzal Khan, Aurangzeb had brought about one important change in his jagir. He had appointed his maternal uncle, Shaista Khan, viceroy of the Deccan. Shaista Khan had experience of governing the Malwa and Deccan regions. But before he could enter the Deccan, Shivaji had to fend off another threat.

Siddi Jauhar was a slave-turned-warlord who had defied Adil Shah to snatch the jagir of Kurnool in present-day Andhra Pradesh. He now wanted to serve Adil Shah in return for royal recognition of his authority over Kurnool. He offered to lay siege to catch Shivaji. On the one hand the Mughals were approaching Pune and on the other Adil Shahi forces led by Siddi were marching rapidly to pin Shivaji down. This was May, at the peak of summer, 1660.

The two-pronged attack forced Shivaji to confine himself to Panhala fort. Siddi laid siege around it, blocking every access point. Shivaji was trapped and could not even send others out. Helpless, he wrote a letter to Siddi pretending to negotiate his exit. Siddi fell for this trap. He promised a safe passage to Shivaji, provided that he accepted Adil Shahi overlordship. Shivaji personally went to see Siddi and pledged his cooperation. However, this left Adil Shah enraged – Siddi was exceeding his brief. As a result, Adil Shah himself thought of undertaking a campaign to teach Shivaji a lesson. But before Adil Shah could reach Panhala, Shivaji, in another audacious act, breached the siege and escaped.

Siddi was enraged when he got to know of Shivaji's flight. He sent two teams after him. Shivaji wanted to reach Vishalgad, another fort that was close by. This was a daunting task as Siddi's men were after him. On the way to Vishalgad was a deep, narrow gorge with steep sides. It was difficult for the cavalry to cross the gorge. Shivaji asked Baji Prabhu Deshpande, his military commander, to block Siddi's approaching army till he reached Vishalgad. Deshpande was left with 5,000 men to defend the ravine and Shivaji. In a gallant act, he fought to the end and died only after receiving a gunfire signal from Vishalgad which indicated that Shivaji had reached safely.

Shivaji had overcome one threat only to be faced with another. Shaista Khan left Ahmednagar with a sizeable army for Pune. His plan was simple – capture all the critical approaches to Pune, forcing Shivaji to come out in the open. By June, Shaista Khan had seized most of the area around Pune without much opposition from the Marathas. As monsoon approached, he thought of spending the rainy season in Pune's vicinity. Meanwhile, he had captured Chakan fort and the surrounding areas. Content, Shaista Khan retired to Pune and made Shivaji's childhood house his home. Being a true Mughal subedar, he had with him his harem and female guards too.

Shivaji used an unprecedented strategy to deal with Shaista Khan. He chose about a thousand of his strongest and bravest men. Two supporting divisions were posted on either side of the Mughal deployment. Legend has it that Shivaji's men joined a marriage procession that was to pass by the place where Shaista Khan was camping. With just around 400 men, Shivaji entered the camp, whose outer ring was manned by a contingent led by Maharaja Jaswant Singh. After midnight they raided the place.

According to one version, it was Ramzan and many of Shaista Khan's men were fast asleep after the day of fasting. Maratha soldiers slaughtered the security guards and Shivaji entered Khan's bedroom with his men. The first to realize something was amiss were the women with Khan who woke him up. In the melee, Shivaji attacked Khan with a sword. Khan kept his life but lost his fingers. Many from Khan's contingent, including his son, were killed in the commotion that followed. Khan was taken away by some women slaves and Shivaji, without wasting any more time, withdrew from the scene along with his men. The Mughals were shell-shocked.

Historians like Jadunath Sarkar hint that Maharaja Jaswant Singh, whose men were manning the outer ring, might have looked the other way when Shivaji was carrying out the raid. After all, Jaswant Singh had a 10,000-strong army with him and none of his men even attempted to prevent the attack. However, there isn't much proof to support this theory. Whatever the factors behind Shivaji's success, it helped his stature grow across the length and breadth of the country. Many were simply bewildered by Shivaji's courage. At the same time, a pall of gloom descended on the Mughal camp. Unsurprisingly, Aurangzeb was upset with Shaista Khan's humiliation. He transferred his uncle to Bengal without even meeting him. Khan left Pune in the first half of January 1664.

The attack on Shaista Khan was a defining moment in Shivaji's life – only to be followed by an even more seminal one.

5

Hindavi Swaraj

Shivaji was not a man to rest on past glory. As Aurangzeb was busy shifting his governors, he sensed another opportunity. He needed money. After being in war mode for well over three years, during which attacks by Afzal Khan and Shaista Khan had caused serious damage to his small empire, now it was time to reinvest. Shivaji did something else that was unheard of.

Before Shaista Khan could depart from the Deccan, Shivaji personally led an attack on one of the richest cities in India then: Surat. He, however, chose not to attack Surat fort, which was guarded well. He set his eyes on Surat city, relatively unprotected and a place of abundant wealth. The fact that the city alone was paying a lakh of rupees every month to the Mughal exchequer is a testimony to its wealth. Despite its riches, it was totally unprotected. Inayat Khan, the governor of the town, was quite laid-back. Shivaji's efficient intelligence system had provided him all the details of the city.

The news of his arrival in the early hours of 5 January 1664 shook Surat. The rich and the powerful of the city made their way to the fort, while the poor fled. Inayat Khan tried to broker a deal with Shivaji by offering him a ransom. The trick didn't work as Shivaji arrested the messenger sent by the Mughal governor. By the time Inayat Khan got wind of this, Shivaji's army was knocking at Surat's doors. Khan too decided to flee. The fire, fury and speed of Shivaji's team hardly gave the people of the city any time to defend themselves. Shivaji, leading a strong cavalry of 4,000 men, hit Surat like a storm.

It is mind-boggling even today if one tries to understand the route he would have likely taken then: from the Deccan descending into Thane and thereafter marching via Mahuli and Jawahar to reach Surat's doorstep within a day. A night before, he sent his messengers to the city with letters asking the rich traders to see him personally once he was in Surat. They carried no demand but an imminent threat: the city would be set on fire if they failed to meet him.

The threat was actually carried out. Surat turned into a ghost town as almost all the residents fled, barring a few exceptions – some English and Dutch men held on to their warehouses and prepared to take on Shivaji's company. But for three days the forces plundered the city, looting house after house and setting it on fire. Some of the mansions of the wealthy were so big and packed with such enormous amounts of jewellery, gold and other riches that it took the Marathas two days to dig the wealth out. Thc only obstacle came from the Englishmen who not only saved their own turf but went on to challenge Shivaji and attack his troops. Though angered, Shivaji ignored their posturing because by then he had enough wealth to carry back home.

There was, however, a small drama before he returned. Inayat Khan sent a mercenary masquerading as a messenger to kill Shivaji. But just as he tried to attack Shivaji with a hidden dagger, the Maratha warrior's bodyguard chopped his hands off as they were slicing through the air. The profusely bleeding assailant, however, did hit Shivaji, drenching him in his blood. In the ensuing melee, the blood-soaked Shivaji started a rumour that he was wounded. Enraged Marathas vowed to kill everyone in Surat. It took a while for Shivaji to convey his well-being to his men and avoid a likely massacre, for Shivaji, unlike past invaders, was not interested in harassing and killing innocent men and women. His aim was money. Having mopped up over a crore of rupees and significant amounts of jewels, he left the city on the fourth day after his arrival. Soon the Mughal army too reached Surat. The shocked citizens, however, refused to return, fearing another raid by Shivaji.

Later in the year, Shivaji looted Ahmednagar, another prominent city under the Mughals. Such was Shivaji's widespread terror that one Englishman wrote about the Maratha having 'wings and airy body' which gave him the ability to be at many places simultaneously. Another one observed that Shivaji had 'an ability to impose strange labour upon himself that he may endure hardship, and also exercises his chiefest men, that he flies to and fro with incredible dexterity'. Rumours also spread that he was going to attack Goa and Vasai next. But he had no such plans. He had his eyes on the Mughals, who were expected to send a bigger army to contain him.

AURANGZEB HAD MIRZA RAJA Jai Singh in mind to take on Shivaji. Jai Singh was a Hindu Rajput known for his commitment to the Mughals. He was the son of Maha Singh and great-grandson of Man Singh, who had served in Akbar's court. Though Aurangzeb had great confidence in him, he was assisted by Diler Khan and many others of his faith, probably to prevent any overtures, should the Maratha warrior play the religion card.

Jai Singh was assigned an army of over 14,000 men. Unlike others who had led attacks on Shivaji earlier, he was very focused and wasn't interested in merrymaking. He left Delhi on 30 September 1664 and reached Aurangabad on 10 February 1665. Having stayed there for a while, he marched to Pune. He was in the Deccan city on 3 March. He strategically spread his army from the Deccan up to a point from where he could easily enter the Konkan region. Though he had no plans of getting there, his move kept two of his rivals guessing: one was Shivaji and the other Adil Shah, who was equally wary of the cool-headed Rajput noble. In reality, he never wanted to open another front with Adil Shah or enter the Konkan, which according to him was just a small limb of Shivaji while the Deccan was the main body. Jai Singh wanted to attack the body.

Simultaneously, he had another plan. He sent out Hindu Brahmin emissaries to various chieftains in the Deccan. The move was aimed at scaring as well as wooing them into a battle against Shivaji. His idea was to create a coalition of the Maratha warrior's enemies. It was not that he needed any military help from them; it was more of a strategic move. He also wrote to the Europeans in Surat and elsewhere who were terrorized by Shivaji. The manoeuvre worked. Many small satraps, like the Mores of Jawali, promised to join Jai Singh to nail Shivaji down.

As he was planning to leave Pune, Jai Singh received news that Shivaji was moving to attack the Mughal territory around Lohagad. This delayed Jai Singh's departure. He extended his stay in Pune to chalk out his next move. He then shifted to nearby Saswad, moving on to Shirwal, where the Mores joined him. He had deputed Diler Khan to search for a place to set up the Mughal camp. Khan approached Purandar fort, where the Marathas too had posts set up, and was welcomed with an attack that led him to ask for reinforcements. Jai Singh sent more troops, along with his son Kirat Singh, to assist Khan. Eager to take on the Marathas, though, Khan launched a counterattack even before the additional troops could join. The ensuing battle prompted Jai Singh too to move towards Purandar.

But around this time he came to know that Shivaji's commander Netaji Palkar was moving towards Paranda fort in Osmanabad. He quickly decided to send a team to engage with Netaji. The idea was to open many fronts and thereby force Shivaji to spreading his men thin. It, however, didn't work as Netaji immediately changed his plan of moving to Paranda once he got to know of Jai Singh's designs. The Mughals had to return to Jai Singh. Now, Jai Singh concentrated fully on Purandar fort. He launched a heavy bombardment that eventually broke its defence, after which Diler Khan led his men to the fort. As a prelude to the massive attack which was to follow, Jai Singh's men had taken control of the small Rudramal fort, also called Vajragad.

The visiting Rajput noble had a two-pronged strategy: on the one hand he allowed Diler Khan to capture small forts around Purandar while on the other he created flying squads to pillage the villages around. The plan was to force Shivaji to come out in the open.

With no sign of Jai Singh loosening his grip on Purandar, and with his flying squads burning villages and fields, killing farmers and reaching up to Rajgad and Rohira, Shivaji was left with no option but to open negotiations with the Mughals. Earlier, even before Jai Singh had reached the Deccan, Shivaji had tried to open a dialogue with him twice, but the Rajput was too strong to budge. Now the situation had turned grim. Diler Khan had attacked Purandar with troops of 5,000 Afghans. Murar Baji, who was in charge at Purandar, tried in vain to prevent Khan. The valour and the grit displayed by him actually stunned Khan, who invited him to cross over with the promise of a high post in Aurangzeb's durbar. Murar Baji not only rejected the offer but went on to attack Khan in a one-on-one fight. One of Khan's arrows finally killed him. Purandar fell to the mighty Mughals, forcing Shivaji to expedite negotiations.

For over five years, Shivaji had been constantly at war, with no space or time to consolidate his gains. And now here was Jai Singh, unwilling to accept anything short of complete surrender. He kept ignoring or rejecting Shivaji's overtures. But he was equally aware that he needed to respect Shivaji because pushing him into a corner could backfire. There was also the danger of Shivaji joining hands with the Adil Shahi forces to challenge the Mughals. Jai Singh's intelligence network had informed him of Adil Shah's promise of every possible support to Shivaji should he decide to take on the Rajput. He sensed the danger and agreed to meet Shivaji.

The meeting between the two took place on 11 June 1665 near Shivapur, which today lies on the Pune–Kolhapur highway. Jai Singh sent his secretaries Udairaj and Ugrasen to convey a clear message: he would meet Shivaji only if he was willing to surrender all his forts. Shivaji replied that he was willing to join imperial service and many of his forts would add to imperial supremacy. On hearing this, Jai Singh sent the paymaster of the army, Jani Beg, to usher in the

Maratha warrior. He had readied his team led by Diler Khan and Kirat Singh to launch a massive attack on Purandar at the same time that Shivaji entered his tent so that he could see his prime fort being demolished. It had its desired effect. Shivaji offered to surrender the fort because many of his men were still camping there with their families and he wanted to save their lives. Jai Singh agreed to Shivaji's plea. Soon some 7,000 Maratha men and women were asked to vacate the fort, which was taken over by Khan's men. Following this, Shivaji's terms of surrender too were finalized. It was quite humiliating, to say the least, for the Maratha warrior.

According to the deal, Shivaji was to surrender twenty-three of his twenty-five forts, along with the land adjoining them that yielded a revenue of 4 lakh *huns*. Moreover, it was decided that Shivaji's son Sambhaji would enter Mughal service and Shivaji himself would perform any military duty assigned to him by the emperor. He sought the emperor's decree for him to retain the forts that he had conquered from Adil Shah and which were never under the Nizam Shahi or the Mughals later. In lieu of this, Shivaji offered to pay 40 lakh *huns* in annual instalments of 3 lakh *huns*. Aurangzeb's acceptance of the proposal gave Shivaji the solace that this territory would not be annexed by the Mughals.

While Jai Singh was negotiating Shivaji's surrender, he had requested Aurangzeb to issue a shahi firman, a royal order, to honour Shivaji, indicating his submission. The fact that the firman and the robe of honour sent by Aurangzeb arrived the day after Shivaji's surrender showed Jai Singh's meticulous planning. Shivaji, respecting royal etiquette, walked barefoot to accept the firman and the robe. Jai Singh and Diler Khan also presented him with an elephant, two horses, a sword and a bejewelled dagger. Soon, starting with Kondana, Shivaji handed over his forts one by one to Jai Singh's men.

It was a complete surrender for Shivaji in less than three months. And that was not all. Soon Shivaji had to offer his services in the Mughal mission against Adil Shah of Bijapur. The interesting point to note is that in all the meetings with Jai Singh and Diler Khan, the Maratha fighter went completely unarmed. It was a deliberate measure deployed to build confidence by a man who had killed Afzal Khan in a similar meeting. Soon, as per the terms of the surrender, over 9,000 Mavales led by Shivaji and Netaji Palkar joined the Mughals as Jai Singh left for Bijapur.

But Shivaji was in for yet another jolt, this time from his trusted lieutenant Netaji Palkar, who defected to the Adil Shahi for the lure of 4 lakh *huns*. Just before that Shivaji had faced a humiliating defeat at Panhala near Kolhapur. His attack was met by Adil Shah's men with equal vigour, and hundreds of Mavales were killed. It was reckless to keep fighting, Shivaji realized. He retracted. And there was the news of Netaji defecting to Adil Shah. By then, Jai Singh too was acquainted with his skills and valour. He tried luring him for the Mughals by offering him cash and a commandership. But then he seems to have asked himself how difficult the situation would become if Shivaji too decided to do that. He must have sensed that a reawakened Adil Shahi and Qutb Shahi joined by Shivaji would spell doom for the Mughals. To prevent that, Shivaji needed to be pampered. Jai Singh had a unique thought. Could the Maratha be induced to visit the emperor? He conveyed his wish to Aurangzeb. And much to Jai Singh's surprise, he welcomed it.

THUS CAME ANOTHER IMPORTANT chapter in Shivaji's life – the time to present himself before Aurangzeb in his court along with his young son Sambhaji. He wasn't sure of Aurangzeb; no one from his team was. A person who had eliminated his own brother and heir to the throne could just as easily pose a huge danger to Shivaji and his son too. Should he be going to meet the emperor at all? Another reason Shivaji didn't want to go to Agra was his total aversion to bowing before the Mughal king. Shivaji was ferociously independent and a man with a tremendous amount of self-respect. For him, it was too much to stand in queue with folded hands and offer *kurnisaat* to the Mughal.

The only reason Shivaji finally accepted the invite was Jai Singh. The Rajput noble wanted Aurangzeb to offer Shivaji the viceroyship of the Deccan. The Maratha warrior was planning to set up his own independent sovereign empire, but he couldn't avoid going to Agra for strategic reasons – even though many of his close associates warned him about the dangers of going into Aurangzeb's durbar. It was unlikely he would return safe and sound, he was cautioned. History is unaware of the likely gains of going to Agra that Shivaji thought of. What is known, however, is a solemn commitment made by Jai Singh about Shivaji's and his son's safety while in Agra. By now, Shivaji and Jai Singh had developed a kind of bond and were comfortable in each other's company. This factor may have finally led Shivaji to acquiesce to the visit. What unfolded next revealed his mind, forethought and organizational skills.

Before leaving for Agra, Shivaji ensured that his officials wouldn't need his guidance or orders in his absence. Such was the system laid down that everything, including the management of forts and so on, would go on uninterrupted even if he was killed or imprisoned. All powers were vested in his mother, Jijabai. She was to be the acting regent in Shivaji's absence. Moropant Pingle was the Peshwa, or prime minister; Niloji Sondev was the majumdar, or the treasurer; and Annaji Datto was entrusted with the responsibility of the seal. The killedars, or those in charge of forts, were directed to be vigilant and to take orders only from Jijabai or Moropant. Shivaji even conducted surprise checks. With all arrangements in place, he along with Sambhaji left in March 1666 for the most awaited – and feared – visit to Agra.

On 9 May he reached Agra. Three days later he was slated to visit Aurangzeb's court. The day happened to be the emperor's fiftieth birthday as per the lunar calendar. The durbar was immaculately decked up in royal splendour. The visiting nobles, retainers and others were dressed for the occasion. Shivaji and Sambhaji were ushered in by Jai Singh's son Kuvar Ram Singh, who was to look after them. Shivaji offered 1,500 gold coins and 6,000 rupees as *nazrana*, a gift, for the Mughal emperor, but was given nothing in return. He was then taken right up to Aurangzeb's throne, where he offered *kurnisaat*, after which he was led to his designated place to stand along with others. Much to Shivaji's surprise – and humiliation – he was placed in the company of mid-level officials and not given the treatment suited to a visiting sovereign.

Ram Singh informed him that he had been given a place alongside commanders of 5,000 soldiers – *panj hazaris*. Shivaji lost his cool right there in the durbar. He pointed out that even his young son was offered *panj hazari* as per the Purandar agreement. Netaji also was one. This was too much for the self-respecting Shivaji. After all, he was an independent ruler. This was not the welcome he had anticipated. What was the need to come all the way to Agra to be given such lowly treatment, Shivaji is known to have thundered.

Ram Singh, alarmed by the breach of royal etiquette, tried to pacify Shivaji. There are two versions of what happened next. According to one set of historians, Shivaji, quaking with anger, fell to the floor. Another set believes that an angry Shivaji left the durbar. Whichever might be true, both agree on how the spectacle ended. Responding to the commotion caused by Shivaji's outburst, Aurangzeb is believed to have ordered Ram Singh to move Shivaji to an adjacent anteroom and sprinkle rose water on him to get him back to his senses. Ram Singh tried explaining to the emperor how the Deccani Maratha was unfamiliar with royal rituals and that he be allowed to leave the durbar.

A furious Shivaji is believed to have said that he preferred death to the utter humiliation. He also accused Aurangzeb of breach of faith. At the same time, the whole episode only antagonized the Mughal emperor, who became more and more wary of the visiting Marathas. Shivaji was placed under house arrest and Ram Singh was given the responsibility of keeping an eye on him, though there were no restrictions on Sambhaji's movements. Now Shivaji had only one thing in mind: how to make an escape along with his son.

Some advised him to offer large tracts of land to Aurangzeb in return for his release, while others advised caution. After all,

Aurangzeb was not a man who could be easily swayed. Shivaji even asked for a one-on-one meeting with the emperor. He tried to woo the prime minister, Jafar Khan, who was married to Shaista Khan's sister. She, with her brother's fate in mind, told Jafar Khan never to meet Shivaji. Nothing worked. And to make matters worse for Shivaji, a large contingent of security guards along with artillery was posted outside his residence. The situation put Jai Singh in an awkward position. It was on his word that Shivaji had come all the way to Agra. He started lobbying for Shivaji's safe release. You are not going to gain anything either by arresting or killing Shivaji, he wrote to Aurangzeb. He was also worried that after a point Shivaji's men would approach Adil Shah or Qutb Shah and gang up against the Mughals. Aurangzeb, however, was willing to wait.

Shivaji, on the other hand, wasn't. He decided to try his own ways. Having consistently failed in getting a pardon from the emperor, he sought permission to send his Maratha contingent back to the Deccan. Aurangzeb was happy. This meant fewer men to keep an eye on, he must have thought. Once his men had departed, Shivaji pretended to have taken ill. He started sending out sweetmeats in huge baskets to Brahmins in Agra every evening. The guards initially searched these baskets but later started allowing them to go out unchecked. This was the moment Shivaji had been waiting for.

On 19 August he sent out a message that he was seriously ill and should not be disturbed. Hiroji Farzand, one of his close confidants, lay in bed in place of him while he and Sambhaji escaped in two of the sweetmeat baskets that went out in the evening. From a remote spot outside the city, Shivaji and Sambhaji made their way to a nearby village where a trusted aide, Niraji Ravaji, was waiting for them with two horses. All of them moved to a jungle close by to discuss the plan further: Shivaji and Sambhaji along with three officials disguised themselves as sadhus with ashes all over and moved towards Mathura, while the rest of their associates made their way towards the Deccan.

Back in Agra, Hiroji lay in bed for well over twenty-four hours pretending to be Shivaji. On 20 August, he and his servants changed their attire and walked out, asking the guards not to disturb Shivaji. After a while the guards realized there was no sign of life inside and there weren't any visitors coming either. It dawned on them that Shivaji had fled. Aurangzeb was informed. Expectedly, the emperor was livid. He sent out large contingents of men to track Shivaji down en route to the Deccan.

Shivaji had anticipated this. So he took a completely different route. Instead of the usual Agra–Malwa–Gujarat/Khandesh route, he moved eastwards to Mathura. And from there to Allahabad, Benares, Gaya, Puri, Gondwana and then towards the Deccan. On the way, he and his associates kept changing their disguise – sadhus, traders or something else. Towards the end of December Shivaji reached Rajgad. Sambhaji was not with him. It was too tough a journey for the young boy. So Shivaji had left him at Mathura with his Brahmin acquaintances and planned his journey back separately. He spread a canard about Sambhaji's death on the way. He went into mourning too for his departed son. The story had its intended impact. Everybody, mainly the Mughals, bought it. A few months later, Shivaji arranged for his safe journey back to the Deccan as a Brahmin from Mathura.

Shivaji's escape from Agra left immense regret and lifelong pain in Aurangzeb's heart. But if Aurangzeb was hurt, Jai Singh was devastated. It was a double whammy for the Rajput. He first failed in invading Bijapur and then had to contend with Shivaji's escape from Agra, for which his son Ram Singh was blamed. This left Jai Singh permanently disgraced in Aurangzeb's eyes.

As the year 1667 began, the political situation in the Deccan was significantly altered: Jai Singh had weakened, Diler Khan had returned and Adil Shah was confused. For over two years, Shivaji didn't do anything to precipitate the situation. He was in no mood to start yet another war. He wanted peace and to set his house in order. Between 1667 and 1669, he built the framework on which his would-be kingdom would rest.

Then war with the Mughals broke out again in January 1670. The first major success was the recapture of Kondana near Pune, which

Shivaji had been forced to surrender under the Purandar treaty. The campaign to conquer Kondana was launched by the legendary Tanaji Malusare, who led a small team of just around 300 Mavales. In an audacious move, they scaled the fort from the less frequented side and surprised the guards up there. Around 1,200 Rajputs were slain and Tanaji too lost his life in the battle. But Kondana came under Shivaji again. In three months, Purandar too was won back. With time Shivaji witnessed differences cropping up among Mughal subedars in the Deccan. And he needed resources to build his kingdom.

Surat proved to be an easy option. In October that year Shivaji launched his second attack on the merchant city. Aurangzeb was aware that Shivaji would revisit Surat. So he had rebuilt the protective wall around the city. But the Mughal guards were lax in their approach. As such there wasn't much resistance and the fact that many merchants had fled before the attack helped Shivaji carry out his plunder.

The only opposition came from the Dutch and English, who were resolute in guarding their godowns. Having looted the city for over three days, Shivaji's men set their eyes on British stations. Shivaji's last experience of tackling Europeans had left bitter memories. This time he was well prepared. The English officials too realized this. As a result, they plied him with lots of gifts. He reciprocated by not attacking them. On 5 October, he left Surat with a warning that he would revisit and burn down the rest of the city if the traders didn't pay him annually. Surat thereafter was in constant fear of Shivaji. Two years later Shivaji's prime minister Moropant Pingle defeated the Kolis of Ramnagar, close to Surat, and demanded huge fees from the city of traders, which witnessed yet another exodus, fearing yet another attack. During these months, Shivaji concentrated on the coastal front. Later, he attacked Burhanpur and Khandesh, to collect a huge ransom.

By then, Aurangzeb had grown more concerned about Shivaji. The second attack on Surat, followed by the raids in Khandesh, had the Mughal emperor worried. Shivaji had another strategy ready. In October 1673 he attacked west Bijapur and looted many provinces till December. The notable fight during these months was put up by Bahlol Khan, who in a bid to protect Miraj Kolhapur tried cutting Shivaji's connections to Satara and Panhala. Had he succeeded, Shivaji would have been in trouble. What followed was a famous battle led by his commander-in-chief Kudtoji Gujar, who strategically cut off Bahlol Khan's water supply. Khan enticed Gujar with the promise of a truce, managed to deceive him and escaped the siege. An upset Shivaji censured Gujar. Hurt by Shivaji's reaction, Gujar followed Khan with just six horsemen and attacked him. All of them were killed in the fight. Gujar's gallant act became a legend that is popular to date. He was then replaced by Hambirrao Mohite as commander-in-chief, who defeated Bahlol Khan in a hot pursuit, chasing him right up to Bijapur. Soon, Shivaji's men defeated Diler Khan too. Between 1664 – when Shivaji had to sign the treaty of Purandar with Jai Singh – and 1675, Shivaji not only recovered what he had had to concede to the Mughals but also went right up to Kanara and Karwar in present-day Karnataka. Shivaji now decided to crown himself as an independent king.

But what was the need for him to do that? He had conquered vast swathes of land, had many forts under him, and led a fairly large army and navy. But, for the Mughal emperor, Adil Shah and Qutb Shah, looking at Deccan from Delhi, Bijapur and Golconda, Shivaji was no more than a mere zamindar, or at most a jagirdar, serving some kingdom or the other. Besides them, many a Maratha also looked at Shivaji's Bhosale clan as rebels not worthy of much respect. So he needed to send out a message on two fronts: one domestic and the second across the Deccan to the north and south. The only way was to coronate himself.

PREPARATIONS BEGAN FOR THIS unheard-of ceremony. The auspicious day decided was 6 June 1674. Gaga Bhatta, a renowned Sanskrit pandit from Benares, was chosen as the head priest. Invitations were sent out to thousands, including British, Dutch and Portuguese officials. Shivaji had chosen Raigad as his capital fort. The who's who of the subcontinent descended there to witness the ceremony. In the early hours of 6 June, Shivaji was given a royal bath with the waters of the Ganga and other sacred rivers, brought specially for the occasion. The coronation hall was decorated with figures from Hindu mythology. On either side of the throne royal emblems were carved. As Shivaji Raje Bhosale mounted the throne, he was showered with flowers. It was picture-perfect – a grand ceremony that left everyone who watched awestruck. According to Dutch records, Shivaji spent around 52 lakh *huns* on this five-day ceremony – a small amount considering the message it sent across.

After the coronation, Shivaji was soon busy tackling the Mughals and Adil Shah once again the following year. In March 1675, he attacked Ponda in Goa, which was under Adil Shah. He arrived in Rajapur, moved to Vengurla and Kudal and laid siege on Ponda, one of the most important of Adil Shah's forts. On 26 April, Shivaji's men visited Karwar. In January 1676, as he was getting ready to tackle Bahadur Khan, sent by Aurangzeb, Shivaji fell ill. For around three months he was bedridden. He chose Satara to get that much-needed rest. By March he was back in action. Unrest in Bijapur offered him an opportunity. He didn't waste it. His army looted Athani, close to Bijapur. The reason was that Shivaji was in dire need of cash.

His coronation, though essential for political reasons, had drained his resources. He was looking for ways to replenish his treasury other than raiding Surat again. He found a land of gold on the Coromandel coast, rich in agriculture but low on security. Shivaji undertook a mission to Tanjore, where his half-brother Vyankoji had founded Maratha rule. To begin with, Shivaji wanted to go to Hyderabad to meet Qutb Shah. At first Qutb Shah was reluctant about the meeting but finally agreed, after which Shivaji began his journey from Raigad in January 1677 and reached Hyderabad the next month.

The city was lit up and brightly decorated to welcome the Maratha king, who reassured Qutb Shah of his intentions by addressing him as his elder brother. The citizens were left awestruck as Shivaji led a Maratha army of over 50,000 men richly dressed for the occasion in colourful outfits. The meeting between the two lasted for over three hours, ending in a pact they signed. Qutb Shah promised to pay Shivaji around 4.5 lakh rupees a month, along with a commitment to send a 5,000-strong army to help the Maratha in his campaign in the Kannada region. Having spent around a month in Hyderabad, Shivaji left in March for his mission further south. He travelled along the banks of the Krishna river, visiting Srisailam, one of the most revered of Hindu temples. From there he marched to Madras, reaching in May.

His men looted English godowns on the way, after which British agents called on him with presents. He then moved further south and reached Thirumalavadi, very close to Tanjore. There, Shivaji demanded a crore of rupees from the ruler of Madurai, an ally of Vyankoji's. To begin with, he was delivered an instalment of 6 lakh rupees, after which Shivaji promised to leave in peace.

Simultaneously, Shivaji had sent a message to his half-brother for a meeting and Vyankoji came calling. The Maratha king got down to business. He demanded three-fourths of what their father had left behind when he died in 1664. Vyankoji's refusal to meet the demand infuriated Shivaji, who blasted him for being subservient to Muslim rulers. The same night a scared Vyankoji fled the camp with just five security men, leaving his fleet of ministers at Shivaji's mercy. Shivaji released them with lots of gifts but captured his entire territory. By October Shivaji had captured South Arcot. Soon, North Arcot too fell into his hands. The next month he annexed Kolar, Bangalore and Balapur, which were part of his father's jagir. From there he returned home via Bellary, Dharwar and Panhala in March 1678. The southern campaign was estimated to have earned him over 20 lakh *huns* along with hundreds of forts, gold and jewellery. He then deployed his men to manage the affairs in the south.

But the jubilation of his successes was to be short-lived. Within six months of his return, Shivaji received the biggest shock of his life. In November 1678 Sambhaji defected to the Mughals. The young lad of just around nineteen, having lost his mother at an early age and left to face a tumultuous life with his father, was bordering on recklessness. Such was the situation that Shivaji had to imprison him at Panhala fort to discipline him but he escaped from there with his wife. An angry Sambhaji then joined the Mughals. The defection pained Shivaji till the end of his life. Sambhaji returned to his father after a year or so when he learnt about his likely arrest and a plan to dispatch him to Delhi. But Shivaji was in no mood to pardon his unrepentant son and jailed him again at Panhala.

Shivaji found it extremely difficult to understand Sambhaji's behaviour. He was also witnessing discord in the family. His second wife Soyarabai, the sister of his former commander-in-chief Hambirrao Mohite, resented Shivaji's love and affection for Sambhaji despite his escapades. She also had serious differences with some of Shivaji's nobles. December 1679 saw a sharp decline in Shivaji's health. Exhausted, more mentally than physically, he never recovered. On 24 March 1680 he developed severe dysentery accompanied by high fever. For the next twelve days his health only worsened and hopes of his recovery faded. On 5 April, his weakened, worn-out body gave up and Shivaji died.

But the spirit of the first Maratha king lives on even 350 years after his death.

6

Why Shivaji Matters

There have been many kings and emperors in India's history but few have been as loved and lionized as Shivaji. The reverence he evokes is close to divinity. What was so unique about him?

To be honest, his kingdom – if it can be called that – was relatively small. And yet Emperor Aurangzeb, who commanded an empire ten times the size of Shivaji's, had to come down personally to the Deccan to try and defeat the Marathas – and failed in spite of spending as many as twenty-eight years on the mission. Another interesting facet of Shivaji's legacy is the admiration he commands among vastly disparate groups of people. Hindus lay claim to him even as Muslims are not antipathic towards him. Brahmins as well as lower castes venerate him with equal zeal. He is respected by people across the political spectrum, from the left to the right.

How is it that he has inspired generations for over 350 years? There are many Shivajis who need to be looked at closely to unravel this mystery.

THE BIGGEST FACTOR – and unfortunately not one that has been looked at keenly – behind Shivaji's success was his extraordinary ability to create a feeling of ownership towards his kingdom in the mind of each and every common person. Remember that the concept of modern democracy as we know it today was not yet born anywhere in the world when Shivaji was planning to set up his kingdom. Though he proclaimed himself king, he was never an autocrat. At the time Shivaji ruled, kings fought many battles. They won some and lost others but commoners hardly had any involvement in them. Shivaji's kingdom was unique in that it made the layman feel like a stakeholder. In his day, a humble tiller would take pride in marching on to the battlefield when needed. Everyone felt the need to protect 'their' state.

And that was because it was truly the first 'indigenous' state the region had witnessed since the time of Gautamiputra Satakarni. This point needs to be understood because many think of Shivaji's as a 'Hindu' state. It wasn't – in the sense in which the religion is looked at today. Nor can he be considered a 'Marathi' king in a parochial sense. He was much more than and above any of that. Religion was never a point of conflict in his life. A good number of Muslims held high posts in his kingdom, including the top naval officials, and he had over 700 Pathans in his army. One of his personal guards too was a Muslim. In his entire life Shivaji never demolished a single mosque. Mughal historian Khafi Khan, one of Shivaji's fiercest critics who went to the extent of calling the Maratha king a 'hell dog', stated that if a copy of the Holy Quran fell into Shivaji's hands, he would keep it with respect and reverence and give it to his Muslim servants. Though, as an individual, Shivaji was a practising Hindu, he kept religion at bay when it came to his politics and social life. He had excellent relations with Qutb Shah, whom he described as an elder brother. Even as he fought Aurangzeb, he can be found reminding him of his great-grandfather Akbar, who was as liberal as Shivaji.

The relationship between Shivaji and religion can be looked at from another perspective: all through his life he had to contend more with his Hindu counterparts than his Muslim enemies. More, Jadhav, Ghorpade, Surve, Nimbalkar and others, with whom Shivaji had running feuds, were not only Hindus but Marathi as well. Thus, painting him with religious and linguistic colours undermines his greatness. On both counts, he can be described as a true liberal. The term 'secular' was yet to come into being but what Shivaji practised was true secularism. He didn't kill Afzal Khan because he was a Muslim; he felt the need to eliminate him because he posed a serious danger to his kingdom. It is easy to perceive everything he did through the prism of religion. And this is often done deliberately to portray him in a particular manner. But had that in fact been the reality, he would have been just another ruler in history. His greatness lies in rising above religious and linguistic considerations. These parameters fall short when assessing a man of his stature.

There is another reason for this. When Aurangzeb, with an army of over a lakh, landed in the Deccan to eliminate Shivaji's relatively small kingdom, the majority in his forces were Hindus and Marathi-speaking. Many of his nobles were Hindus. And so neither Aurangzeb nor the Marathas viewed the battle ahead as a Hindu-versus-Muslim one. One more point to be noted is that Aurangzeb was also fighting against Adil Shah and Qutb Shah, who were Muslims. It makes no sense to give Shivaji's battle a religious colour; it was always invaders against locals.

And thus comes the important point: that Shivaji's was a truly indigenous state. Many quote him describing his kingdom as 'Hindavi Swarajya' to ascribe religious motives to his political thoughts. But what he meant by Hindavi Swarajya was its indigenous nature. To be clear, Aurangzeb and quite a few of his forefathers too were born and brought up in Hindustan, but they never considered themselves Hindustani. They were the conquerors and India the conquered land. The difference between the Mughals and Shivaji is this. For the latter, his region was his homeland and setting up an independent kingdom meant freeing it from the clutches of foreigners. This is what he meant by dubbing his state 'Hindavi Swarajya' – and also the reason why Aurangzeb spent his life trying to overpower Shivaji and his people more than any other local king. For, fighting him meant fighting the spirit of freedom.

Shivaji was the first Indian king of the time to think of and execute language reforms. At a time when Persian had become the de facto official language thanks to the Mughals, he made special efforts to raise his mother tongue's stature. The Marathi in use then was heavily Persianized, even to the extent of its literature. Shivaji took a decision to purify the language. In 1677, he published the *Rajya Vyavahar Kosha*, a kind of thesaurus that provided Marathi substitutes for Persian words. Historian V.K. Rajwade has compiled the following data: before the advent of Shivaji, the number of Marathi words in circulation vis-à-vis Persian was just about 14.4 per cent. The figure rose to 93.7 per cent after Shivaji. Earlier there were 202 Persian words which were frequently used in official business as against just around 34 Marathi ones. Due to Shivaji's efforts, the number of Persian words fell to just 8 while the number of Marathi ones rose to 119.

At the same time, Shivaji never considered himself to be the leader of Marathi-speaking people alone. He saw himself as a Hindavi king – native, indigenous, born of the soil. He expanded his kingdom up to Tanjore in the south and wanted to stretch its boundaries up to Kashi in the north. No ruler of the Marathi region before or after Shivaji, with the sole exception of Gautamiputra Satakarni, dreamt of spreading his empire over such a vast area. Limiting a ruler of Shivaji's calibre to a particular religion or region means confining him to the margins. And that would be grossly unfair to the great man.

TURNING TO SOME OTHER striking aspects of Shivaji's life, it is interesting to note that he took a public pledge to set up a Hindavi Swarajya in 1645. This means he was just fifteen when he first expressed his desire to do so and must have been thinking along those lines for some time before that. He started handling his father's jagir from 1642 under the guidance of Dadoji Konddev. He spent the five years from 1642 to 1647 streamlining the regional systems of Bara Maval, a province near Pune. Constant wars had ravaged the region, with its agricultural land too becoming completely uncultivable. Shivaji revitalized the whole area, providing seeds and saplings to farmers along with the necessary equipment. Once the land became cultivable, he also set rules regarding how much the farming community should be contributing back to the state. As he was laying the rules, he ensured that the farmers' ready-to-harvest crops would not be looted by thugs, a practice which was rampant during those days. In a way, it was hands-on experience for Shivaji in how to administer. By the time he was seventeen, he knew what an ideal, sensitive administration should be like.

This, incidentally, was the region and the time that connected Shivaji with lifelong partners. Yesaji Kank, Baji Pasalkar, Baji Prabhu Deshpande and many others who stayed by Shivaji's side all along were from the same region. None of them came from any royal lineage. Most were from the farming community. A look at the kind of people Shivaji attracted suggests how magnetic his persona must have been. Along with many Marathas like Tanaji Malusare and Hambirrao Mohite, he had Brahmins like Moropant Pingle and Annaji Datto, and Kayasthas like Deshpande. Each one of them was willing to die for the cause Shivaji espoused.

From 1645 to 1649 was the period of Shivaji's first uprising. He snatched half a dozen forts either from the Adil Shahi or the Mughals, but the bigger challenge was from within. During those days, many Marathas were happy serving the various sultanates that had allowed them to create their own fiefdoms in return. Almost all of them belonged to Shivaji's community. His dream of carving out an independent empire posed an existential threat to these local satraps. Initially, overcoming them was the bigger task for him. And to that end he played a simple trick: that of winning over common men and women and using their goodwill against the traditional fiefs. There are some prominent examples to explain this.

As early as 1645, two Maratha sardars were set on Shivaji by Adil Shah: Khandoji and Baji Ghorpade. Adil Shah had ignored Shivaji's activities as long as they were confined to Shahaji's jagir in and around Pune. The moment Shivaji stepped out of it, the Ghorpades were sent to curb his activities. Both lost to him. The very next year, another powerful regional satrap, Nimbalkar of Phaltan, made an attempt and met the same fate. The point to be noted is that all three of them were Shivaji's relatives but he didn't spare them. Commoners must have sensed the difference between Shivaji and the other Maratha sardars, who were happy exploiting the common man in the name of either Adil Shah, the Nizam or the Mughals later. He also became the first ruler to bring about a systemic change in favour of the common man. The system he created was transparent, just and based on farmers' income unlike the prevalent practice of extracting a certain percentage of produce from them irrespective of their harvest.

Another significant impact was in the area of land reforms. Shivaji ensured that the land in every province under him was measured and the area calculated. To ensure this, he standardized the measure and took care that each and every village had detailed land records, based on which estimates about agricultural produce and each farmer's contribution to the state were prepared. Shivaji also created a system to provide capital for buying seeds, cattle and so on which was to be recovered in two to four instalments. In doing so, he did away with the system of middlemen, who were known for amassing wealth for themselves. These local officials, mainly appointed by Adil Shah and the Mughals, had become very powerful, with some of them even maintaining armies. He compensated them and dismantled the entire structure.

Also noteworthy is Shivaji's reform in scrapping the special powers of military officials. These officials used to exercise political powers over their tenants or the villages they represented. Some collected revenue in the form of agricultural produce from farmers in lieu of their military services. Shivaji revoked these special powers. He started paying all military officials a special allowance from the state exchequer depending on their grades and position held. This gave great relief to the farming community, which had to face the brunt of the whims and fancies of the local rulers and military officials. All these measures make Shivaji the first king to lead a real civil government.

In addition to farming, he brought about a significant change in law and order as well. In one instance, he ordered that the right hand and left leg of one Ranze Patil be chopped off as he kept misbehaving with the women from a village in Shivaji's jagir despite warnings. Every such case helped Shivaji widen his support base among the common man. He lived by the modern dictum that justice should not only be given, it should be seen to be given. In return, the commoners became not only great sympathizers but also active supporters of Shivaji in his mission. This act of Shivaji's – of preparing the common man for a bigger struggle – can only be compared with what Mahatma Gandhi did in the twentieth century by empowering the common man in the fight against the British.

THERE WASN'T MUCH ACTION between 1649 and 1656. Shivaji utilized these seven years to strengthen the systems in the territories he had won. He also concentrated on his armies and intelligence networks. There have been many tales about his secret service chief Bahirji Naik's adventure. It was he who did a recee of Surat as a fakir and provided perfect information to Shivaji before his first raid. Another excellent example of the efficiency of the secret service is Shivaji's daring raid on Shaista Khan – he had all the information he required, down to Khan's bedroom. Later in life too, after Shivaji plundered Jalna near Aurangabad in 1679, he managed to escape successfully thanks to Bahirji's knowledge of the different routes from there.

Shivaji annexed Jawali in 1656, fully aware that Adil Shah would send his strongest noble to get him. So, he was mentally prepared to face Afzal Khan. Many feel Shivaji should not have killed Afzal Khan and ask if it was ethical to do so and who attacked whom first. But the fact is that Khan was not on a charity mission to the Deccan. Had he not been killed by Shivaji, the latter would have certainly met the same fate at his hands. What is more important is that the win over

Afzal Khan didn't make him complacent. From 1659 onwards he fought many battles, with the only setback coming from Jai Singh. By 1666, the year in which he escaped from Agra, his stature had grown in leaps and bounds – while he had been a local phenomenon earlier, he was now a figure with much wider resonance.

A look at Shivaji's army is also instructive. Initially it comprised just around 1,200-strong cavalry and 2,000 horsemen with their own arms. In 1655, as he launched and led the successful Jawali mission, it had swelled to a 7,000-strong cavalry, 8,000 horsemen and a 10,000-strong infantry. He also added over 700 Pathans. In 1680, at the time of his death, Shivaji's army had a cavalry of 45,000 led by twenty-nine colonels, 60,000 horsemen, and an infantry of over 1 lakh men. He also had 32,000 horses and 1,260 elephants. He also possessed 200 guns that were ready and an equal number were mounted at various forts.

Simultaneously, Shivaji concentrated on raising his naval forces too – for three years from 1649 onwards. Again, he was the first Indian king to understand the importance of having a strong navy. Indian kings since the year 1000 had consistently ignored the coastline, which resulted in forces from faraway European lands coming and firming up their presence on Indian soil. Shivaji could stand up to them because of his focus on the navy. In fact, he had employed Portuguese technicians to help him develop his fleet. His navy had two main varieties of ships: gurabs and galbats. Gurabs were large ships ranging between 150 and 300 tonnes, propelled only by sails. Each had a minimum of two masts, with two large sails and five to seven cannons on both sides. At least fifty to sixty sailors were required to run gurabs, which were capable of carrying around the same number of soldiers. As compared to gurabs, there were two ways to navigate the galbats: sailing and rowing. Each could carry twenty-five to thirty sailors and an equal number of soldiers. Small cannons could be deployed on the galbats.

In 1670 Shivaji pressurized Englishmen in Bombay into selling him war material for his fight against the Siddis – he always had in mind ways to strengthen his naval forces. He had as many as 400 vessels of various sizes and classes, including gunboats. They were divided into two squadrons of 200 vessels each. Both were led by two Darya Sarangs, or admirals. Shivaji's navy often went on expeditions to places as far as Karwar, Goa, Surat and Daman, among others. Besides building major seaports such as Sindhudurg and Janjira, he did many things to strengthen his rule on the coast. His was the first navy to have a strong presence on the western coast.

At the time of his death, Shivaji's kingdom stretched from Ramnagar near Surat in the north to Karwar in the south, Baglana in the east to Pune district through Nashik in the west, along with all of Satara and most parts of Kolhapur. He had as many as 240 forts all over. A small stretch from the Kannada-speaking Belgaum to Bellary too was recognized to be under Shivaji.

His kingdom was divided into three zones, each led by a viceroy. The northern one comprising Surat, Dang, Konkan and parts of the Deccan was led by Moropant Pingle. Regions of the south such as Konkan, Sawantwadi and North Canara were entrusted with Annaji Datto. The rest, including Satara, Kolhapur and parts of Karnataka, was under Dattaji. These regions yielded around 9 crore rupees to Shivaji's exchequer annually. Accounts of his collection of gems, jewellery, and gold and silver coins vary.

Shivaji had an eight-member council of ministers to run his kingdom. Known as the Ashta Pradhan, the system cannot be compared with the modern-day cabinet as most of them were advisers. However, Shivaji never interfered in their day-to-day operations such as revenue collection. What is interesting to note in the context of Maharashtra politics of today is that all of them, except the army chief, were Brahmins.

Shivaji also had a well-defined structure for the armed forces. Each fort was under three officers, of whom two were Marathas and one Brahmin, and they all had equal cadres. The granary, provisions, stationary and so on were under the control of Kayasthas. In the cavalry, each unit comprised twenty-five men led by one havaldar. Five havaldars were put under one subedar, and ten subedars under one hazari. Over and above them were panch hazaris and sarnaubats.

The structure of the infantry was similar. Everyone in the army was instructed to adhere to the guidelines laid down by Shivaji himself. Anyone found violating them met with strict punishment. Shivaji never took lightly any complaints regarding the harassment of commoners, especially women, by members of the army. He was extremely respectful towards women and wanted his military to respect them too.

Every year, on the day of Vijaya Dashami, the army was sent out on a mission. At the time of departure, a detailed list of their belongings was made. No one was exempted. No woman, female slaves or dancing girls were allowed to accompany the forces. Shivaji had rules framed even for mundane things such as how his infantry should behave with villagers while camping in unknown territories. He did not tolerate anyone misbehaving with civilians. This helped him create a wide support base and also generated considerable faith among the masses in him. There were strict instructions not to take any woman or child hostage along the way. Anyone violating these rules didn't get a second chance as the punishment prescribed by Shivaji was beheading. He was extremely ruthless in such matters. This also helped Shivaji maintain a lean army that was quick to respond, unlike the armies of his Mughal counterparts who were known for taking their harems even on war campaigns.

Shivaji was a genius in war games. Having developed an excellent intelligence apparatus, he could always stay ahead of the curve vis-à-vis his enemies. His missions were normally of seven to eight months and came back on Gudhi Padwa, the Hindu new year. On their return, each and every person, irrespective of his position, was checked again and his belongings were compared against the list made at the outset. Anything found to be in excess of the list was confiscated and the person concerned fined. Top generals were given an audience by Shivaji to present detailed accounts, after which they were duly rewarded. The next four to five months were typically meant for staying at home and for agricultural work.

THE FOUNDATION OF SHIVAJI'S governance was his moral character, which all through his life remained impeccable. A devoted son, a caring father and a considerate husband, he had no vices. Passionate about religious scriptures but truly liberal, he had respect for holy men of all faiths. One of the saints Shivaji was close to was Ramdas, fondly called Samarth Ramdas. That Shivaji had high regard for Samarth can be ascertained from two facts. One is that the Ramdasis, the followers of Ramdas, were the biggest beneficiaries of grants made by Shivaji. The other is Shivaji's letter, dated 22 July 1672, that directs his commanders to let Ramdas stay at Sajjangad near Satara and look after him. There is no other instance of Shivaji extending similar privileges to anyone else. He was always extremely respectful towards Ramdas, whom he considered his spiritual guru – and not his political mentor, as some like to portray.

There is no proof available that indicates Shivaji was ever in need of a political guru. He was a born leader who could get the best out of his colleagues. It is not for nothing that many were willing to die for Shivaji and his dream. His ability to involve everyone around and make his goal theirs was extraordinary. He truly exemplified the rule of law, wherein all were treated as equals.

The greatness of Shivaji's character has kept him alive in people's minds 350 years after his death. His life and legacy show how a leader's personal attributes can shape the society they want to build. That was the differentiating factor between Shivaji and the other rulers who came before and after him.

He continues to be the only leader this region has produced who dared to dream big and proved that, regardless of one's lineage or circumstances, one can take on the mighty. This is the reason why, even today, Shivaji is considered a fount of inspiration that refuses to dry.

7

Deccan After Shivaji

What happened in the Deccan after Shivaji underlines the importance of the departed Maratha warrior. Before Shivaji, the Marathas were mostly subordinates of their respective masters. Shivaji taught them how to become masters themselves. He was the first to challenge Bijapur's Adil Shahi and the Delhi-based Mughals. After his passing, however, it was as though all hell broke loose, and no one, including his son Sambhaji, could stem the Deccan's steady decline.

Sambhaji was in prison when Shivaji died. His stepmother, Soyarabai, declared her son, Rajaram, as Shivaji's heir with the help of some of his ministers who were not comfortable with Sambhaji. But her success was short-lived. As Sambhaji got wind of the coup, he mobilized his supporters, killed the Panhala fort commander and escaped. In a couple of months, in June 1680, he captured Raigad and the very next month ascended the throne. Rajaram ended up in prison along with Soyarabai and wife Janaki. Sambhaji initially tried to make peace with them by pardoning them all. It, however, didn't work as Soyarabai was too ambitious. Shivaji's tightly held inner core was split in two after his death, Soyarabai on one side and Sambhaji on the other. In between were many of Shivaji's close confidants. Finally, Sambhaji put an end to the succession issue by killing Soyarabai along with those loyal to her, some of whom had been prominent members of Shivaji's Ashta Pradhan Mandal. The bloodshed also took away an invaluable talent pool that Shivaji had groomed. Later, Sambhaji would pay a heavy price for it.

But, for the moment, he emerged victorious from the internal battle. Fired up, he went on to attack Mughal regions. His raids in places such as Burhanpur, however, were unlike Shivaji's, whose army never committed atrocities on civilians. The same couldn't be said about Sambhaji's actions, which bordered on the reckless. Sambhaji, though extremely courageous, lacked his father's patience and diplomatic skills.

He was soon put to the test as within two months of Shivaji's death a huge Mughal contingent descended on the Deccan hoping to wipe off the Maratha empire. Aurangzeb was in Rajputana, a region spread over present-day Rajasthan and Madhya Pradesh. He sent Bahadur Khan with a large army. A few months later, Shahabuddin, another of his senior commanders, was also asked to open a front against Sambhaji. The regions around Nashik witnessed heavy Mughal activity to rein him in. In 1681, Mughal general Husain Ali Khan too descended on the Deccan to pin Sambhaji down. None of them were successful. The Maratha forces under Sambhaji fought every battle valiantly. Finally, Aurangzeb himself decided to take the plunge. In March 1682, he along with his sons Shah Alam, Azam Shah and Kam Bakhsh as well as all of his important commanders landed in the south. He had two dreams: to finish off the Marathas and later annex the Adil Shahi and the Qutb Shahi. With Shivaji gone, he thought his dream was just a few years away. He even had plans to retire in Delhi. This was, however, not to happen, thanks to Sambhaji and his men.

Sambhaji had to battle on three fronts: with the Mughals, Siddis and Portuguese. All those who had been hammered by Shivaji in the past were active now with a vengeance. However, almost all of them, including Aurangzeb, miscalculated Sambhaji's strength. He very well knew that his men had no chance in head-on battles with any of Aurangzeb's forces. The emperor was in the Deccan with all his might at his command: a 2,00,000-strong army and cavalry, along with battalions of elephants and camels. The situation forced Sambhaji to adopt a hit-and-run strategy.

It was more than mere guerrilla warfare. His light cavalry was divided into many small teams. Each led by a Sambhaji loyal, they launched indiscriminate raiding and looting of Mughal forces. When challenged, they would run away. In the event of Mughal forces laying siege, Maratha commanders would hand over their forts to them, only to come back, catch the enemy's forces off guard and attack again. The Marathas took to cutting off the Mughals' supply chains, making their lives extremely difficult with so many to feed. The Mughals didn't know how to stop the blitzkrieg. It was so effective that Aurangzeb's forces couldn't win a single battle even after four years. The emperor started losing his cool and his faith in his forces. He is known to have flung his headgear on the floor out of anger in 1684, taking a pledge not to wear it again till he defeated Sambhaji. As it happened, that moment never came. His dream of defeating Shivaji's small, worn-out kingdom without much effort was nowhere near reality.

In the meantime, Aurangzeb received another major blow – from within his family. His son Muhammad Akbar, revolting against him, joined the Rajputs. He issued a statement 'dismissing' Aurangzeb and appointing himself as the emperor, and marched towards Ajmer to take on the Mughal forces. But Aurangzeb was too shrewd for the young man, who was soon completely outfoxed by the father. Aurangzeb wrote a letter to him congratulating him for his plot to deceive the Rajputs and saw to it that it fell in the Rajputs' hands. That was around 1681. The leak had its desired effect. The Rajputs feared that he may have been sent by his father and desisted from supporting him openly. The situation forced Muhammad Akbar to flee to the Deccan, where he stayed with Sambhaji for around five years.

He thought Sambhaji would lend him support to defeat his father. Unfortunately, Sambhaji failed to grab the opportunity –

either because he too smelled a rat like the Rajputs, or he was too busy fighting his own battles. Eventually, he could only help the exasperated Mughal rebel flee to Persia, where he died a few years later. The fact that in Persia he used to daily pray for his father's early death underlined the animosity between the father and son, as also the opportunity of exploiting the rift that the Marathas had wasted.

This notwithstanding, the Maratha forces gave an unexpected fight to Aurangzeb. He found it so tough to overcome them that he was forced to halt his campaign and look at other options. He changed directions and planned to defeat Bijapur and Golconda. Sambhaji went to Adil Shah's and Qutb Shah's rescue. But that was not of much help. Aurangzeb pocketed the two weakened empires within two years and returned to the Deccan in 1687 with renewed vigour to defeat Sambhaji. The two-year break gave the Marathas too time to restructure and rejuvenate their forces. In the hiatus, Sambhaji undertook as many as seventeen campaigns against the Mughals. He went to Bharuch in the west and also to the Kannada region, which Aurangzeb had recently won by defeating Adil Shah.

But Sambhaji's coffers were nearly empty. He faced a serious financial crisis. From 1681 onwards, he had been constantly at war on several fronts. This had ravaged the region and destroyed its agriculture. The strength of his forces had come down to a mere 30,000. He had to spend a significant amount on maintaining his naval force too. The dire situation forced him to leave his men to fend for themselves. The flow of revenue to the state exchequer shrank considerably. The financial crunch meant that the warring Maratha fiefs that had been held together for long began to fall apart.

The vatandari system that Shivaji had successfully got rid of started showing signs of revival. Vatandars were landowners who were allowed to employ locals. The land was offered to them in lieu of their service to the king. Shivaji, having realized the nuisance caused by these vatandars who eventually became local fiefs, had demolished the system. Aurangzeb slowly won them over by offering Maratha sardars vatandari. Sambhaji's lack of authority also failed to prevent defections from the top ranks of Maratha sardars. Many in his own camp were found to be spying for Aurangzeb. Shivaji's success lay in his ability to keep the Marathas' large egos in check and make them work for one goal: setting up of the first Hindavi Swarajya. Unfortunately, Sambhaji failed on this front. The fact that he had eliminated many of Shivaji's lieutenants didn't help either.

In 1687, Sambhaji won the battle of Wai against the Mughals but lost his commander, Hambirrao Mohite, whose death brought about an early disintegration of his forces. Soon, in February 1689, Sambhaji and twenty-five of his advisers were captured by the Mughal forces in a battle at Sangameshwar in the Konkan region. Stories of what happened after that vary widely. All, however, are unanimous on one point: Sambhaji was tortured horribly and killed in the most inhuman way.

He and his men were taken to Bahadurgad in Ahmednagar, where they were subjected to insults by Mughal soldiers. Sambhaji was asked to surrender his forts and his treasures and bow before Aurangzeb, which he refused. The courage he showed in refusing to give in to Aurangzeb's demands is unmatched in history. His tongue was cut off and his nails and hair plucked. Adamant even in captivity and having faced tremendous physical torture, Sambhaji was offered one last chance to save his life on the condition that he converted to Islam. With his tongue slit, Sambhaji couldn't reply, so he wrote down his answer, telling Aurangzeb that he would convert provided the emperor married his daughter to him. A furious Aurangzeb ordered his killing.

On 11 March 1689, he was beheaded at Tulapur near Pune. According to some accounts, his body was cut into pieces, preventing his last rites.

SAMBHAJI'S DEATH REVIVED AURANGZEB'S dream of conquering the Maratha empire. But he was to be disappointed yet again.

After Sambhaji, his half-brother Rajaram took over the reins of the kingdom. He was large-hearted and tried to build bridges with his generals. He knew that the real heir-apparent to the throne was Sambhaji's elder son Shahu, who had been in a Mughal prison from 1689, after Sambhaji's killing. He decided to hold fort till Shahu was released. Rajaram lacked the qualities of his father and his brother. For nine years, from 1680 to 1689, he had also been in captivity, imprisoned by Sambhaji. Soon after he was crowned, he had to leave Raigad as Aurangzeb's forces were planning to lay siege. He and Sambhaji's widow Yesubai went to Pratapgad near Satara and from there to Jinji in Tamil Nadu as the Mughals chased them. Keladi Chennamma, the warrior queen of the Keladi kingdom of Karnataka, formed after the fall of the Vijayanagar empire, helped them on the way by foiling the attempts of Aurangzeb's forces to capture them. Rajaram was then confined to Jinji for over nine years and died in 1700.

Though Rajaram couldn't do much, two of his commanders, Santaji Ghorpade and Dhanaji Jadhav, kept the Maratha flame burning. They continued carrying out flash attacks on Aurangzeb's forces, displaying unbelievable courage. In March 1690, Santaji led a most audacious attack on a Mughal camp where Aurangzeb himself was spending the night. The emperor escaped but Santaji's forces decamped with an urn from Aurangzeb's tent. His personal guards too were killed by the Marathas. This daredevilry terrorized the Mughals. Santaji–Dhanaji became the subject of folklore. Legend has it that just a mention of them would agitate Mughal horses.

Around this time, a realization started dawning on Aurangzeb that the war he had started was much more difficult than he had anticipated. He wanted to win Jinji and arrest Rajaram – it had been more than seven years. But the brave Maratha forces thwarted every attempt. Finally, Jinji fell, but not before Rajaram was escorted to the Deccan by the valiant Santaji–Dhanaji. The campaign made a big hole in the Mughal treasury. Besides, Aurangzeb's forces were fatigued having spent over a decade in the Deccan's difficult terrain. The prolonged stay away from Delhi had left them exhausted. They were in no mood to fight more.

A statue of Gautamiputra Satakarni in Amaravathi in Andhra Pradesh. He was a ruler of the Satavahana Empire who lived around second century BCE and can be said to be the most important historical political figure for Maharashtra until Shivaji.

A statue of a young Shivaji along with his mother, Jijabai, in Mumbai. Jijabai had a strong formative influence on the seventeenth-century leader.

All photos in this section have been sourced from Wikimedia Commons

A painting of Chhatrapati Shivaji Maharaj, who lived from 1630 to 1680 and established the Maratha Empire.

A mural in Mumbai's Shivaji Park depicting the coronation of Shivaji, which took place in 1674 at Raigad fort.

A painting showing Chhatrapati Shivaji in the court of Mughal Emperor Aurangzeb. Shivaji is known to have felt humiliated that the treatment accorded to him was not suited to his stature.

A view of Torna fort in Pune. It is historically significant as it was the first fort captured by Shivaji at the young age of sixteen.

Some of Shivaji's other popular forts: (from top to bottom) Shivneri near Junnar in Pune, his birthplace; Pratapgad in Satara, the site of the battle in which the Marathas defeated Adil Shahi forces led by their general Afzal Khan, the Marathas' first significant victory against a major regional power; and Raigad in the Konkan, here Shivaji was coronated and which became the capital of his empire.

Balaji Vishwanath, the first of a series of Peshwas (prime minister) who gained effective control of the Maratha Empire during the eighteenth century even as Chhatrapati Shahu, Shivaji's grandson, remained the ruler.

A view of Shaniwar Wada in Pune, the seat of power of the Peshwas.

A painting depicting Peshwa Baji Rao I, who lived from 1700 to 1740. He was one of Maharashtra's greatest generals and can be compared with the likes of Napoleon Bonaparte or the Duke of Wellington. He was the first Marathi warrior who dared to take on Delhi and it was under him that the Maratha Empire reached its peak.

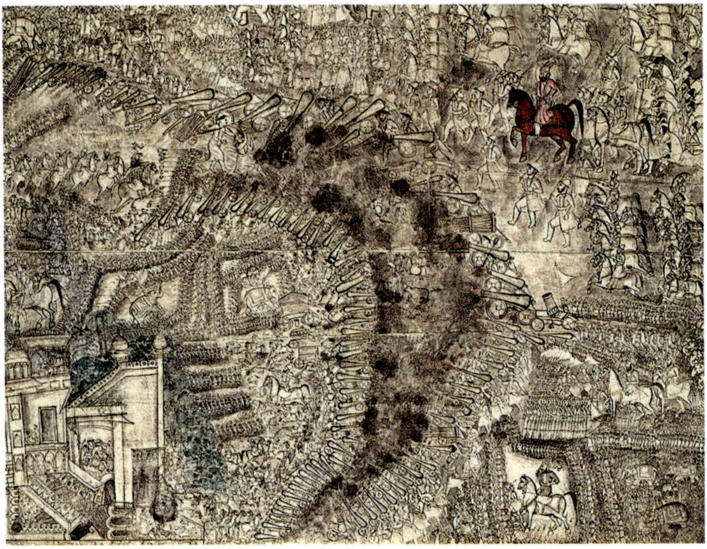

A Faizabad-style drawing of the Third Battle of Panipat, which took place in January 1761. The Durrani Empire led by Ahmad Shah Durrani and supported by the Mughals defeated the Marathas. The loss can be said to have left a deep impact on the psyche of the Marathi Manoos for centuries to come.

A portrait of Nana Fadnavis, an influential sardar under the Peshwas, who was called the Maratha Machiavelli by the British.

A painting showing Peshwa Baji Rao II, the last Peshwa, signing the Treaty of Bassein (Vasai) with the British in 1802, which proved decisive in the dissolution of the Maratha Empire.

Unfortunately, this was also the time when the Marathas were left rudderless. Rajaram was weakened and Shahu still in jail. With no one to lead, differences between many Maratha sardars came to the fore. The most unfortunate was the rift between Santaji and Dhanaji themselves. Santaji was the commander-in-chief, the post Dhanaji was eyeing. He convinced Rajaram to sack Santaji. His removal robbed one of the finest Maratha warriors of everything and he died an ordinary man's death in a forest, believed to be plotted by Dhanaji. The incident also exposed the Marathas' vulnerability to differences. It also antagonized Santaji's two sons, who later went on to support an anti-Rajaram faction.

Dhanaji became commander-in-chief and continued to lead the Marathas. After Rajaram died in 1700, his widow, Tarabai, anointed herself as the regent. She wanted her son Shivaji II to be king. Not everyone was convinced, but the opposition was too weak and Tarabai had her way. Dhanaji, on his part, kept the battle against the Mughals alive. Aurangzeb by then had lost all hope of defeating the Marathas. He opened talks with Dhanaji to release Shahu. But they failed, following which Dhanaji launched a massive attack on Surat and went on to conquer today's Gujarat, right up to Bharuch and Vadodara. Around this time, Aurangzeb is believed to have had a premonition that he would not return to his throne in Delhi. His dream of taking over the Deccan by defeating the Marathas was to remain a dream. He had spent twenty-six years chasing it but in vain. Worn out, he retired to Ahmednagar. To make matters worse, a full-blown succession war had erupted between his sons, who were all staking claim to his legacy. Frustrated, exasperated and completely fatigued in his eighty-eighth year, Aurangzeb lost his battle for life too on 3 March 1707.

Soon after the last rites were performed, Aurangzeb's son Azam Shah stepped into his shoes at Ahmednagar. At the same time, news came that another of his sons, Shah Alam, who had been in Afghanistan, was on his way to Delhi to take control of the empire. Azam Shah too marched to Delhi to take on his brother. This was an opportunity for Tarabai and Dhanaji as the Mughals were busy with their family feuds. Both of them independently launched wide-ranging raids on various forts held by the Mughals and won almost all of them. Azam Shah was in a fix. Though he had his eyes set on Delhi, the situation in and around Pune and Ahmednagar turned grim. At this juncture, he played a move that guaranteed a split among the Marathas. He released Shahu.

Released on a clear understanding that he would work for the Mughals, Shahu landed in the Deccan sometime in June 1707 with his 200 men. The Mughals kept his mother Yesubai hostage to ensure that he stuck to the script. The news that Sambhaji's son was returning to rule had its desired impact. He was given a hero's welcome all over, and many Marathas who had been loyal to Sambhaji extended their support. His first act after returning to the Deccan was to write to Tarabai, claiming that he was the real heir to the Maratha kingdom. This, obviously, was not acceptable to her. She first claimed that Shahu had been sent by Azam Shah to deceive the Marathas, but it didn't hold water. She then made another argument: that Shahu was the son of Sambhaji, who had failed to save the Maratha kingdom, and that it was saved by Rajaram, so Rajaram's son and not Sambhaji's should be the natural successor. This too failed to cut much ice. Tarabai had nothing really going in her favour. Her son Shivaji II was a maniac and incapable of ruling. He spent twelve years of his youth in jail and eventually died in captivity. But Tarabai was keen to see him occupy the throne, which was beyond people's comprehension. War was the only way to end the impasse.

It did end, but not before the legendary Shivaji's legacy was split in two. One faction led by Tarabai and the other by Shahu decided to battle it out at Khed near Pune. Dhanaji was to fight on Tarabai's behalf but, as the war began, he simply walked over to the other side and joined hands with Shahu. Many others went with him. Tarabai lost the battle even before it started. She, however, wasn't willing to concede defeat. She couldn't wrest what Shahu had but was successful in dividing the kingdom. She set up her own seat of power, while Shahu, in January 1708, went on to pronounce himself Chhatrapati like his grandfather Shivaji.

But he was nowhere near Shivaji in stature. The big difference between the two was that Chhatrapati Shivaji was a self-made person and a sovereign ruler, which was not the case with Shahu, who ruled on behalf of the Mughals. He was one of many nobles in the Mughal court and was entrusted with the responsibility of running the Maratha kingdom. It was a big climbdown for a descendant of Shivaji.

Shahu fought on two fronts. He was locked in a battle of nerves with the Mughals, from whom he was trying to break free. And he also had to contend with Tarabai, who kept rejecting his claims. Though he had the Mughals' recognition, she too kept expecting similar prominence. She wasn't alone. All the top Maratha families that had once worked under Shivaji had made a beeline to serve the Mughals. Their egos were bigger than their capabilities and they didn't think of coming together to recreate the Shivaji era. It was a free-for-all as it became extremely difficult to know who was working for whom.

AMONG ALL THE REGENTS working under Shahu was one Brahmin. Originally from Shrivardhan in the Konkan, he moved to the upper lands of western Maharashtra while serving Dhanaji as a clerk. When Shahu and Yesubai were imprisoned, he showed loyalty and served both with total dedication. After Shahu's release too he stayed by his side, helping him negotiate with many regents serving Tarabai. And so this was the man Shahu thought worth promoting.

He was Balaji Vishwanath, the Peshwa, or the prime minister, who would go on to rule the Deccan.

He had been serving as subedar of the Pune region from 1699. He was no warrior, nor a war strategist. But the qualities he possessed were a complete rarity then. He was diplomatic, a sweet talker, had an impeccable sense of timing and was extremely suave. In an era when most of the Maratha sardars were ill-tempered and impatient, Balaji's qualities stood out. He could easily find a way out when many of his contemporaries were locked in bitter feuds. Shahu used him to arrange many a defection from Tarabai's camp. Incidentally, it was Balaji who had convinced Dhanaji to switch to Shahu's side in the battle with Tarabai. Needless to say, Balaji soon became a key player for Shahu.

Around this time, in 1707, as the succession dispute worsened, the Maratha kingdom was divided into two: Satara and Kolhapur. Balaji faced his first major challenge in Chandrasen Jadhav, Dhanaji's son. After Dhanaji's death in June 1708, Shahu appointed Chandrasen as senapati, or army general. But he lacked his father's many qualities, loyalty being the most important. He opened negotiations with Tarabai even while serving Shahu. The Mughals too kept wooing him. He even tried to bring together other Maratha defectors and planned to attack Shahu. At this juncture, he sensed that the person who could come in his way was Balaji Vishwanath. He tried to arrest Balaji, who fled to Satara. He then conveyed to Shahu that he should surrender Balaji, failing which he would not be able to serve him. Incensed by his arrogance, Shahu asked one of his nobles, Haibatrao Nimbalkar, to arrest Chandrasen. Haibatrao defeated Chandrasen, after which he switched loyalties to Tarabai. Interestingly, Haibatrao too defected to Tarabai's camp.

It was one of the lowest points in Shahu's life. Almost all his experienced generals gone, Shahu turned to Balaji and assigned him the task of raising a fresh army. In recognition of his service and also to underscore the importance of his new responsibility, he gave him the title of senakarta, or organizer of Maratha armies. This development that took place in August 1711 also had huge social significance. It was not only the beginning of the rise of the Peshwas, it was also the first time since Shivaji's reign that a Brahmin was entrusted with the responsibility of raising an army.

Balaji had his task cut out for him. He set his eyes on Tarabai, who posed a major challenge to Shahu. He mopped up all the disgruntled elements in her court to hatch a conspiracy against her. She was defeated in the battle that followed at Kolhapur in 1712. He then went on to win over Rajaram's other widow, Rajasbai, by staging a coup against Shivaji II, Tarabai's son, and installing Rajasbai's son, Sambhaji II, on the Kolhapur throne. This move, in a way, checkmated Shahu too, who had become extremely vulnerable.

Then came one of the most important challenges in Balaji's life. He wanted to win over the Angres. Tukoji Angre had commanded Chhatrapati Shivaji's navy and was succeeded in 1690 by his son Kanhoji, who was made sakhel, or admiral, of the Maratha fleet by Rajaram. Later, he served Tarabai. Like many other Maratha warriors, Kanhoji too thought of setting up his own empire, thanks to the constant war between Tarabai and Shahu. In a bid to free himself from both, he seized the major trading centre of Kalyan, along with the forts of Rajmachi and Lohagad near Pune. This was in 1713 and Balaji was yet to be officially appointed Peshwa then. Shahu deputed then Peshwa Bahiroji Pingle to address the challenge. Kanhoji was too powerful for Pingle, who was not only defeated but also imprisoned at Lohagad.

An emboldened Kanhoji had Satara on his mind, Shahu's capital. It would have been the end for Shahu had Kanhoji attacked Satara. The responsibility of stopping him from advancing fell on Balaji, who agreed but hinted that he should be appointed the Peshwa formally so as to tackle Kanhoji from a position of authority. Shahu agreed. Although he got the designation he wanted, Balaji was well aware that he could not defeat Kanhoji. As a result, he chose the path of negotiations and opened a dialogue with the admiral. He called on Kanhoji at his camp at Lonavla near Pune. He charmed the admiral by recalling his family's commitment to Hindavi Swarajya and argued how he should play a key role in rebuilding the Maratha kingdom. Such was Balaji's skill that Kanhoji agreed and became the admiral of Shahu's navy, with full control over most of the Konkan. Balaji ensured that his birthplace of Shrivardhan too came under Kanhoji's rule. He then joined Kanhoji in an attack against the Siddis of Janjira, whose combined forces had captured most of the Konkan coast. This enormous success turned Balaji Vishwanath into a major power player of the day.

The Peshwa had arrived. Initially, his ascent created quite a rift in Shahu's camp as not many were willing to accept him. There were many Brahmins serving Shahu – Krishnarao Khatavkar, for example – who were upset with his rise. The Khatavkars were a family of Sanskrit scholars and had served the Maratha kingdom for generations. After Sambhaji's death, Aurangzeb had given Krishnarao the jahagiri of Khatav near Satara. There were many such instances of men who were happy to serve the Mughals but couldn't get along with a fellow Maratha. Shivaji had been successful in uniting people of various castes and social standing but that legacy had waned with time. After his death, there were regular skirmishes between Marathas. And then Shahu was no Shivaji. Though he tried to unite the scattered Maratha force, he lacked initiative. Especially with a man like Balaji, who had showed tremendous capability in handling internal and external affairs, he could have struck a fatal blow to the warring and weakened Mughals. But he didn't. 'Had Shahu maintained the zeal and courage he showed in the initial days, Maratha history would have been different than what it is,' writes eminent historian G.S. Sardesai. Unfortunately, it was not to be.

On his part, Balaji later won many accolades. A Maratha–Mughal treaty, signed in 1718, was another example of his diplomatic skills. As part of the treaty, he extracted chauth and sardeshmukhi, a tax and an additional levy, over the rich provinces of Gujarat and Khandesh, and the return of the regions conquered by Chhatrapati Shivaji in Karnataka. In exchange, Shahu acknowledged the nominal overlordship of the Mughal emperor, and agreed that the Marathas would provide a force of 15,000 armed horsemen to the Mughal empire. A faction of Mughals readily agreed to the demand, hoping to have Maratha soldiers at their disposal when needed in some crucial battle. A triumphant Balaji returned to Satara from Delhi, having also successfully negotiated the release of Shahu's mother

Yesubai, wife Savitribai and half-brother Madansingh from Mughal captivity.

But the journey and the constant power struggles took their toll. His health began to fail. In October 1719, he retired to the village of Saswad near Pune which Shahu had gifted him. In its peaceful environs, he breathed his last on 12 April 1720.

His son Baji Rao I was to take the Peshwai to greater heights thereafter.

8

The Peshwas

If there is anyone in history who matches up to Shivaji, it is Peshwa Baji Rao. He was one of Maharashtra's greatest generals and can be compared with the likes of Napoleon Bonaparte or the Duke of Wellington. In his short life of less than forty years, Baji Rao fought as many as forty-one battles and won them all. He was the first Marathi warrior who dared to take on Delhi. It was under him that the Maratha empire reached its peak. Extremely innovative in tactical planning, brilliant with logistics and a brave soldier himself, it is unfortunate that the lion-hearted Baji Rao is identified today more with his escapades with Mastani than his valour and statesmanship.

Fortunately, historians are not so unkind. Almost all of them have nothing but lavish praise for him. In his book *A History of the Mahrattas*, historian James Grant Duff notes, 'Bred a soldier as well as a statesman, Bajirao united the enterprise, vigour and hardihood of a Maratha chief with the polished manners, the sagacity and address which frequently distinguish the Brahmins of the Konkan. In this respect, the genius of Bajirao enlarged the schemes which his father devised; and unlike most Brahmins, of him it may be truly said – he had both – the head to plan and the hand to execute.'

Even more generous is Sir Jadunath Sarkar, who says, 'Bajirao was a heaven-born cavalry leader ... he was unequalled for the daring and originality of his genius and the volume and value of his achievements. If Sir Robert Walpole created the unchallengeable position of the Prime Minister in the unwritten constitution of England, Bajirao created the same institution in the Maratha Raj at exactly the same time.'

Baji Rao was renowned for his extremely rapid cavalry movements. Quick in gaining knowledge of the local topography, he would use local landscapes to his advantage. He consistently took his rivals by surprise either by attacking them from behind or encircling them and cutting their supply lines with rapid troop movements. Known to be constantly on the move, the great Peshwa was compared to the American Civil War's General William Sherman by Field Marshal Bernard Montgomery, a legendary British army officer who served in both the world wars, in his book *A History of Warfare*. According to him, Baji Rao's victory at Palkhed was a 'masterpiece of strategic mobility'. He goes on to describe him as the 'finest cavalry general ever produced by India'.

Signs of being a warrior were visible in Baji Rao from early childhood. When his father Balaji Vishwanath was arrested by a local army chief, Damaji Thorat, Baji Rao chose to accompany him to prison and stayed with him for two years until his release. He had also been with his father on the expedition to Delhi in 1716. When Balaji died in 1720, Shahu wasted no time in appointing Baji Rao as the next Peshwa. He was only twenty years old at the time. This led to major resentment in the Shahu camp. Many veterans, incidentally all Brahmins, were upset for being passed over. In an attempt to avoid friction, the situation prompted Baji Rao to scout for young lieutenants. Two of them were Malhar Rao Holkar, who later went on to set up Indore state, and Ranoji Scindia, who founded Gwalior state – both in their teens when they began assisting Baji Rao. Unlike his fellow Brahmins, Baji Rao was extremely aggressive – the first Maratha ruler to show the ambition to expand into north India.

By the time he was appointed Peshwa, the Mughals and Nizams had regrouped and were busy reviving their empires. At the time, Mughal emperor Muhammad Shah had acknowledged the Marathas' right to collect taxes, known as 'chauth' or 'chauthai', in the Deccan. Incidentally, this was a system that Shivaji had demolished, for he knew that legitimizing local satraps would eventually be detrimental to statehood. But the situation changed after his death and the fiefdoms were active again, thanks to weak rulers. Later, the Mughals too encouraged the practice in order to weaken the Maratha state. When they allowed the fiefs to collect local taxes, Baji Rao took it as a sign of Mughal decline and wanted to strike them where it would hurt the most: the north. Unfortunately, not many in Shahu's court supported him. They felt he was too young to be allowed to launch such a campaign.

But the opportunity came soon enough.

THE MUGHAL GOVERNOR OF the Deccan, Nizam Asaf Jah, challenged Shahu's right to collect taxes in the region. He even refused to acknowledge Shahu as Shivaji's legitimate heir. In January 1721, Baji Rao had a failed meeting with him at Chikhalthan to settle their disputes through a mutual agreement. Incidentally, Asaf Jah's growing stature and arrogance had upset Emperor Muhammad Shah, who transferred him from the Deccan to Awadh. But Asaf Jah rebelled against the emperor's order and refused to accept the transfer. Angered by his defiance, the emperor sent an army to fight him, which Asaf Jah defeated in the Battle of Sakhar Kheda in 1724. Helping him take on the emperor's forces was Baji Rao, who used the opportunity to widen the wedge between the governor and the emperor. His tactical help forced the Mughal emperor to recognize Asaf Jah as the viceroy of the Deccan.

Once settled, Asaf Jah was back to his old ways of spreading his influence. He expanded his empire to Karnataka and tried to venture into the regions of Gujarat, Malwa and so on. He started sending out missives to all the Muslim governors of different regions in a bid to unite them against the Marathas. At the same time, he also tried to woo both Shahu and the Mughal emperor. He always knew that the Marathas were a bigger challenge than his own emperor, and so he applied the time-tested tactic of divide and rule to defeat the Marathas. The time was just ripe for such a move.

Sambhaji II of Kolhapur was emerging as a challenger to Shahu. He too wanted to be recognized as a Maratha Chhatrapati. Asaf Jah realized that he could use these rumblings to his advantage. He refused to pay the chauth or sardeshmukhi to Shahu, citing divisions between the two. His argument was that he didn't know who it should be paid to, since it was unclear who the real Chhatrapati was. He offered his services to settle the dispute between the warring factions. He took the help of Brahmin Parshuram Pant Pratinidhi – a staunch foe of Baji Rao's – to talk to Shahu, and of yet another rival, Chandrasen Jadhav, to talk to Sambhaji II. This gave Baji Rao all the more reason to take him on.

On 27 August 1727, he launched a massive campaign against Asaf Jah. His men plundered Burhanpur and many places in Khandesh which were under him. While Baji Rao was away, Asaf Jah invaded Pune and installed Sambhaji II as Chhatrapati, by now a pawn in his hands. It was now an all-out battle between the two. On 28 February 1728, their armies faced each other at Palkhed near Aurangabad. Baji Rao defeated Asaf Jah hands down and forced him to a complete surrender. This was his first major victory as a warrior and is a landmark in Maratha history – the first time that Mughal forces were defeated comprehensively and made to plead for mercy by any Maratha king.

How Baji Rao moved his forces – from Karnataka to Palkhed in Marathwada – to corner the enemy is a lesson in war logistics. Baji Rao, much like Shivaji against Afzal Khan, chose a battleground that was suitable for him and ensured that the Mughals were drawn to it. In the end, on 6 March, Asaf Jah signed a treaty recognizing Shahu as the Chhatrapati and agreeing to the Marathas' right to collect taxes in the Deccan. After the victory, Baji Rao moved his army from

Saswad to Pune and laid the foundation stone for the magnificent fort of Shaniwar Wada.

After this episode, Baji Rao helped many local rulers who were willing to challenge the Mughals. Notable among them was Maharaja Chhatrasal of Bundelkhand. Having been defeated and imprisoned with his family by the Mughals, Chhatrasal sought Baji Rao's help in saving his kingdom, which was under attack from Muhammad Khan Bangash, the Nawab of Farrukhabad. Baji Rao went to his rescue and restored him as the ruler of Bundelkhand after defeating the Mughals. The victory earned Baji Rao two gifts: a very large jagir from Chhatrasal and the love of his life, Mastani.

Mastani was Chhatrasal's daughter, who married Baji Rao as a tribute to the Maratha king. Sadly, the two of them could not spend more than a few months together. She had a son from Baji Rao who was denied the rights of a legitimate offspring by Pune's blimpish high society of the time. This forced the parents to raise him as a Muslim, and change his name from Krishna Rao to Shamsher Bahadur. Interestingly, he was raised by Kashibai, Baji Rao's first wife, following Mastani's death in 1740. Shamsher fought and died in the Battle of Panipat along with the Peshwas.

BAJI RAO'S CREDENTIALS AS a warrior king had been established by the time of his Bundelkhand campaign. Along with his younger brother Chimaji Appa, he had annexed many regions. As he was set to expand the Maratha empire, he faced a major hurdle within.

Upset with him was Trimbak Dabhade, Shahu's army chief. He was jealous of Baji Rao's successful expeditions in Gujarat, which until then had been his monopoly. He rebelled against Baji Rao along with the Gaekwads of Gujarat. Sambhaji II joined forces with them too. All three then got together with Nizam Asaf Jah to take on Baji Rao. But the Peshwa proved too strong for them. In a historic battle in Baroda, he killed Dabhade. Before the battle, Chimaji Appa had written to Shahu that Dabhade and the Gaekwads could be tolerated as long as they didn't join hands with the Nizam. But if they did, it would be unacceptable to the Peshwa, who remained true to his word. Not only was the trio defeated, but the Nizam was forced to commit that he would no longer interfere in the Maratha kingdom. Baji Rao also demarcated the regions under Shahu and Sambhaji II. This victory too was a feather in his cap. There were two more to come.

First was his historic win over the Siddis of Janjira in the Konkan. The Siddis had been slowly expanding their base after Shivaji's death. Their spread was halted due to a war of succession in 1733 after the death of Yakut Khan, their chief. One of the feuding sons sought Baji Rao's intervention, which gave the Marathas a much-needed opportunity against the Siddis. Baji Rao dispatched Sekhoji Angre, son of the legendary Kanhoji, to help the younger Siddi. As the Maratha forces returned after completing the mission, the Siddis were out again to reclaim Maratha territories. At this juncture, Chimaji Appa launched a surprise raid, catching the Siddis completely off guard. It had its desired effect. The Siddis went back and agreed to be confined only to Janjira.

Even grander was the Peshwas' success in Vasai against the Portuguese, who had been troubling them for some time. Having captured many places in and around Vasai, the Portuguese had refused to honour their agreement with the Marathas to allow them access to Salsette island. Besides, the Portuguese were also committing atrocities against Hindus. Finally, in March 1737, Chimaji Appa launched a major offensive against them and won the crucial battle. The Peshwas also gained control of Salsette soon.

However, there cannot be a better example underlining Baji Rao's greatness as a commander than his ambitious mission to Delhi – the first of its kind for anyone from the Marathi region until then. It was monumental in terms of every aspect of war: logistics, strategy, planning and execution. Baji Rao started for Delhi on 12 November 1736 from Pune and on 22 November he was in the Mughal capital, riding for ten days at a stretch. This in itself must have been exhilarating. The reports of the Peshwa attacking Delhi set off alarm bells. The worried Mughal emperor directed Saadat Ali Khan of Awadh to launch a counter-offensive to halt the Maratha forces' advance. Meanwhile, the Maratha duo of Malhar Rao Holkar and Pilaji Jadhav had crossed the Yamuna and started plundering Mughal territory. They were challenged and subsequently defeated by Saadat Khan with a huge contingent of over 1,50,000 men. Happy that he had halted the Maratha advance, he retired to Mathura. He seemed to be under the impression that Baji Rao would now have second thoughts about his Delhi plan. He was right. Baji Rao did rethink his plan, but only to attack Delhi within the next four days.

On 28 March, Baji Rao and his men crashed on Delhi, taking the Mughals by surprise. This time the emperor asked another commander, Mir Hasan Khan, to take on Baji Rao. The Marathas proved too strong for him and he faced a humiliating defeat. Such was the terror of Baji Rao and his forces that Emperor Muhammad Shah had plans to flee Delhi by sailing on the Yamuna as Maratha forces were all over the land. Interestingly, he never came face-to-face with Baji Rao as he was advised that the emperor should not take on a mere sardar. But the situation forced him to seek help from the Nizam, who set out from the Deccan with a vow to eliminate the Marathas from the north. On reaching Delhi, he was joined by other Mughal chiefs and a massive army took on the Peshwas.

The size of the theatre of this war can explain its enormity: it was 1,000 miles long and 500 miles wide. The Mughals had forces of over 1,20,000 men, while the Peshwa had 80,000 soldiers. Baji Rao had left some 10,000 men with Chimaji to guard the Deccan, and with the rest he was set to take on the Mughals. The two armies clashed in Bhopal in December 1737 and the Mughals were comprehensively defeated. The tactics adopted by Baji Rao were commendable to say the least. The manner and the speed with which he moved his forces and reached Bhopal even before the Nizam could realize it proved to be the clincher in the battle.

The Nizam's son, Nasir Jung, had planned to go to his father's rescue from the Deccan. But he was blocked by Chimaji Appa. Another branch of the Mughals that set out for Bhopal from Delhi was attacked and sent back by sardars Scindia and Holkar. The situation demanded nothing less than complete surrender from the Nizam and the Mughals. Yet again, the Nizam was forced to sign a peace agreement, this time formally ceding the province of Malwa to the Marathas, while the Mughals were forced to cough up 50 lakh rupees as indemnity. Such was the aftermath that the Nizam was compelled to take an oath on the Holy Quran to not indulge in anti-Peshwa activity ever again. Thus, on 7 January 1738 ended the two-and-a-half-year war Baji Rao had launched against the Mughals and the Nizam that proclaimed the Peshwas invincible all over India. This was when the Marathas were at their peak.

The moment had arrived to tackle the Nizam once and for all. Baji Rao had intended to do it. He also wanted to put an end to Mughal rule. It is possible he would have been successful as both were extremely weak at the time. But Shahu's lack of vision prevented him. First, he directed Baji Rao not to attack the Nizam as he felt it was unnecessary, and later he stopped him from launching any more campaigns against Emperor Muhammad Shah. Not much is known about Shahu's decision to save the Nizam, though for the emperor, it appears, he had a soft corner. Shahu was raised in Delhi by Aurangzeb's second daughter, Zeenat-un-Nissa, who was very kind to him. Shahu regarded her 'in place of his mother' and her brothers like maternal uncles. His sympathy towards the Mughals came in the way of Baji Rao's grand dream.

AFTER REACHING HIS PEAK, Baji Rao died on 28 April 1740, probably due to a sunstroke or a viral fever. He was just thirty-nine years old.

Shahu continued his legacy by appointing Baji Rao's eldest son, Balaji Baji Rao, alias Nanasaheb, as the next Peshwa. Like his father, Nanasaheb too was young – around nineteen – when he was appointed the Peshwa. And he too encountered stiff opposition from others in Shahu's court for that reason. But those opposing Nanasaheb were not Brahmins; they were Marathas who were opposed to sharing power with others. Prominent among them was Raghoji Bhosale. Around this time, the Shahu family also witnessed major divisions.

The one responsible for this was Tarabai, who now wanted to mend fences with an ageing Shahu. In his last days, Shahu adopted Rajaram II, Tarabai's grandson. After his death, she tried to grab power by claiming that Rajaram II was the real heir to Chhatrapati Shivaji's legacy. Having ensured the throne for him, she wanted Rajaram II to arrest Nanasaheb and dislodge him as the Peshwa. But Rajaram II refused. A furious Tarabai then tried revolting by dubbing him an impostor. She failed as no one from Shahu's court supported her. Nanasaheb's initial years were wasted on this front. He also lacked his father's skills.

The late Baji Rao had always had his eyes set on one mission: uniting the Hindus against invaders. With that goal in mind, he had won over the Rajputs. His son, however, squandered away the alliance by alienating the Rajputs. When Rajput-ruled states like Jaipur faced wars of succession, Nanasaheb chose to side with those offering higher revenue to him, instead of looking at the bigger picture. Revenue was a perennial headache for Shahu and, hence, also for the Peshwa, who was his major fundraiser. Moreover, in some instances, Malhar Rao Holkar and Nanasaheb were seen supporting opposing factions, which also led to strife amongst the Marathas.

Also spoiled during his rule was the Maratha–Jat relationship. In this case, Nanasaheb and his younger brother Raghunathrao sought compensation from the state of Bharatpur, which had interfered in settling family disputes in the Jaipur clan. Raghunathrao and Malhar Rao Holkar were on one side, while Nanasaheb was on the other. Raghunathrao attacked Bharatpur for failing to pay the amount he had sought. This antagonized Suraj Mal, the ruler of Bharatpur. All of this notwithstanding, Nanasaheb was soon to face his real challenge.

Afghan king Ahmed Shah Durrani had been knocking on India's doors for a while. Interestingly, the Mughals would be the first to face his attack and had to, eventually, seek help from the Marathas. The situation forced the Mughals to sign an agreement with the Marathas in 1752 in exchange for Nanasaheb getting the governorship of Agra and Ajmer. They also had to give the Marathas the right to collect taxes from places as far as Lahore, Sindh and Multan. However, the Mughal emperor had simultaneously conceded some of the same regions to Durrani in an effort to make peace. And though he had promised the Marathas governorship over certain regions, those were never actually transferred. By fooling the Marathas, the Mughals successfully deflected Durrani towards the Marathas.

At this point, it so happened that Raghunathrao, fighting on behalf of Nanasaheb, defeated Durrani in a major battle and drove him away from Lahore and Peshawar. At this time, the Marathas were so powerful that they overshadowed the Mughal empire. Nanasaheb, Raghunathrao, the likes of the Holkars and others made for a formidable combination that took the Maratha empire to its zenith – to the extent that Nanasaheb Peshwa was in a position to instal his son Vishwasrao on the Mughal throne. Alarmed by the possibility of the Peshwas taking over the empire, the Mughals, in turn, approached Durrani – against whom they had fought – to save them from Maratha aggression.

This encouraged Durrani to launch a fresh attack on Lahore. Supporting him in his mission were Najib ad-Dawlah and Shuja-ud-Daula, two Rohilla nawabs from the present-day Uttar Pradesh region. Nanasaheb sent a large contingent led by commander Sadashivrao Bhau, the son of Chimaji Appa, to take on Durrani. Helping him actively were the Holkars of Indore, Scindias of Gwalior and Gaekwads of Vadodara. For a while they were successful in winning over Suraj Mal of Bharatpur too but couldn't retain him.

This was around 1759. For the next two years, the Marathas were engaged in fighting Durrani. Unfortunately for the Marathas, it ended in defeat in the Battle of Panipat on 14 January 1761, one that was so comprehensive that the Marathas could never recover from it. It pushed them back by at least a century. All the gains made by Shivaji, Baji Rao and Nanasaheb – and Maratha supremacy on the whole – were washed away completely in this battle of nerves.

There were many reasons for this debacle. Durrani proved supreme in every aspect of war. Not only did his army outnumber Sadashivrao's, but he was excellent with tactics as well. Though the Marathas possessed some of the best French-made guns of the time, they lacked the flexibility in manoeuvring displayed by the Afghan forces. Against the Marathas' guns, Durrani had strong, long-range cannons. And, aside from these machines, what let down the Marathas was their man management.

The Maratha chieftains had egos coming in the way of the larger goal of defeating Durrani. Each one of them – Holkar, Scindia and others – had his own fiefdom in mind and not the interest of the Maratha state as a whole. They never factored in the reality that the theatre of war was far away from their familiar geography – it was over a thousand miles away from the Deccan. Moreover, the decision to make Sadashivrao the commander proved to be short-sighted because the geographical and political situation of the north was alien to him. Veterans such as Raghunathrao and Malhar Rao Holkar were ignored in this crucial battle.

The Marathas lost over 40,000 of their men. An entire generation was lost in Panipat. Many of them were publicly beheaded by the Afghan forces, and their wives and other family members were taken as slaves. Nanasaheb was in Vidisha, in present-day Madhya Pradesh, when he received the news of the defeat on 24 January 1761. He was busy planning reinforcements to be sent but it was too late. It came as a personal blow to Nanasaheb, who, along with his senior generals and thousands of men and women, also lost his son Vishwasrao and cousin Sadashivrao Bhau. A shattered Nanasaheb died on 23 June 1761 in Pune.

Succeeding him was his second son, Madhavrao, who led the Marathas' efforts to recover from the losses inflicted on them at Panipat. It was during his rule that the Maratha empire shone again briefly. Unfortunately, he did not live long enough to arrest its decline.

9

The Beginning of the End

With Madhavrao began the final act of the epic tragedy called Peshwai. Today the word has assumed a different connotation. Implying an upper-caste bias, it is now associated with all things bad about Brahminism – which was not the case till Madhavrao Peshwa I was at the helm.

Madhavrao was only sixteen when he donned the Peshwa's hat. At the time, the Maratha empire was shattered and in huge debt. But the Peshwas remained almost oblivious to the situation, continuing with their grand religious rituals. Madhavrao's first task was to streamline the systems. The toughest challenge was the resurrection of Maratha power in the aftermath of the Panipat debacle. This difficult task proved even harder because of Raghunathrao, his uncle, who had harboured a dream of becoming the Peshwa himself but could never achieve it. The relationship was so soured that he even deserted Madhavrao midway in his mission against the Nizam. Soon enough, Madhavrao also attempted to build his own army. Wary of waging a war against his own uncle, he offered a truce, which Raghunathrao accepted. Although the agreement was to not attack each other, Raghunathrao didn't keep his end of the bargain.

Madhavrao was caught completely off guard by Raghunathrao's assault on his forces. Raghunathrao even had plans to seek help from the Nizam to run the state. Fortunately for the Marathas, wisdom prevailed. Madhavrao too pointed out the dangers of aligning with the enemy. It resulted in the uncle and nephew joining hands, albeit the peace was again short-lived. Wary of Madhavrao's growing clout, Raghunathrao backed off from his ambitious campaign against Hyder Ali of Mysore in 1764. Instead, he chose to go to Nashik to perform some religious rituals. Perhaps as a result of this, Madhavrao's first campaign yielded no results. In 1767, he organized another expedition against Hyder Ali and made significant gains. Incidentally, that was the year British officers called on Madhavrao in Pune to seek his support in setting up their bases in Vasai and Sashti in return for their assistance in conquering Hyder Ali. But young Madhavrao was an astute politician and clearly understood their intentions. He firmly rejected their proposal.

Around this time Raghunathrao's desire to dethrone Madhavrao resurfaced. But just as he was preparing his army to attack Madhavrao, the Peshwa launched a full-fledged attack on him. In June 1768, Raghunathrao was captured and put under house arrest in Shaniwar Wada along with his adviser Sakharam Bapu Bokil, another Brahmin. The following year, while returning home from Pune's Parvati temple, Madhavrao was attacked by one of his own soldiers on the instructions of Raghunathrao. Although he only sustained a shoulder injury, it brought to the fore the deep divisions between the uncle and nephew. The situation only got worse with time as Madhavrao was diagnosed with tuberculosis. The news revived Raghunathrao's hopes, who then tried to escape but got caught. The incident took a toll on Madhavrao, who was already weak and extremely lonely. On the one hand, his mother, Gopikabai, had deserted him following his decision to fine his maternal uncle for dereliction of duty in protecting the city of Pune. On the other, his paternal uncle Raghunathrao was after his life. He could not survive for long and gave up his fight on 18 November 1772 at the age of just twenty-seven. After the Panipat disaster, this was yet another setback for the Marathas.

In his short life, Madhavrao had proved to be a capable leader and administrator and was able to bring back the derailed Maratha empire on track briefly. Known to be a strict disciplinarian, he plugged loopholes in the revenue system. He also revived public flogging as the punishment for corrupt government officials. As a result, he earned the common man's respect and goodwill. He is also credited with establishing an extremely fair judicial system led by Ram Shastri Prabhune. It was unfortunate that his untimely death expedited the end of the Maratha empire.

AFTER MADHAVRAO'S DEMISE, HIS younger brother and Nanasaheb's third son, Narayanrao, ascended the throne. Having lost two elder brothers – Vishwasrao in Panipat and Madhavrao to tuberculosis – Narayanrao now had to contend with his extremely ambitious and bitter uncle Raghunathrao, who was unwilling to concede the post of Peshwa to his younger nephew. Narayanrao was also compelled to place him under house arrest. But Raghunathrao soon created an opportunity for himself.

Narayanrao was killed in a ruthless coup executed at Shaniwar Wada itself. Raghunathrao and his wife Anandibai used the services of the guards, who hacked Narayanrao to death in front of his wife Gangabai. A hapless Narayanrao's cries of 'Uncle, save me' did not help. The murder was so brutal that his body parts were carried away in an urn, which was buried by the river in Pune the same night.

After eliminating his nephew, Raghunathrao finally became the Peshwa. But his reign did not last long. He too faced a royal revolt as many of the Peshwa sardars opposed his ascent. At the time of Narayanrao's death, Gangabai was pregnant. She delivered a boy, named Sawai Madhavrao, who was installed as the next Peshwa. The responsibility to groom him lay on the shoulders of Nana Fadnavis, an influential sardar, a back-room operator who came to be known as the Maratha Machiavelli – a title he earned from the British for his skills.

Nana, a Brahmin from Wai near Kolhapur, was secretary to Sadashivrao Bhau and was one of the few to have survived the Battle of Panipat. His grandfather, Balaji Bhanu, had saved the Peshwas from the Mughals, which earned him the title of Fadnavis. They soon put him in charge of finance, and the legacy continued. Nana went on to become a close confidant of Madhavrao and played an important role under him in streamlining the Peshwai. He was one of the key opponents of Raghunathrao. After Narayanrao's death, it was he who led a coalition of twelve sardars that dethroned Raghunathrao. The group, called 'Baarbhai', also protected the infant Sawai Madhavrao, who was made the Peshwa when he was only forty days old. He later imprisoned Anandibai and her two sons after Raghunathrao's death in 1783 due to unknown reasons. Needless to say, Sawai Madhavrao was just a puppet figure at the time, while real power lay in the hands of Nana Fadnavis and the Baarbhai.

Such were his governance skills that the British developed a strong dislike for him and tried to get rid of him. But he was smart enough to read their designs. When Raghunathrao sought help from the British in taking over Pune, Nana showed amazing shrewdness in forging an alliance with the Nizam and the Bhosale branch of the Maratha empire from Satara. The British were forced to sign a treaty with the Marathas in 1775. When they attempted to strike, Nana counterattacked and inflicted a crushing defeat on them in 1779 at Pune.

As Sawai Madhavrao grew up, he too developed animosity towards Nana for his high-handedness. He himself lacked leadership skills and was a mere pawn in Nana's hands. Frustrated with his inability to achieve anything significant in life, he committed suicide in 1795 at the age of twenty-one in Shaniwar Wada. After that, it was only a matter of time before the Maratha empire's ultimate collapse.

Nana Fadnavis died in 1800, and the British, waiting in the wings until then, wasted no time in dividing the feuding Maratha sardars one by one. Some of them – the Scindias of Gwalior, the Holkars of Indore and a few others – tried to hold on for a while. But they were too scattered and lacked the vision and wherewithal to manage an empire.

Soon it was curtains for the glorious Maratha empire. It was a rapid decline from the peak it had scaled under the Peshwas, with the Chhatrapati as the titular head, in the 1750s, when it stretched from Thanjavur in the south to Peshawar in the west and Bengal in the east. The empire did not fall because the enemy was any stronger. It folded up because the Marathas failed to overcome their petty internal differences, which prevented them from seeing the bigger picture. They never had a problem serving an outsider if there was even the smallest chance of defeating a rival from their own clan. Over 200 years, they recorded some truly great victories but invariably failed at creating a robust system that could outlive individuals. With the honourable exceptions of Chhatrapati Shivaji and Baji Rao I, they also could not keep their sardars from turning into looters and plunderers. In the final analysis, all of these factors resulted in the Marathas wasting their valour.

THE EMPIRE WAS NOW a thing of the past but individual fiefdoms held on. Finding its administration unmanageable, Madhavrao I had given a kind of autonomy to many of his knights. They ran their empires, though small, in their own right. These autonomous states included those ruled by the Gaekwads of Baroda, the Holkars of Indore, the Bhosales of Nagpur, the Scindias of Gwalior and others, along with small princely states such as Sangli (under the Patwardhans), Aundh (Pant), Phaltan (Nimbalkars) and so on. However, after the death of Madhavrao I, when central rule weakened, these satraps started flexing their muscles. This further enfeebled the Marathas as a unified force.

But there were some glorious military victories in this period too, though sporadic. For example, in the Third Battle of Panipat in

1761, Malhar Rao Holkar single-handedly took charge of Rajasthan by defeating the Rajputs. Another heroic attempt was from Mahadji Scindia, who successfully defeated the Jats and the Rohilla Afghans and went on to take over Delhi. His army was so strong that he also went on to take control of present-day Haryana. Meanwhile, small feudal states had grown in the Malwa and Bundelkhand regions which tried to avoid paying taxes to the Scindias. Mahadji ended their reign by sending his army to conquer states such as Bhopal, Datiya, Chanderi, Narwar, Salbai and Gohad. It was the ruler of Gohad, Chhatar Singh, who controlled the magnificent Gwalior fort. The Scindias' association with Gwalior began when Mahadji's men conquered it. Later he turned to Delhi again and kept his firm grip over it for over twenty-five years. But Jodhpur and Jaipur were two prominent Rajput states that were outside Maratha domination. In time, Mahadji sent his French military official General Count de Boigne, who crushed the Rajputs. Later, Marwar too was captured by the Scindias. Meanwhile, another branch of the Marathas, the Holkars of Indore, had taken on Tipu Sultan of Mysore, Hyder Ali's successor. Tukoji Rao Holkar, the adopted son of Malhar Rao, faced Tipu in Gajendragad in the Gadag district of present-day Karnataka and defeated him.

Yet another branch of the Marathas flourished in the south for over two centuries. This was the Bhosales, who were the descendants of Shahaji. Venkoji, the half-brother of Chhatrapati Shivaji, was the first raja of Thanjavur from the Bhosale dynasty. He ruled until 1684. After Venkoji's death, his eldest son, Shahuji I, ascended the throne at the age of twelve. His regime witnessed the Mughals occupying the Cholamandalam coast along with Tiruchirappalli. Around 150 years later, this branch of the Marathas too was significantly weakened and eventually annexed by the British.

The final nail in the Maratha empire's coffin was struck by Mountstuart Elphinstone, who came to Pune as the British Resident in 1811. He remained in the Deccan till 1827, perfectly exploiting the divisions between the feuding Maratha sardars – the Gaekwads of Baroda, the Patwardhans from Sangli and Baji Rao II, the son of Raghunathrao. In 1812, the Patwardhans went under British protection, while the Gaekwads had a running dispute with the Peshwa over the payment of arrears. In 1815, the Gaekwads sent their representative, Gangadhar Shastri, to Pune to settle the dispute. Considering the animosity between the two groups, Elphinstone stepped in to mediate and offered Shastri protection during his stay. By the time he reached the Peshwas' seat of power, it was Aashadhi Ekadashi – an auspicious day in the month of Aashadh which marks the beginning of the holy season for devout Hindus. The day also witnesses congregations of warakaris walking down around 185 kilometres from Dehu–Alandi in Pune to Pandharpur, the home of Lord Vithoba, to commemorate the day. Exploiting Shastri's religious sentiments, Baji Rao II offered him a yatra to Pandharpur.

Unmindful of Baji Rao II's motives, Shastri went to Pandharpur, where he was caught completely unawares and killed by the Peshwa's confidant Trimbakji Dengale. The news came as a rude shock to Elphinstone, who was at Ellora near Aurangabad at the time. He immediately rushed to Pune and asked Baji Rao II to hand over Dengale, which the Peshwa refused to do. It provided the perfect opportunity for the British officer to intervene, which he did not waste. Elphinstone laid siege to Pune on 8 May 1816 that forced Baji Rao II to completely surrender while declaring Trimbakji Dengale as the traitor. Dengale was the last of the Maratha sardars to show courage in trying to save the dying empire, but in vain.

IN 1817 BEGAN THE British assault on the Maratha empire. Baji Rao II was not a warrior. He chose to run away and tried seeking help from the Holkars, the Scindias and the Patwardhans. None obliged. Finally, in 1818, he was arrested by the British forces. To save himself, he accepted their condition that he would spend the rest of his life at a place chosen by them and not return to Pune. He was also forced to give up all his claims to the empire and relinquish the title of Peshwa. He was sent to a small place near Kanpur, where the

British had a substantially large military base. The man who once ruled most of the Deccan lived a faceless life for over thirty-three years and died in captivity there in 1851.

The last years of the Peshwas had become synonymous with complete lawlessness. Baji Rao II had ascended the throne in 1796 following Sawai Madhavrao's death. For the next twenty-two years, the Peshwas faced a rapid decline every passing day, resulting in the demise of the Maratha empire by 1818. The last Peshwa was known as 'palputa' or 'runaway' Baji Rao because of his timidity and incapability. In the end, the Union Jack was unfurled on the magnificent Shaniwar Wada, the seat of Peshwa power in Pune.

After defeating the Peshwas comprehensively, the first thing Elphinstone did was to reinstate the Satara-based King Pratapsingh Bhosale, one of Chhatrapati Shivaji's descendants, as the head of the Maratha kingdom. It was a precursor to the British divide-and-rule policy as it delegitimized the Brahmin Peshwas and painted them as usurpers of power from Shivaji's heirs, who were Marathas. They were so successful that the rift they created continues to widen even in the twenty-first century.

Helping Elphinstone was a young British officer, James Grant Duff. He had joined the British infantry at the young age of eighteen. Efficient and quick to learn, he was soon noticed by Elphinstone, who deployed his services just as the Peshwas were winding up. It was his first-hand experience during this period that helped him write his magnum opus, *A History of the Mahrattas*, one of the most essential books covering the developments after Shivaji. As a veteran, Elphinstone personally hand-held him in wading through the complex history and making sense of it. It's no wonder, then, that Duff became the first Western writer to analyse the 'Mahratta' character. He candidly noted that the Marathas of the time had failed to live by the vision laid down by Shivaji and that they were inconsistent. According to him, the Marathas could hold on for as long as they did not due to their strategic planning but because their enemies were even weaker. He was not the only one to have thought so. 'Considering the consistent decay in the moral character of the last two to three generations of rulers, the end was inevitable and not at all surprising,' wrote historian V.K. Rajwade.

The point to be noted is that in the final years of the empire, the region was bereft of a leader worth his name. There were many Maratha satraps around, but none of them succeeded in arresting the decline, whether singly or unitedly. Their collective failure was not only monumental but also unparalleled in history.

The fall of the Maratha empire removed the last hurdle in the way of the East India Company's rule over India. From 1600 to 1757, British operations in India had been mainly confined to trade through the company. The Battle of Plassey of 1757, in which it decisively defeated the Nawab of Bengal, changed its course. The Company then took over Bengal, which had until then been in the hands of various regional kings. Slowly, it took away the powers of most of them.

But the Marathas, even at their weakest, denied the East India Company unchallenged access to its prized possession, India. By the end of the eighteenth century, all of the north and east had come under Company rule. The only hurdle it faced was from the Maratha fiefs and the Deccan, which was under the Peshwas. The Marathas wanted to set up a 'Hindupadpatshahi', a kind of empire run by indigenous rulers after freeing the land from invaders. Unfortunately, their knowledge of economics, modern warfare and global developments did not keep up with their desire. The Marathas operated in silos. They could at times overcome rivals such as the Nizams, the Mughals and others but were totally exposed before the British.

The British fully gauged the strengths and weaknesses of the Marathas. They saw Indians as uncivilized, undisciplined, oblivious to global developments and as a people who could be won easily. They realized that there did not exist a single ruler, thinker or philosopher who held an appeal across the subcontinent and who could kindle a nationalistic spirit in his countrymen. Most of the rulers at the time were highly ignorant and self-serving, confined to the boundaries of their own fiefs.

Having decimated the Marathas, the British were keen to win over the common man, who had suffered under the state of complete lawlessness in the last few years of the Peshwas. The arrival of the British and the promise of a rule of law offered a ray of hope to the harried locals. It is little wonder, then, that they embraced the 'firangs', as the British were called, with open arms and quietly slipped into a state of subservience.

10

Renaissance State

It may seem surprising but the inglorious end of the Peshwas was largely welcomed by two sections of Maharashtrian society. The first were the poor, who had found themselves at the receiving end of the overall lawlessness during the last few years of the Peshwas. The other were the upper-caste Hindus, who were the first to sense the opportunity in aligning with the British.

Europe was going through the industrial revolution at the beginning of the nineteenth century and England was its epicentre in a way. Machines had started replacing men, machine tools were being invented and, most importantly, the steam engine had multiplied the horsepower manyfold. Several inventions were taking place in England then, the most important among them being mechanized spinning. It revolutionized the textile sector, and brought about unbelievable changes in the way Indians conducted their business.

India, even before the advent of the British, was robust in textiles. In the mid-eighteenth century, it dominated the global textile business, thanks to its cheap labour. But by the early nineteenth century, it had been converted into a British colony. The British started sourcing raw materials from India and dumped finished textile products back here. It changed the way Indians ran their business.

Another major technological innovation that came to India was printing. Although Johannes Gutenberg, who lived in the fifteenth century, is considered the father of modern printing, the industrial revolution brought rapid changes to the technology. Steam power began to be used to run the mechanical parts of printing machines, and flat printing beds were replaced by rotary cylinders. It speeded up the printing process.

Around this time, a small piece of legislation helped India adapt to Britain's modernizing influence more easily. About five years before the regime of the Peshwas came to an end and the East India Company established its rule, the Parliament of Great Britain passed the East India Company Act in 1813, also known as the Charter Act of 1813, directing the company to encourage modern education in India by spending a sum of one lakh rupees every year to educate Indian masses. A section of British officers in India had originally thought of strengthening the traditional Sanskrit schools here. But the first person to advocate modern education in India was the Bengali reformer Raja Ram Mohan Roy, according to whom Western education was the key to 'the treasures of scientific and democratic thought of the West'. But before British politician Lord Thomas Babington Macaulay could lay the foundation of modern education in India with his 'Minute on Indian Education', one relatively lesser-known and unacknowledged Maharashtrian took a giant leap in that direction.

Balshastri Jambhekar (1812–46) was a brilliant academic and the father of Marathi journalism, who launched the weekly *Darpan* (Mirror) as early as 1832 to spread modern values. Priced at one rupee then, *Darpan* was a bilingual newspaper with English and Marathi writings in two columns. The newspaper was a completely new idea in India in those days. It took a while for people to understand its importance. Balshastri was also an assistant professor in Bombay's Elphinstone College. Mathematics, astronomy and physics were his areas of interest. He was also equally proficient in Greek, Latin, French, Arabic, Farsi, Bengali, Gujarati and Kannada.

Balshastri founded the Bombay Native General Library. He also started the Native Improvement Society, on which was modelled the Students' Literary and Scientific Society that went on to inspire intellectual giants such as Dadabhai Naoroji and Bhau Daji Lad. Incidentally, he was also the first Indian to have published research papers in the quarterly journal of the Asiatic Society. It was he who is known to have published *Dnyaneshwari* in 1845.

Balshastri was the first intellectual from Maharashtra to speak against child marriage. He was an equally strong proponent of widow remarriage. One can only imagine the debate and controversy his stand must have triggered in Maharashtra's orthodox society then. Unlike his Bengali counterparts like Raja Ram Mohan Roy, who were primarily interested in subjects such as philosophy, theology and so on, Balshastri was solely focused on social issues. He consistently wrote critically on the prevailing social ills in his columns in *Darpan*. He was a man with interests in various issues.

He also happens to be the first to flag the issue of unfair taxation by the British. It is interesting to note that while he was impressed by the modern, scientific attitude of the British, he was equally aware of their exploitative ways at the same time. In his columns, he exposed the discriminatory taxation policies adopted by the British and explained how they were designed to destroy India's agriculture. In 1840, he launched the first Marathi monthly, *Digdarshan* (Direction), and published articles on various subjects, including physics, chemistry, geography and history. Besides, he also authored books like *Neetikatha* (Stories on Morality), *Encyclopaedic History of England, English Grammar, History of India* and *Mathematics Based on Zero*. Unfortunately, Balshastri died at the young age of just thirty-four. But he left behind a lasting impression on Maharashtrian society, which went on to produce brilliant public intellectuals one after another.

Around the same time as Balshastri, another Maharashtrian came down heavily on the British with his sharp critique of Company rule. Bhaskar Pandurang Tarkhadkar (1816–47) was the first intellectual who, in eight long letters published in the *Bombay Gazette* as early as 1841, put forward the 'drain theory' to explain how the British were exploiting India's wealth. The fact that his proposition was later expanded by Dadabhai Naoroji on a much wider scale shows his importance. His elder brother, Dadoba Pandurang (1814–82), was also a social reformer, besides being a linguist whose major work, *Maharastra Bhasheche Vyakaran*, published in 1836, made a significant contribution to the grammar of the Marathi language. Another one of the Tarkhadkars, Atmaram Pandurang (1823–98), was a physicist and one of the founders of the Prarthana Samaj. A student of the first batch at Bombay's Grant Medical College – incidentally along with Dr Bhau Daji Lad – Atmaram ran a smallpox vaccination campaign and later helped frame Article 14 of the Contagious Diseases Act in the 1860s. Like his brothers, he too was a bitter critic of many Hindu traditions, including child marriage. He was at the forefront of demanding twenty years as the minimum age for a girl's marriage. Balshastri Jambhekar is considered the pioneer of the intellectual awakening that Maharashtra witnessed during that period and Dadoba offered it an organizational structure by founding the Paramahansa Mandali in 1849, a secret socio-religious body with a mission to demolish all caste distinctions. Interestingly, none of the three Tarkhadkars used their surname.

Following in their footsteps was Gopal Hari Deshmukh (1823–92), also known as Lokhitwadi (champion of people's welfare), another influential social reformer. He didn't mince his words while describing the state of the natives: 'The lack of knowledge in Hindus, and amongst Brahmins, is the biggest curse,' he wrote. 'The society is caught in a time warp: how Lord Vishnu sleeps on a giant cobra, Rahu and Ketu capturing the moon and the sun – this is the standard of knowledge of this society. It's far, far away from modern physics, geography, astronomy...'

At the age of twenty-five, while working as a translator under the British and later as a small causes judge, Deshmukh started writing on social issues under his pen name in the weekly *Prabhakar* edited by Govind Vitthal Kunte, who was popularly known as Bhau Mahajan. In the first two years, he wrote over a hundred such articles on topics ranging from child marriage, women's education and polygamy to the importance of modern education. These have been compiled in the book *Lokhitwadinchi Shatpatre* (The Hundred Letters of Lokhitwadi), a gem in Marathi literature that continues to inspire even today. He had a clear target in mind: the Brahmins, whom he found resistant to change. It was also quite courageous on his part to prescribe English education while denouncing Sanskrit in those days. But he did it all.

He was the first to come down heavily on the caste system while challenging the power the Brahmins enjoyed. The point to be noted here is that he was critical of Brahminism while being a Brahmin himself. He was one of the pioneers of the social reform movement in Maharashtra. He was actively involved in launching periodicals like *Dnyan Prakash, Indu Prakash* and *Lokhitwadi*. Later, having been appointed as a judge in Ahmedabad, he worked in Gujarat too in various areas, including widow remarriage. Considering that Gujarat was more backward than Maharashtra at the time, his decisions to launch a weekly, *Hitechchhu,* in both Gujarati and English and to start the Gujarati Budhhi-Wardhak Sabha are considered far ahead of their time.

BALSHASTRI JAMBHEKAR AND LOKHITWADI set the stage for one of the most important social reformers that India has seen: the anti-caste thinker and activist Mahatma Jyotirao Phule (1827–90). Scholar Hulas Singh writes in his book *Rise of Reason: Intellectual History of 19th-century Maharashtra*, '[Phule] represented a radical departure from the mainstream movement ... he condemned caste with utter abomination single-mindedly.' Mahatma Phule wasn't happy with the small social measures suggested by reformers until then; he wanted a complete, revolutionary transformation. He was the first to propose a social system based on the modern European principles of equality. His three books – *Gulamgiri* (Slavery), *Shetkaryancha Asud* (The Whipcord of Cultivators) and *Sarvajanik Satyadharma*

Pustak (A True Religion of Public Life), published posthumously – are considered the solid foundation for social reforms in India.

Along with the eradication of untouchability, Mahatma Phule is considered the pioneering champion for the emancipation of women. He and his wife, Savitribai, were among the first native Indians to open a school for girls in India. While he was in his early twenties, he visited the first girls' school in Ahmednagar, run by Christian missionaries, in 1848. The same year he read Thomas Paine's *Rights of Man*, which helped him develop a keen sense of social justice. Then onwards the education of those belonging to the lower castes and women became the mission of his life.

On 24 September 1873, Phule, along with his followers, formed the Satyashodhak Samaj (Society to Seek Truth) to demand equal rights for the lower castes. Phule's approach to social issues was fundamentally different in every respect. He tried to restructure the Aryan invasion theory by saying that they were responsible for the subcontinent's social divisions, which they achieved mainly by subjugation. According to him, Lord Rama symbolized the social oppression brought in by the Aryans, and the Vedas, which are dear to Hindus, created a 'false sense of consciousness'. He held Muslim rulers guilty too of being equally repressive. It led him to suggest that British rule over India was a blessing of sorts. He publicly celebrated the failure of the 1857 uprising against the British as he felt the Brahmins would return to rule otherwise.

It was Mahatma Phule who coined the term 'Dalit' to encapsulate the situation of the oppressed classes, and it went on to assume huge importance in India's political and social lexicon. Therefore, it is no wonder that he became the inspiration for one of the most groundbreaking social reformers Maharashtra and India have ever produced: Dr Bhimrao Ramji Ambedkar.

IN 1857, JOHN WILSON, a Scottish Christian missionary and founder of Wilson College in Bombay (now Mumbai), set up one of the most premier educational institutions in the country, the University of Bombay. It helped strengthen the intellectual fibre of Maharashtrian society, which was witnessing the emergence of a plethora of scholars who went on to become the leading lights of India. Sociology, mathematics, astronomy, philosophy, economics – there wasn't a single sector not led by a Maharashtrian. The rise of Bombay University coincided with the birth of journals such as *Vividh Dnyan Vistar* and *Marathi Dnyan Prasarak*, which helped spread modern Western values.

It is not a coincidence that the second half of the nineteenth century produced a spectacular array of intellectuals from different walks of life. Maharashtra with its many scholars – such as Pandit Vishnu Parasuram Shastri (1827–76), Ramakrishna Gopal Bhandarkar (1837–1925), Narayan Mahadev Paramanand (1838–93), Mahadev Govind Ranade (1842–1901), Vishnushastri Chiplunkar (1850–82), Kashinath Trimbak Telang (1850–93), Ganesh Vasudev Joshi (1828–80), Narayan Ganesh Chandavarkar (1855–1923), Gopal Ganesh Agarkar (1856–95), Pandita Ramabai (1858–1922) and Dhondo Keshav Karve (1858–1962), among others – became the cerebral powerhouse of India.

Unfortunately, many of them have been forgotten. What's more interesting is the fact that these reformers, scholars and intellectuals came from all over Maharashtra and not just the cities of Bombay and Poona (as Pune came to be called in the colonial times). It's worth recalling the contribution of some of them here.

Pandit Vishnu Parasuram Shastri: In 1855, Pandit Ishwar Chandra Vidyasagar raised the issue of widow remarriage in Bengal. He sought the government's permission to let widows enter into matrimony again. A year later, the law was amended and widows were allowed to remarry. This triggered a major movement in Bengal and Maharashtra for widows' rehabilitation. Pandit Vishnu Parasuram Shastri was among the few who took the initiative in Maharashtra.

Having studied English and worked in the government's education department, Shastri published a book called *Brahman Kanya Vivah*

Vichar (Thoughts on the Marriage of Brahmin Girls). It was quite extraordinary for its clarity of thought. He put forward a rational idea behind matrimony at a time when society believed that marriages were made in heaven. He proposed a kind of agreement that mature brides and grooms should consider entering into before finalizing an alliance.

Following his mission, Shastri also translated Ishwar Chandra Vidyasagar's book *Vidhava Vivah* (Hindu Widow Marriage) into Marathi. The book created quite a stir in a society that was happy worshipping old values. There were heated exchanges between the conservatives and those proposing modern changes. Later, Shastri joined the newspaper *Induprakash* in Bombay to spearhead his mission against child marriage, widows' right to remarry and against 'jarath-kumari vivah', a practice that allowed aged men to marry young, even pre-pubescent, girls. Shastri's speech in Bombay on 'Striyanche Adhikar' (women's rights) was quite fiery.

Sir Ramakrishna Gopal Bhandarkar: He was another leading light of society, fondly known as 'Pitamaha', the grand old man, of Indology. He came from Malvan, a tiny town in the Konkan, to Bombay for higher education and was part of the first batch of graduates from the university, along with Mahadev Govind Ranade. He then went to get a PhD from a German university. A top-class orientalist and Indologist, Bhandarkar became a professor of Sanskrit at Elphinstone College in Bombay and later at Deccan College, Poona. He also went on to become the Vice Chancellor of Bombay University. Such was his scholarly persona that he was invited as a keynote speaker to many international forums.

Bhandarkar is credited with restructuring the history of the Deccan of the Satavahanas, and also of Vaishnavism and other sects. Like Shastri, he too was a vocal advocate of widow remarriage and criticized the evil tradition of child marriage. He actively participated in a campaign to educate girls and took the lead in setting up a school in Poona exclusively for girls. He and a few other liberals came together to push for social reforms, which resulted in the founding of the Prarthana Samaj in Bombay. The well-known Oriental Research Institute in Poona, set up in 1917, has been named after Bhandarkar as a tribute to the orientalist par excellence. The British too acknowledged his scholarship by knighting him in 1911.

Narayan Mahadev Paramanand: Popularly known as Mama Paramanand, he came from an extremely poor family in Mangaon near Sawantwadi in the Konkan. Like many of his contemporaries, he too joined the teaching profession after his graduation in Bombay. A progressive, Mama taught many students who went on to make a mark, the Indologist and judge Kashinath Trimbak Telang being one of them. He then entered the field of journalism and edited newspapers such as *Induprakash*, *Native Opinion* and *Indian Spectator*. He wrote extensively on social issues in English and started criticizing the British for their exploitation of India. He was greatly influenced by Benjamin Franklin and propagated social and religious reforms.

Because of his knowledge and commitment to social reforms, many important personalities including Maharaja Sayajirao Gaekwad of Vadodara (Baroda during colonial times), Mahadev Govind Ranade and others were regularly in touch with him to seek his advice. Mama was at the forefront of raising aid for Mahatma Phule when he was in dire need, including writing to Maharaja Gaekwad for financial help. He was also one of the founder members of the Prarthana Samaj and an editor for its mouthpiece *Subodh Patrika*.

Mahadev Govind Ranade: Volumes have been written about Justice Ranade's immense contributions to India's intellectual and social fields. On his 101st birth anniversary celebrations on 18 January 1943, Dr B.R. Ambedkar spoke of him thus:

> Nobody can question that Ranade had intellect of a high calibre. He was not merely a lawyer and a judge of the High Court, he was a first-class economist, a first-class historian, a first-class educationist, and a first-class Divine. Indeed, it would be difficult

> to find in the history of India any man who could come up to Ranade in the width of his learning, the breadth of his wisdom and the length of his vision. There was no subject which he did not touch and in which he did not acquire profundity. His reading was on the scale of the colossal and he was every inch a scholar. He was great not merely by the standard of his time, but he was great – measured by any standard.

Justice Ranade was undoubtedly one of India's foremost scholar-reformers. Like many others, he too denounced the caste system and untouchability and pushed for widow remarriage, the liberation of women and emancipation of the oppressed classes. He was among the first few nineteenth-century intellectuals, along with Dadabhai Naoroji, to extensively criticize the British for their economic policies. But unlike Naoroji, who blamed only the British for India's poverty, Justice Ranade felt, 'State help is after all a subordinate factor in the problem [of India's poverty]. Our exertion and our own resolution must conquer the difficulties which are chiefly of our own creation.'

In his career as a judge, he rose from the rank of a presidency magistrate in 1871 to Justice of the Bombay High Court in 1893. As a judge, he exercised his powers to promote equality of the sexes, spread education, rescue children and widows from social injustices, and protect agricultural workers and land tenants from exploitation. He always advocated constitutional and legal means for attaining freedom and bringing about social reforms. Later in life he became involved in the working of a number of institutions aimed at the social, economic and political advancement of India, such as the Poona Sarvajanik Sabha, Social Conference, Industrial Conference and Prarthana Samaj.

He was also considered to be a great historian, who published books on Marathas as well as on Indian economics. He considered Western education as a vital element in the formation of a new and progressive India. A reformer, lover of justice and a believer of equality among all, he inspired many other Indian social reformers through his works. Among his many contributions, there is one more, though it has been largely forgotten: he was a founder member of the Indian National Congress.

Vishnushastri Chiplunkar: 'Nothing can compensate a nation for the loss of freedom', 'All the native princes in India are mere puppets in the hands of respective political agents', 'The condition of the natives is not better than that of the lower animals' – these are some examples of the fiery writings of Vishnushastri Chiplunkar from Poona. Born to Sanskrit scholar Krushnashastri, Vishnushastri was an excellent writer both in Sanskrit as well as English. He is the one who famously compared the English language to a tigress: 'Whoever is brought up on her milk cannot be a pushover.' Though he appreciated the modern values that came with the British, he was equally critical of their rule for taking away India's freedom. He was proud of his Chitpavan Brahmin lineage and, although he was a social reformer too, he had his differences with Mahatma Phule.

Known for his razor-sharp and caustic writing style, Vishnushastri launched scathing attacks on the British. Two of his essays, 'Amchya Deshachi Sthiti' (The State of Our Nation) and 'Mudranswatantrya' (Freedom of the Press), are remembered even today. Having earned a degree from Deccan College, Vishnushastri initially worked as a schoolteacher and later joined hands with Bal Gangadhar Tilak and Gopal Ganesh Agarkar to launch the Marathi daily *Kesari* and the English *Mahratta*. He also opened two printing presses and a bookstore. Before that, he had started a monthly, *Nibandhmala* (Series of Essays), to enlighten Marathi readers on various issues.

A voracious reader and prolific writer, Vishnushastri has a large collection of writings to his name. Besides his original works, he also translated Samuel Johnson's *Rasselas*, Edward Lane's *The Arabian Nights* and the seventh-century Sanskrit scholar Banabhatta's *Kadambari* into Marathi. He accomplished all this and more before he died of typhoid at the young age of thirty-two in 1882.

Kashinath Trimbak Telang: A brilliant lawyer, Indologist, Sanskrit scholar, accomplished translator and social reformer, K.T. Telang was elevated to the Bombay High Court at the age of just thirty-nine. He was the first Maharashtrian to have been appointed a permanent high court judge. He also held two other high-profile posts – Vice Chancellor of Bombay University and head of the Bombay branch of the Royal Asiatic Society.

Telang lived for only forty-three years, but the range of his accomplishments is nothing short of amazing. Albrecht Weber, a German Indologist and historian, was the first to underline the social philosophy of Buddhism as well as compare the Ramayana with Homer's epics. It was Telang who analysed and criticized Weber, in a most erudite way, unknown to the Marathi audience then. As a reformer, it was he who strongly argued in favour of keeping religion separate from education. A strong votary of educating children in native languages, Telang also undertook a mission to write the glorious history of the Marathas. Unfortunately, his untimely death deprived us of what could have been a great scholarly work.

Around the end of the nineteenth century, the Maharashtra region, as well as India as a whole, was witnessing a serious issue: what should be the minimum age for consensual sexual intercourse for girls? The battleground for this issue was Bombay, as the trigger for the debate was eleven-year-old Rukhmabai Arjun, the stepdaughter of physician Dr Sakharam Arjun, who was refusing to consummate her marriage with her nineteen-year-old husband, Dadaji Bhikaji. In March 1884, Bhikaji sent her a legal notice saying she had refused him his conjugal rights. This led to a major debate as it was the first time the interpretation of Hindu law vis-à-vis its traditions became an issue.

Fighting on behalf of Rukhmabai was Telang, who along with Justice Ranade was in favour of upholding girls' rights. The debate over whether girls should be allowed to deny husbands their 'legitimate right' in the first place and, if yes, what the age should be below which a physical relationship should not be enforced on them stirred society like never before. On the one hand there were people opposing girls' rights and on the other were reformists like Ranade and Telang. In between was the British government trying to frame a suitable law, which was seen as an interference in the 'Hindu way of life' by many, including Tilak.

Rukhmabai became the first woman in India to stand up for her rights. After a series of court cases that did not go in her favour, she took the issue all the way up to Queen Victoria, who then overruled the courts and annulled the marriage. Not just that, Bhikaji was also ordered to pay Rukhmabai two thousand rupees. The case eventually led to the Age of Consent Act of 1891, which raised the minimum age for consensual sexual intercourse for all girls, married or unmarried, from ten to twelve. The whole issue is a glorious – and unfortunately forgotten – chapter in Maharashtra's history.

Dhondo Keshav Karve: If there is one area that sets Maharashtra apart from the rest, it is women's empowerment. Much of the credit for that goes to Dhondo Keshav Karve, who resolutely fought for women's causes his whole life with a missionary zeal. A professor of mathematics at Poona's Fergusson College, Karve was inspired by the thoughts of Vishnushastri Chiplunkar and Pandita Ramabai and decided to take up the issue of women's rights and education. Today it is difficult to imagine the backlash he had to face from society when he decided to marry a widow after his first wife had passed away. The widows of those days were tonsured and compelled to live a celibate life. They were objects of ridicule and abuse even within their own families.

When Dhondo Keshav, a Chitpavan Brahmin, married a widow, he was ostracized for 'his sin' and forced to live outside the city limits. Even as he was caught in the eye of this storm, he undertook a mission to educate women. He opened India's first school exclusively for widows in Hingane, a small village on the outskirts of Poona. In a few years, he went on to set up India's first women's university, which was named Shreemati Nathibai Damodar Thackersey (SNDT) after the philanthropist Thackersey family donated a sum of fifteen lakh rupees in 1920 for the cause. He also set up the Samata Sangh for abolishing the caste system and spreading primary education.

Pandita Ramabai: 'What Mahatma Phule was to Shudras, Pandita Ramabai was to womanhood…' writes Hulas Singh in *Rise of Reason* aptly. Like Mahatma Phule, Pandita Ramabai too was a rebel with a cause, and like him she too was disenchanted with Hinduism. Her act of embracing Christianity shook Hindu society.

Born as Rama Dongre to Sanskrit scholar Anant Shastri Dongre, she followed in her father's footsteps in learning ancient Indian scriptures. In 1878, she was invited to Calcutta University to lecture on Sanskrit. It was there that her knowledge earned her the title of 'Pandita'. She married Bipin Behari Medhvi, a Bengali from a lower caste. Her marriage created controversy at the time as it was inter-caste and inter-region, and so unacceptable to many. This was her first challenge to the religion she was born into. The couple wanted to start a school for widows. But that couldn't happen and Bipin died two years after the marriage. Rama returned to Poona with their daughter Manorama and founded the Arya Mahila Samaj. Her endeavour was to fight women's oppression and she worked towards it tirelessly.

Her second challenge to religion came about when she decided to travel to England. Ramabai was undeterred when she crossed the seas, something that was total anathema to Hinduism. The next shocker was her conversion to Christianity during her stay in London. The move was the logical next step of her consistent, thoughtful denunciation of Hinduism. It shook society back home. Ramabai, Mary Rama after conversion, was so ferociously independent that she kept fighting even with the clergies for women's rights. 'I shall by no means let others lay hand on my liberty,' she would tell her fellow Christians. She did not mind being accused of lawlessness in her constant quest for freedom.

'Even animals have the freedom to establish male–female relationships according to their own wishes. Why then should human beings not have this freedom?' she asked in her famed work

Stri Dharma Niti (A Code of Conduct for Women), the other being *The High-Caste Hindu Woman*. Both books are considered to be the first indigenous intellectual articulation of feminism. Ramabai never resorted to 'male-bashing' in her feminism, and in fact rebuked women for their 'foolishness' and for being 'slothful'. She continued to struggle on a personal as well as social level after returning to India. In 1921, she lost her daughter, heir apparent and principal of the school she had established in Gadag in Karnataka. Shaken and tired after the constant struggles all through her life, Pandita Ramabai died nine months after Manorama. In a male-dominated world, the actions and thoughts of Pandita Ramabai are considered trailblazing even today.

In between Rukhmabai and Pandita Ramabai is the equally glorious chapter of Anandibai Joshi (1865–87), the first Indian woman to study Western medicine. She was born in a middle-class family in Poona and married off at the age of nine to Gopalrao Joshi, who was older than her by twenty years. He was a clerk in the postal department and, after the marriage, the couple moved to Calcutta. Unlike other men of the era, Gopalrao was a progressive, forward-thinking Brahmin, who allowed his wife to travel all the way to Pennsylvania in the US to study medicine after their son died when she was fourteen. Upon Anandibai's arrival back in India, the Kolhapur principality appointed her as a physician. Sadly, she couldn't serve for long. She met with an untimely death at the age of just twenty-one.

THERE ARE MANY MORE such examples of social warriors whose work helped Maharashtra become an intellectual hub in the second half of the nineteenth century – when other regions of India, with the exception of Bengal, lagged far behind in their struggle even for the basics.

The era also witnessed an unprecedented proliferation of publications, mainly newspapers. Journalism is an easy tool to trigger political and social debates. Towards the end of the nineteenth century, Bombay Presidency alone had as many as 133 newspapers, mostly owned by Indians. Even a cursory look at some of them, several of which have already been mentioned in this chapter, gives a sense of the high-powered intellectualism of the state.

Balshastri Jambhekar started *Bombay Darpan* in 1832, followed by the only Marathi magazine of the time, *Digdarshan*, eight years later. Bhau Mahajan launched *Prabhakar* in 1844. Lokhitwadi's popular *Dnyan Prakash* came in 1849, followed by the Anglo-Marathi *Indu Prakaṣh*, in Poona and Bombay respectively. Vishvanath Mandlik founded *Native Opinion* in 1864. A decade later came Vishnushastri Chiplunkar's *Nibandhmala* and Mahatma Phule's *Deenbandhu*. Not to forget Tilak and Agarkar's most impressive venture, the Marathi weekly *Kesari*, and the English weekly *Mahratta* beginning in January 1881. However, the duo parted ways over the question of what should be given precedence – political or social issues. In 1888, Agarkar launched his landmark initiative *Sudharak*, an Anglo-Marathi weekly with a social cause.

This was the era when the Maharashtra region clearly provided the country intellectual leadership in the social sphere. From here onwards, four Marathi men led the nation on the political front too while maintaining the region's eminent position in the social domain. Gopal Krishna Gokhale (1866–1915) and Bal Gangadhar Tilak (1856–1920) shaped India's politics while Gopal Ganesh Agarkar (1856–95) and Bhimrao Ramji Ambedkar (1891–1956) led the social dimension. After Independence, Ambedkar's leadership moulded the politics of India. Along the way, these men and women made the region the nation's cerebral powerhouse. The late eighteenth century can undoubtedly be described as Maharashtra's renaissance.

11

The Starry Sphere

The nineteenth century gave Maharashtra its distinct identity. It was the period when the region witnessed the remarkable rise of reason that made it intellectually strong. Social and political leaders of impeccable integrity and extraordinary cerebral power took it to such enviable heights that it became the powerhouse of the nation – be it in the realm of politics, economic theories or social movements. But that did not mean that the men and women leading on these fronts were always on the same page. They fought, argued, differed – but within the architecture of an intellectualism that allows us to aptly describe nineteenth-century Maharashtra as a starry sphere.

The second half of the nineteenth century witnessed the freedom movement coming into its own. The Indian National Congress was formed in 1885, and Maharashtra provided it with a slew of brilliant leaders. Maharashtra also set the agenda for the nation with developments down the years across the intellectual spectrum: from atheism to religiosity in political movements; capitalism to Marxist thought; from inspiring Mahatma Gandhi's non-violence to leading an armed movement against the British; and, interestingly, from the birth of the Congress to a call for a 'Congress-*mukt* Bharat' today.

MAHARASHTRA IS THE BIRTHPLACE of the movement for national education, which later spread throughout Bengal, as well as to Benares, where Pandit Madan Mohan Malaviya (1861–1946) set up the private Banaras Hindu University in 1916. The two leading lights of this movement were Bal Gangadhar Tilak and Gopal Ganesh Agarkar.

Understanding Agarkar's importance is necessary for many reasons. A true atheist, he steadfastly demolished the prevailing notion that linked an individual's situation to divine forces. Completely rejecting the role and importance of religion in shaping the morality of humans, he single-handedly brought atheistic rationality to the Indian intellectual tradition. He was the first to logically put forward the argument that religion was not an essential part of culture and was not needed to define morality. According to Hulas Singh, 'It was Agarkar in contemporary Indian history who raised reason to an unprecedentedly high intellectual pedestal.' Justice Ranade rightly termed that era as one of 'national awakening' while addressing the fourth Indian National Social Conference in Calcutta in 1890. A significant part of the credit for this awakening goes to Agarkar.

Born into a poor Chitpavan Brahmin family in 1856, in Tembhu in Satara district, the generous assistance of some relatives helped Agarkar pass his BA and MA examinations in 1878 and 1880 respectively from Deccan College, Poona, where he became a fellow for about a year. In a letter that he wrote to his mother while in college, he articulated his resolve to dedicate himself to social service for the rest of his life. Agarkar, his friend Tilak, and some others realized that education was the only available means for national resurrection. These young men, backed by veterans such as Ranade and Chiplunkar, launched the New English School in Poona on 1 January 1880 with thirty-five students on its rolls, a figure that increased to 336 by the end of that year. It was one of the first native-run schools offering Western education in Poona. (Incidentally, one year later, on 2 January 1881, appeared the English weekly *Mahratta*. Two days after that was launched the Marathi weekly *Kesari*.

Journalism, Tilak and Agarkar believed, was a powerful medium to influence the administration and educate the masses.)

They launched the Deccan Education Society on 24 October 1884 and, on 2 January 1885, the society established Fergusson College. It was named after the then governor of Bombay Presidency, Sir James Fergusson, who hailed it as 'a social fact – unquestionably of great political importance'. Among the professors were Tilak and Agarkar themselves.

Within three years, though, in October 1887, Agarkar severed his connection with *Kesari* as its editor owing to increasing differences between him and Tilak over what should be given precedence: social reforms or the political struggle against the British. In 1888, Agarkar started his own weekly, *Sudharak*. He wrote the Marathi columns for it himself and the English ones were written by another intellectual, Gopal Krishna Gokhale. In 1890, Tilak resigned from the Deccan Education Society. Agarkar became the principal of Fergusson College in 1892 and held that office till his death in 1895. Although he argued valiantly in favour of Western education as the agency of social progress and equality of opportunity, he was equally opposed to British rule. He stated that no nation should be ruled by another forever, and that India was bound to be ruled by Indians one day. He was among the first leaders to call for unity among Hindus and Muslims as a prerequisite for political liberation, and was critical of the British policy of divide and rule. He also exhorted his countrymen to set up representative assemblies for governance at all levels – from the local to the central.

He was one of the first leaders to understand the economic implications of losing freedom to the British. He pointed out the vast disparity between the per capita income and expenditure of India and other countries like Great Britain. He cited India's extremely low salt consumption as an indicator of its economic situation and demanded gradual industrialization. It was quite remarkable of him to point out the abysmal state of agriculture in those days and how having 86 per cent of the population dependent on agriculture made for unsound economics. He openly welcomed machinery and wanted at least ten students to be deputed annually to foreign countries to gain technical skills. It is astonishing that Agarkar, along with Tilak, underlined the importance of small-scale industries in the nation's development while raising issues such as administrative expenditures, budget deficits and so on even though neither of them had studied economics.

TILAK AND AGARKAR WERE great friends but, while they shared many similarities, they had big differences too. They were both known for their simple and austere private lives and impeccable moral character. Equally dedicated to the country, both were driven by solid intellectual commitments. While Tilak was unemotional, clinical, lawyer-like and argumentative, Agarkar would touch the emotional chord, was imaginative and near poetic in arguments. Tilak almost always came across as an angry man and intimidating, while Agarkar was more persuasive and approachable.

Tilak was a proud, studious commentator on India's great legacy. Agarkar never liked dwelling on India's past glory. Tilak had a penchant for mathematics but also wrote a book like *Gita Rahasya*, a critical explanation of the Bhagavad Gita. Agarkar, on the other hand, was blunt in criticizing the India of the time as a degraded and fallen nation and minced no words when dealing with those who tried to glorify its past. He didn't even spare Justice Ranade, who, in a speech in Poona, was critical of Christianity while eulogizing early Hindus for developing what he saw as the best belief system. Agarkar asked him to stay away from such morbid illusions as they may be excusable only for the satisfaction of the emotional part of man's nature. He was candid enough while stating the futility of recollecting with pride the past achievements of forefathers when they have least resemblance of greatness.

These differences apart, the duo complemented each other in their cause and led the region to glorious heights. As Vishram Bedekar, a well-known Marathi author of yesteryear, rightly notes,

'Watching Tilak and Agarkar differ is like witnessing a race of stars that illuminates the path it passes through.' Unfortunately, the rivalry – if it could be called that – between the two, which had sparked many debates and set the tone for the national political movement, abruptly ended with the untimely demise of Agarkar at the age of just thirty-nine on 17 June 1895.

Like Agarkar, Tilak too was a Chitpavan Brahmin. Agarkar came to Poona from the Western Ghats, while Tilak was from the Konkan city of Ratnagiri. Incidentally, Tilak shares his birth year with Agarkar. Born to Gangadhar Shastri and Parvati Bai in 1856, he moved to Poona due to the transfer of his father, a noted Sanskrit scholar and schoolteacher in Ratnagiri. Tilak was a very bright student. After graduating from Deccan College in 1877 in Sanskrit and mathematics, he went on to get an LLB degree from the Government Law College, Bombay. Although he was part of the first generation of Indians to receive a modern college education, he also strongly criticized the British educational system. He raised his voice against the unequal treatment meted out to Indian students compared to their British peers and the total disregard of the system for India's cultural heritage.

There were two Maharashtrians who played a key role in the formation and expansion of two important organizations: the Indian National Congress, formed in 1885, and the Indian National Social Conference, formed in 1887. The two men were Tilak and Ranade, the latter playing a role in both bodies. The Indian National Congress was formed by the British civil servant Allan Octavian Hume with the aim of bringing together a group of educated individuals on a common platform to influence policymaking. It was Ranade who suggested the name 'Indian National Congress' to Hume. Ranade was an institution builder and, as Justice M.C. Chagla put it, 'his greatest quality was that he was the maker of great men, the greatest of whom was [Gopal Krishna] Gokhale'. Ranade was the driving force behind setting up the Poona Sarvajanik Sabha in 1870, which was a precursor to the Indian National Congress. A socio-political organization, the Poona Sarvajanik Sabha offered to be a bridge between the British government and the natives on a variety of issues, the most important of them being peasants' rights. With over 6,000 members, the sabha had a galaxy of intellectuals – from Ranade and Chiplunkar to Lokhitwadi and Tilak. The sabha was very active during the famine of 1875-76.

Nearly ten years after the famine, the Congress came into being. In its initial days, it made no demands for independence from the British. The first conference of representatives was convened on 25 December 1885 by the union of Poona, but the meeting was held in Bombay due to a plague outbreak in the former. Eventually, the meeting took place from 28 to 31 December in Bombay's Gokuldas Tejpal Sanskrit College. Womesh Chunder Bonnerjee was the president of the first session. A total of seventy-two delegates from all parts of the country took part.

Maharashtra was a fertile ground for a strong political movement arguably because of the history of the first national war of independence of 1857. The Marathi region had played an important role by offering able leaders such as Nanasaheb Peshwa, Tatya Tope, Rani Lakshmibai of Jhansi and others. An important point to note is that the Maharashtra and Karnataka regions were not immediately affected by the rebellion that began in the north, and yet they saw a slew of valiant, nationalist revolutionaries springing up.

As the Congress was being formed, there were raging debates over what should be given precedence – political or social reforms – which split the intellectual classes into two. The Congress had a purely political agenda, while the Social Conference, as the name suggests, was out to push for social reforms. The person who opened up the debate on these lines was Justice Telang. In an address to the Students' Literary and Scientific Society in Bombay, he gave a clear call for social reforms. While addressing the gathering on 'Must Social Reform Precede Political Reform in India?' he said, 'A nation so low on the social front cannot be great politically.'

There was another group of leaders, known as the Rationalists, who wanted a unified approach on these issues. Efforts were on to bring both the political and the social factions under one roof. The idea was to hold sessions of the Congress and the Conference in the same pandal. But Tilak thwarted any such attempt. A staunch supporter of the political movement, he wanted to use social movements only to mobilize people for a political push. The divide continued when Dadabhai Naoroji chaired the second session of the Congress held in 1886 in Calcutta as he too preferred a political to a social movement. His argument was that political issues should be taken up as everyone was united on that front, while there wasn't unanimity when it came to most social issues. His insistence on political issues silenced the other factions, and the following year, at the third session in Madras, the members avoided discussing the matter further.

The age of consent issue brought the division to the fore, with Tilak and Ranade seen as leading two opposite fronts and bitterly attacking each other. A couple of years later, in 1891, at the Conference's fifth year, Justice Ranade took a conciliatory approach by describing the Congress and Conference as 'two sisters' and suggesting simultaneous pursuance of the two. According to him, 'Cause of the Conference was the cause of the well-being of the people and cause of the Congress was the cause of their country's progress.'

Tilak, however, was in no mood to relent. He was consistent in criticizing social reform initiatives. He used the platform of the Poona Sarvajanik Sabha to deny the Conference a place in the same pandal as the Congress. He took up the issue before Pherozeshah Mehta, president of the Congress session in Calcutta in 1890, asking him to reject the Conference's proposal to use the Congress pandal for its session. Later, he stepped up his criticism of social reformers to such an extent that it forced Justice Ranade to organize the Conference at a different venue during the Congress's eleventh session in Poona in 1895. That year, Ranade held the Conference meet at Fergusson College.

Interestingly, Tilak had initially stayed away from the Congress and joined the organization only in 1890. And it was from 1892 that he started taking an active part in it. Until then, he was politically proactive through *Kesari*, reporting and commenting on the Congress's developments. It's not that he hadn't wanted to join earlier, but he was critical of its lukewarm attitude towards the fight for self-governance. Having said that, giving the Congress a pro-people outlook was completely Tilak's doing. He led the peasants' movement in Maharashtra, and his speeches, writings and addresses at innumerable conferences and meetings sowed the seeds of Indian nationalism. Until then, the Congress was a congregation of well-intended, soft-spoken gentlemen helping the British regime, directly or indirectly, in streamlining the administration. With Tilak storming the organization, it changed completely. In the early days, Tilak was devoted to widening the Congress base across India. He can be credited with kindling the nationalistic spirit in the minds of common people by reviving India's great legacy.

In those days, Tilak confined himself to two types of issues. One was cultural and the other economic and political. The first was espoused in the form of Ganesh and Shivaji festivals, the second was raised and pushed by taking up issues such as farmers' plight during the famine, the inept and inhuman handling of the plague by the British, and so on. The plague outbreak had started towards the end of 1896 in Bombay, followed by Poona. By January 1897, in a matter of months, it took a serious turn. British troops were brought in to handle the situation. They resorted to entering people's homes and hunting down the diseased. Their forceful evacuation triggered a major unrest. Responding to the situation, Tilak wrote fiery articles in *Kesari* against the British, which eventually led to the murder in Poona of Indian Civil Service (ICS) officer W.C. Rand, heading the Special Plague Committee, and his military escort Lieutenant Ayerst. The British charged Tilak with 'incitement to murder' and sentenced him to eighteen months in prison. By the time of his release, Tilak's stature had grown to that of a national hero. And by then he had also coined his famous slogan: 'Swaraj is my birthright and I shall have it.'

TILAK'S IMPORTANCE LAY IN his ability to stoke the nationalistic fire through regional issues. Credit must also be given to him for his skill in using religion, which until then had been confined to social causes, to push a political agenda. His deft use of Ganesh and Shivaji festivals showed how culture could ignite nationalism.

Today it's almost fashionable to attribute Brahminical motives to Tilak's work and to accuse him of a Hindu bias. It is an ignorant position to take, for it was Tilak who once wrote, 'Shivaji was born in Maharashtra, but a future leader may be born anywhere and who knows may even be Mohammedan.' Tilak was clear in his mind about every symbol he used to light the fire of Indian nationalism. According to him, 'The Shivaji festival is not celebrated to alienate or even to irritate Mohammedans. Both [Mohammedans and Hindus] are sailing in the same boat as far as the situation of India is concerned. We are not against if someone wants to start a festival in honour of Akbar or any other hero from Indian history.' The greatness of Tilak's leadership lay in invoking popular symbols to tell the larger national story. Using the platforms of the Shivaji and Ganesh festivals that attracted large crowds, he categorically stated, 'The English government has been established for the benefit of the Englishmen. They have not come here all the way for our salvation.' He successfully used regional issues to mobilize political movements. After his release from prison in 1889, he fully focused on matters facing the nation.

It was around this time that he gave a unique, solely indigenous weapon to the common man in his fight against the British. The Swadeshi movement was meant to encourage people to use domestically produced goods – in today's context, he can even be called the father of the 'Make in India' initiative. It also entailed boycotting foreign goods. The Swadeshi movement, along with the national education movement that Tilak had launched earlier by setting up various educational institutes, proved to be extremely effective and went a long way in India's struggle for independence.

Tilak's leadership reached even greater heights when Lord Curzon, the Viceroy of India, decided to partition Bengal in 1905.

The move was aimed at weakening the nationalist movement, which was at its peak then, and Tilak made the point bluntly in his hard-hitting editorials and speeches. Some accuse him, due to his politics during Bengal's partition, of alienating the Muslims in the Congress. Tilak, in fact, went to the extent of asking the British to hand over the reins of the government in Bengal to a group of Muslim representatives instead of partitioning the presidency. This move of Tilak's can only be compared to a similar call given by Gandhi during the 1942 Quit India movement.

Along with the Swadeshi movement, around this time Tilak also launched the Home Rule League movement. It offered him and his followers an independent platform other than that of the Congress while consolidating his own follower base. He used the situation to exert more pressure on the Congress to own the Home Rule demand and put it before the British government. It is important to look at who comprised the Home Rule movement in order to understand Tilak's genuinely secular leadership. Joseph Baptista of Bombay was the league's president and N.C. Kelkar and Gopal Krishna Gokhale were secretaries. The league's membership was drawn from people of different religions and various castes. It gained momentum as the First World War broke out, and Annie Besant, leader of the Theosophical Society, formed another league.

But before that, during the annual session of the Congress in Surat in 1907, tension erupted between the moderates and the radicals over the selection of the future president of the Congress. Needless to say, Tilak was leading the radicals. The session witnessed the Congress splitting into the 'Jahal Matavadi' or the radicals, led by Tilak, Bipin Chandra Pal and Lala Lajpat Rai, famously called 'Lal-Bal-Pal' of the Congress, on one side and the 'Maval Matavadi' or the moderates, led by Gopal Krishna Gokhale, on the other.

A year later, on 30 April 1908, two young revolutionaries, Prafulla Chaki and Khudiram Bose, tried to assassinate the Chief Presidency Magistrate, Douglas Kingsford, by throwing a bomb at a carriage in Muzaffarpur that they believed he was in, but instead there were two women inside who were killed. Chaki committed suicide to escape arrest while Bose was caught and hanged. Tilak dared to defend the attack by the two men and called for immediate Swaraj. The British government wasted no time in arresting Tilak and slapping sedition charges on him. He was also accused of glorifying violence and killings. It resulted in his being sentenced to a six-year jail term from 1908 to 1914 in Mandalay in Burma. He used his time in jail to sharpen his thoughts on Indian nationalism and write his magnum opus, *Shrimadh Bhagvad Gita Rahasya*.

However, Tilak was exhausted by the end of his jail term in June 1914. Also troubling him was his diabetes. But it was hardly a deterrent for Tilak's zeal and commitment. He played a decisive role in the Lucknow Pact of December 1916 that witnessed the Indian National Congress and the Muslim League agreeing on the representation of religious minorities in provincial legislatures. The pact came against the backdrop of the British government's promise to have at least half of the members of the executive council elected from among the people, along with having a majority of elected members in the legislative council. Both the Congress and the Muslim League had realized by then that, to get further concessions from the British, they needed greater cooperation between themselves. The merits and demerits of the Lucknow Pact can be debated, but the event ought to put all doubts regarding Tilak's genuinely secular leadership to rest. A fiery orator and a true patriot, he spoke and stood for the entire nation and not for any particular community or region.

As part of his Home Rule activities, and as president of the league at the time, Tilak visited England in 1918. His understanding of international affairs was fascinating. He had an eye on the developments in Russia and was aware of the post-First World War situation. He was among the first to introduce Karl Marx and his theory of class conflict to Indians way back in 1881. Another important contribution of Tilak's that remains largely ignored is his push for the labour movement, which played a crucial role in the freedom struggle. While in England, he sensed the Labour Party's growing clout in British politics and wanted to establish a firm relationship with its leaders. He proved to be right. It was a Labour government that eventually granted independence to India in 1947.

By the time Tilak returned home from England in late 1919 to attend the Congress session at Amritsar, he did not have enough energy left to oppose Gandhi's decision to boycott elections to the legislative councils, which were part of the Montagu–Chelmsford Reforms of 1918. In a move that indicated a major change in his politics, Tilak instead advised the delegates to follow his policy of 'responsive cooperation' in implementing the reforms that allowed a limited degree of Indian participation in regional governments.

Tilak, however, was not to live long enough to give the new reforms a decisive direction. He breathed his last on 1 August 1920 in Bombay. It was not only the end of an era but with him also ended Maharashtra's dominance in the national political leadership. He was the tallest leader Maharashtra has produced, and nobody else matches up to him even a hundred years later. 'His patriotism was a passion with him. He knew no religion but love of his country. He was a born democrat ... No man preached the gospel of Swaraj with the consistency and the insistence of Lokmanya [Tilak],' said Gandhi in a befitting tribute to him. According to him, Tilak was 'the maker of modern India', while Jawaharlal Nehru was 'the father of the Indian revolution'.

AS THE CURTAIN CAME down on the Tilak era, it was time for the rise of Mahatma Gandhi. With the arrival of Gandhi on the Indian political horizon, Tilak had sensed that the new leader was someone India should look up to. Such was the greatness of the man that he even wrote to this effect, asking his followers to help Gandhi, in his preface to Avantikabai Gokhale's biography of Gandhi in Marathi – the first in any Indian language – that was published in 1918. Many of Tilak's staunch supporters such as S.M. Paranjape (1864–1929), Senapati Bapat (1880–1967), Veer Nariman (1883–1948) and others joined hands with Gandhi after Tilak's death. Maharashtra has since never attained a position of pre-eminence in national politics. Though the irony is that it was another Maharashtrian, Gopal Krishna Gokhale, who played an important role in shaping Gandhi's thoughts. Gokhale was the face of the highly intelligent, educated Indian, exposed to English education and Western philosophy, and went on to become the backbone of the independence movement. Another Chitpavan Brahmin, he was a mentor to Muhammad Ali Jinnah as well. Like his political adversary, Tilak, Gokhale too was born in Ratnagiri. After earning a degree from Elphinstone College, Bombay, in 1884, he became a teacher at Poona's Deccan Education Society, which was packed with stalwarts such as Tilak, Agarkar, Chiplunkar, Ranade and others. Gokhale was influenced by Ranade's personality, his insistence on reason and logic, which eventually resulted in his becoming Gokhale's mentor. In 1894, Gokhale visited Ireland to woo the Irish nationalist Alfred Webb to lead the Indian National Congress as its president, a mission in which he proved successful. The following year, Gokhale became the Congress's joint secretary along with Tilak. Interestingly, Tilak's and Gokhale's early careers were almost parallel – both studied at Elphinstone College, loved mathematics and taught it as well, and were actively involved in the Deccan Education Society. The two had equally strong but different opinions on how to improve the lives of Indians. In 1889, Gokhale joined the Congress and later became a member of the Bombay Legislative Council, and then of the Imperial Legislative Council.

It was in 1905 that Gokhale became Congress president. The same year he quit the Deccan Education Society to set up his own association in Poona, called the Servants of India Society, with the aim of creating educated and dedicated volunteers to promote human and social development while fighting to oust the British. 'The Society will train men prepared to devote their lives to the cause of the country in a religious spirit, and will seek to promote, by all constitutional means, the national interests of the Indian people,' Gokhale said. Supporting him was a small group of educated Indians such as Natesh Appaji Dravid, Gopal Krishna Deodhar, Anant Patwardhan and many prominent others who chose to stay away from political activities and organizations like the Congress. It was the first strictly social organization formed in the country to uplift the underprivileged and the backward irrespective of their caste or ethnicity. Gokhale was also the first to demand free universal primary education. All members of his society were trained for five years and were sent out to serve its cause on extremely meagre wages.

An erudite scholar, Gokhale was an influential speaker who had the great ability to weave data and logic into his audience-friendly speeches. In some of them he can be found taking on great economists such as John Maynard Keynes. The speeches conclusively demonstrated how British policies were hurting India. A collection of Gokhale's speeches on topics ranging from budgets to social reforms are widely read even today for their scholarly nature and sheer class.

Like his mentor Ranade, Gokhale too differed with Tilak. Among other things, he was against Tilak's call for passive resistance as a strategy against the British. Logical and articulate but also a constitutionalist, Gokhale was always in favour of wider dialogue with the British to demand more and more representation for the natives in all arms of governance – elected assemblies, the judiciary and academia. Gokhale may have opposed Tilak's ideas of passive resistance and non-cooperation, but it was his own disciple, Mohandas Karamchand Gandhi, who later went on to master the same ideas and put them to use across the country.

Gokhale first met Gandhi in 1896 in Poona. His advice to Gandhi was to 'tour the length and breadth of the country, with eyes and ears open, but mouth shut' – with an aim to absorb, learn and digest but not to react. In *Gokhale: My Political Guru*, which is a collection of Gandhi's writings on his multilayered association with his mentor, he describes Gokhale thus: 'But Gokhale was the Ganges. One could have a refreshing bath in the holy river. The Himalaya was unscalable, and one could not easily launch forth on the sea, but the Ganges invited one to its bosom. It was a joy to be on it with a boat and an oar.' He even referred to Gokhale as 'Mahatma', calling him 'the most perfect man in the political field, as pure as crystal, as gentle as a lamb, as brave as a lion'.

The two leaders spent a month together during the Calcutta session of the Congress in 1901, where Gokhale first proposed that Gandhi return to India. It, however, took another decade and a half for Gandhi to finally return in 1915, which was also the year Gokhale's life came to an abrupt end. Gokhale was so fond of him that he had even financed many of Gandhi's initiatives in South Africa. He was probably the only person to influence two completely divergent but towering leaders: Mahatma Gandhi and Muhammad Ali Jinnah, both of whom held him in high regard.

Very active on social and political fronts with equal zeal and ease, Gokhale also travelled abroad extensively for political reasons. But the constant and excessive stress, along with ailments such as asthma and diabetes, started taking its toll on him. He breathed his last on 19 February 1915, at the age of just forty-eight. It was only a month before his death, in January, that his most distinguished, eminent disciple, Gandhi, had returned to India to lead the freedom struggle.

Over the years, the differences between Gokhale and Tilak have been unnecessarily and unjustifiably magnified. But this was the rich tribute Tilak paid his fellow Congressman from Poona: 'This diamond of India, this jewel of Maharashtra, this prince of workers is taking eternal rest on the funeral ground. Look at him and try to emulate him.' And many did do that.

Tilak and Gokhale were two poles of Indian politics. The former was aggressive and radical, while the latter was a moderate. By 1920, both had left the stage. An important point to note is that both of the Congress's factions then were led by Maharashtrians – Tilak and Agarkar. Maharashtra's firmament was brightly lit with many such stars. And when Gandhi arrived on the political scene, the Maharashtrians diversified into many other areas.

12

Magnificent Maharashtrians

Bal Gangadhar Tilak was undoubtedly the brightest star not only in Maharashtra's firmament but the entire nation's. There were of course many others too who helped the region become truly a 'Maha Rashtra'. They were not necessarily from politics but other fields such as economics, science, filmmaking, circus and even airplane-making. They are – and continue to remain – the unsung heroes of the state. One of the most important among them was Mahadev Ballal Namjoshi (1833–96).

When Tilak and Agarkar were igniting the national spirit, and when newspapers such as *Indu Prakash*, *Native Opinion*, *Dnyan Prakash*, and so on were taking up the social cause, Mahadev Namjoshi launched *Kiran* to take up the economic issues of the region. A bilingual periodical that was published in Marathi and English, its first issue was released on 26 August 1877.

Around this time, Europe was witnessing the Russo-Turkish war. It was a time when the Ottoman empire was witnessing a decline. On 12 April 1877, Romania gave permission to the Russian troops to pass through its territory to attack the Turks, resulting in Turkish bombardments of Romanian towns on the Danube. Russia declared war on the Ottomans on 24 April and its troops entered Romania via the Prut river. On 10 May, the Principality of Romania, which was under formal Turkish rule until then, declared independence. Soon, Russia sent a large army to take on the Ottomans on the Balkan peninsula. The Russo-Turkish war changed the demographic structure of Europe, affecting Britain and the rest of the world. During this period, Mahadev Namjoshi thought of having a special section in every issue analysing the Russo-Turkish war, such was his awareness of global affairs.

That, naturally, wasn't his sole intention behind launching *Kiran*, though. His mission was to spread economic literacy. In one of the issues, he wrote: 'We Indians though these days are burdened with overall rising taxes, one item being taxed heavily should be a major cause of concern to us. And that is salt. Salt is the most common ingredient in food and heavy taxation on it is impacting common Indians' economy.'

He further explained the plight of the local community that produced salt – their reduced income due to additional taxes vis-à-vis the high revenue the British were mopping up. Some five decades later, in 1930, Mahatma Gandhi would pick up the same issue to launch the Dandi March. A young man from Maharashtra was the first to understand and explain the economic importance of salt.

Helping Namjoshi financially in the endeavour was a steel merchant from Poona, Keshav Sathye. However, the Vernacular Press Act of 1878 made the venture unviable. The Act was aimed at curtailing the freedom of publications in Indian languages. Modelled on the Irish Press Laws, it gave the government extensive rights to censor reports and editorials. Namjoshi had to close down *Kiran*, but the enterprising young man launched *Deccan Star*, an English daily, in 1879. It ran for two years, after which it merged with Tilak's *Kesari* and *The Mahratta*. The very first issue of *Kesari* carried the announcement of the merger. From then onwards, Namjoshi became a regular contributor to both publications, writing on economic issues. Soon he launched another, *Shilpa Kalavidnyan*, dedicated exclusively to the importance of industry and wealth creation.

In its very first issue, Namjoshi wrote:

> Why we don't have quality goods like those that come from the West? Because we have forgotten the importance of industry. Our Indian industrialist brothers have lost their business due to superior quality of imports. Our industries are closing down and our agriculture is no longer remunerative as it was a few years ago. It's unfortunate that we Indians live with only two options in mind: to do agriculture or get employed. We have no vision to become entrepreneurs ourselves. The situation of the natives won't improve unless we start giving importance to industrialisation ourselves.

Namjoshi was not just a preacher, he was active on the ground as well. Thanks to his vision, Poona held the first industrial exhibition and conference back in 1889. He carried on with his mission till 1893. He was also associated with Tilak, Chiplunkar and Agarkar in setting up the Deccan Education Society, which went on to set up the first commerce college in Poona. The preparatory work to establish it began in 1942, when India was witnessing Mahatma Gandhi's Quit India movement. The following year, the Brihan Maharashtra College of Commerce, popularly known as BMCC today, was established. Its first principal was the well-known economist Dattatreya Gopal Karve, former deputy governor of the Reserve Bank of India (RBI), who, along with his mentor in economics Professor V.G. Kale, had written the first well-researched Marathi book explaining the principles of modern economics as early as 1927. He was also one of the first commentators on the cooperative movement in India.

ANOTHER MAVERICK MAHARASHTRIAN OF that era was Shivkar Bapuji Talpade (1864–1916). Most of the other Marathi activists and scholars of the time had been Chitpavan Brahmins from Poona, but Talpade belonged to the Pathare Prabhu community – one of the few original Mumbaikars. Having completed his education at the Sir J.J. School of Art, Talpade learnt about ancient Indian aeronautics under his teacher Chiranjilal Verma, who encouraged him to read Swami Dayanand Saraswati's works such as *Rigvedic Bhashya Bhumika* and *Rigved ani Yajurveda Bhashya*. Inspired by his readings, Talpade decided to learn Vedic Sanskrit to know more about the Vedic Vimana. He also read about Thomas Alva Edison and his experiment of flying in a balloon. An inspired Talpade created his own unmanned aircraft named Marutsakha, meaning 'friend of the wind'. According to a report in the *Kesari*, it was supposed to have been inspired by Vimana, and flew in 1895 – some eight years before the Wright brothers' successful flight in the United States.

Although there isn't much written material available on Talpade's experiment, there is no dearth of hearsay about it. Some believe his aircraft didn't reach very high and came down quickly. The full technical details of his flying machine – which was made of bamboo, with liquid mercury as the fuel – aren't known either. However, the experiment is believed to have been witnessed by Justice Ranade and Maharaja Sayajirao Gaekwad III of Baroda state, along with some of Talpade's friends and a few onlookers. According to Pratap Velkar, who has chronicled Talpade's experiment in his book *Maharashtracha Ujwal Itihaas*, the test flight was more like a sporting event and nothing more should be read into it. Velkar's father was one of the spectators when Talpade flew his machine. Talpade later tried to raise funds to build another aircraft but wasn't successful.

Recognition eluded India's first flying machine and the man behind it. But unlike Talpade, another alumnus of the Sir J.J. School of Art wasn't so unlucky. Dadasaheb Phalke (1870–1944) went on to be celebrated as the father of Indian cinema.

DHUNDIRAJ PHALKE WAS BORN in a Chitpavan Brahmin family in Nashik. Like many other Brahmins of the era learned in Sanskrit, his father, Dajishastri, also made a living by performing religious ceremonies. Young Dhundiraj too followed in the father's footsteps and started performing *pujas* and *yajnas*. Things changed when he got a chance to teach Sanskrit at Bombay's Wilson College. Once he started living in Bombay, Phalke took admission at the Sir J.J. School of Art to study drawing. He later moved to Baroda, where his elder brother was serving in the princely state of the Gaekwads as the diwan, and joined Kala Bhavan to study oil and water-colour paintings.

It was during his time in Baroda that he decided to explore photography, bought a film camera, and taught himself the art of film processing and printing associated with photography. Enterprising as he was, Phalke did short-term courses in block-making, photolithography and three-colour ceramic photography. Ratlam, a major business centre then, was his next destination. He soon founded the Shri Phalke's Engraving and Photo Printing Studio. But it failed to provide him a steady livelihood. He then moved to Godhra, which too failed to offer him a break. Worse still, he lost his wife and a child to the plague there. An exasperated Phalke returned to Baroda to try his luck with the camera.

In Baroda, he was faced with a typically Indian conundrum of the time. People were scared of the click of a camera because they believed it would suck away their energy and spirit, and so they did not want to stand before one. Even the prince of Baroda believed that people who were photographed did not live long. Phalke had to fight this superstition but his perseverance finally won and he started getting steady business. Meanwhile, he had also started working in drama companies in various capacities, including performing small-time roles on stage, for additional income. He also learnt magic tricks from a German magician who was touring Baroda then. He would put to use all of these experiences in fulfilling his dream of making a feature film eventually.

Phalke kept experimenting. He set up a printing press with the well-known orientalist and scholar Sir Ramakrishna Gopal Bhandarkar at Lonavla, near Poona. Phalke Engraving and Printing Works mostly printed the artist Raja Ravi Varma's works. The printing business brought a little stability to his life. With a steady source of income, he shifted his press to Dadar in Bombay, with his new partner, Seth Purushottam Mavji, a well-known collector of antiquities who later became a major contributor to Bombay's Prince of Wales Museum, later renamed as the Chhatrapati Shivaji Maharaj Vastu Sangrahalaya. The following year, in 1909, Phalke went to Germany to purchase colour printing machines. But soon serious differences arose between the two partners, and he eventually quit the printing business. Although he had offers from other printers, he was not interested any more in the same business. He had his eyes set on just one dream: filmmaking.

The film that triggered his ambition was *Amazing Animals*, which he went to watch with his son in Bombay's Girgaum at the American-Indian Cinema owned by P.B. Mehta. Later, he also watched *The Life of Christ*, which inspired him to show Hindu deities on screen. Phalke wrote about his inspiration in Ganesh Vitthal Kulkarni's magazine *Navyug* in 1918:

> I happened to watch *The Life of Christ* in a picture palace called American-Indian in Bombay in 1910. I must have seen movies a number of times earlier, must have often gone there for recreation with friends or family, but that day changed my life forever! There are millions of big and small businesses in the world, but that day a poor Brahmin like me from a priestly family laid the cornerstone in India, on a scientific basis, of the business of cinema, which occupies the fifth place in the world!

Those were the days of the Swadeshi movement spearheaded by Tilak. Phalke wanted to contribute to the movement in his own way: by making a 'swadeshi film'. The idea, however, was ridiculed and scoffed at by his friends. But that didn't deter Phalke.

The Life of Christ gave Phalke the mission of his life – to make films. From that point onwards, he got seriously involved in the film business, including importing the necessary equipment from Europe. Obsessed with filmmaking, Phalke created a makeshift studio at home. At his disposal were some used rolls, candles and a magnifying glass, and his family members were the captive audience. He was so passionate that he would be at it hour after hour for days, which even made him temporarily blind. He developed cataracts in both his eyes and was advised to stay away from the eye-straining work. But he paid no heed to the doctor's advice. He got a special set of spectacles made for himself, which offered some relief. Completely dedicated to his dream, he wanted to travel to London to learn more about filmmaking. But he was out of business and without any major source of income. And so he mortgaged his family's insurance policies of Rs 12,000 to raise a loan and borrowed Rs 10,000 from acquaintances. A determined Phalke left for London on 1 February 1912.

He arrived in the city without a set agenda. The only reference he had was *The Bioscope*, a cine-weekly whose subscription he had in Bombay. He knew the journal's office was somewhere near Piccadilly Circus. Once he arrived in London, he went straight to see the weekly's editor, who advised him against the idea of filmmaking in India. He also pointed out the hostile climate in India, which, according to him, was detrimental for films. But Phalke wasn't willing to give up. He persuaded the editor to guide him. He also got references to film studios in London. Along the way, he spent some £50 to buy a camera and place an order for Kodak film. When he returned to India after spending more than two weeks in London, he founded Phalke Films on 1 April 1912.

In his office, Phalke built a small studio along with a dark room that had arrangements for film processing. The equipment he had ordered from abroad also arrived the next month. His target then was to raise funds for filmmaking. He made *Ankurachi Wadh* (Growth of a Plant), a short film portraying the progression of peas planted in a pot, observing them until they grew into a climber. He showed the film to a few would-be financiers, and two of them, Yashwantrao Nadkarni and Narayanrao Devhare, offered him a loan.

Encouraged by the response to his short film, Phalke chose another topic for his first feature film: King Harishchandra, a Hindu mythological king who gave away his kingdom, including his family, and agreed to be a slave in order to fulfil a promise he had made to the sage Vishwamitra. Those were the days when it was anathema for women to perform in public, and so Phalke cast some of his male friends in the female roles. He looked after all the aspects of filmmaking, such as scriptwriting, directing, editing, film processing and even the make-up. It took him nearly seven months – 207 days to be precise – to complete the film, whose rolls were around 3,700 feet long.

On 21 April 1913, *Raja Harishchandra* premiered at the Olympia Theatre in Bombay for the press and a select few. Unsure of how the response to the invite would be, Phalke advertised the screening in a unique way: 'A performance with 57,000 photographs. A picture two miles long. All for only three annas.' He also arranged for a dance performance by two European girls for the first few days before showing the film.

History was made. *Raja Harishchandra* became India's first feature film. Ramchandra Gopal alias Dadasaheb Torne is believed to have made the first film, *Shree Pundalik* (1912), before Dadasaheb Phalke made his, but the Government of India considers Phalke as the father of Indian cinema, perhaps because Torne sent his film overseas for processing, unlike Phalke, who did everything by himself in India. Torne's *Pundalik* was twenty-two minutes long, while Phalke's *Raja Harishchandra* ran for over forty minutes.

This was followed by Phalke setting up a company, Hindustan Films, in partnership with a few Bombay-based businessmen. He also set up a model studio and trained technicians and actors but ran into insurmountable problems with his partners very soon. In 1920, he resigned from Hindustan Films, made his first announcement of retiring from cinema, and wrote *Rangbhoomi*, an acclaimed play. Without him in charge, Hindustan Films ran into deep financial losses and he was finally persuaded to return. However, Phalke felt constrained by the business and, after directing a few films for the company, once again withdrew from it. In time, silent films became passé with the arrival of sound films.

He couldn't cope with the talkies. The father of Indian cinema became obsolete. His last silent film, *Setubandhan*, was released in 1932 and later re-released with dubbing. After producing his last film, *Gangavataran* (1937), Phalke retired to Nashik, where he died on 16 February 1944.

The Government of India instituted an award in his honour in 1969, considered the highest recognition for film practitioners. The irony is that while the father of Indian cinema was Maharashtrian – and Mumbai continues to be the centre of the Hindi and Marathi film industries – it is difficult to think of a Marathi Manoos who can be said to be its flagbearer today.

FILMMAKING WAS NOT THE only domain in which the Marathi Manoos made early strides. When Tilak, Agarkar, Ranade, and others were busy igniting political and social movements in Poona and Bombay, there was a relatively unknown man in faraway Kurundwad in Kolhapur district who dreamt of setting up India's first circus. He was Vishnupant Chatre (1840–1906).

Chatre, though a multifaceted personality, was primarily a horse trainer, a stuntman of sorts and head of the stables of the princely state of Kurundwad. How he came to create India's first circus makes for an interesting story.

Chatre once accompanied his king to watch the Royal Italian Circus by the legendary Italian equestrian Giuseppe Chiarini (1823–97). Chiarini is considered the most influential circus director of the nineteenth century and was also responsible for popularizing the skill show. He conducted circuses for almost sixty years, with extensive tours all over the world – from Europe to the Americas, and from Asia to Australia. Just as in his other destinations, Chiarini's was the first circus the locals had ever seen in India too. Chatre and the king of Kurundwad were part of one such audience. Hugely impressed by Chiarini's craft, Chatre got an opportunity to meet him. During their conversation, he expressed his desire to do something similar in

India. But Chiarini's response was discouraging as he believed India wasn't at a stage where it could think of setting up its own circus and it wouldn't be ready even in the next ten years.

This annoyed Chatre and he vowed to set up a circus of his own. Helping him in his endeavour was his wife and, partly, the king. His wife was a trapeze artiste and could also train wild animals. Together they founded the Great Indian Circus in Tasgaon, a small village in Miraj district, and held their first show on 20 March 1880. A select few came to watch the maiden show, including the king. Soon the Great Indian Circus started travelling all across the length and breadth of the country. It is quite remarkable to note that Chatre travelled to South and East Asian countries and even to the US with his circus. Unfortunately, he returned home a little distraught on realizing that he could not match up to the standards of the big circus companies such as the Barnum & Bailey Circus. He then decided to stay domestic, with his first indigenous innovation coming about during a trip to Kerala.

Like everywhere, in Tellicherry (now Thalassery) too the Great Indian Circus attracted large crowds. One of its spectators was the famous gymnast Keeleri Kunhikannan Master, who was working as a trainer in the Basel Mission School then. He was immediately attracted to the circus and signed a deal with Chatre, who had seen remarkable acrobatic performances while touring abroad. It was a win-win deal for both. Kunhikannan committed to supply his trained gymnasts to Chatre's circus. Over the next few years, he trained a number of fine acrobats. The partnership was so successful that, in 1901, he inaugurated a circus school in Chirakkara near Quilon (now Kollam). The school became extremely popular and went on to train scores of performers – the reason behind the many Malayali girls and boys joining Indian circuses for several decades to come. Later, a number of Chatre's performers set up their own circus companies. One of the biggest and most successful of them was Kamala Three Ring Circus, which, despite its humble beginnings, went on to become a giant American-style, six-pole, three-ring circus, the first of its kind in Asia. Along the way,

Kunhikannan too gained international acclaim apart from becoming an entrepreneur himself.

Chatre wore many hats. One of them was that of a music maestro – not as a singer but a kind of encyclopaedia of music. According to Janaki Bakhle, associate professor of history at Columbia University and author of *Two Men and Music,* such was Professor (no one, however, knows why or since when Chatre had that title) Chatre's authority that he once argued with legendary classical singer Abdul Karim Khan saheb on the purity of gharana pedigrees.

Not much is known about Chatre's demise. But what we do know is that like many other Marathi men and women, he remained an unsung hero.

Incidentally, there is another Chatre that Maharashtrians should be proud of. He was the mathematician Kero Lakshman Chatre (1824–84). Keronana, as he was fondly known, was born near Bombay. He was one of the few students of the first batch to graduate from Elphinstone College under the tutelage of Balshastri Jambhekar. He was fond of mathematics and went on to explore astronomy and earth science. His academic prowess provided him the unique opportunity of working at the Bombay Observatory at the young age of sixteen. He later moved to Poona as an assistant professor of mathematics at Deccan College. Just ten years later, Keronana, having studied astronomy, wrote a brilliant book in Marathi called *Grahasadhanchi Koshtake* (Equations and Formulas) to study planetary structures. It was a landmark publication that discussed the solar system in great detail.

Later, he went on to study and make almanacs and has quite a collection of books on the subject to his name. He wrote books for schoolchildren, explaining complex subjects like physics, arithmetic and earth science way back in 1860. His brother Lakshman (1830–64) is credited with writing and compiling notations of Indian classical music. He was a musicologist and a Sanskrit scholar. As a hobby, he used to teach music at various girls' schools in Bombay. His compilation of 'Strigeete', traditional songs of women, is considered a landmark work in cultural history. He also devised and explained a simple method to decode notations of any song. It is still relevant today, even after over 150 years.

BESIDES MATHEMATICS, THE MARATHI Manoos showed equally high calibre in science and technology as well. One such prominent name is that of Dr Shankar Abaji Bhise (1867–1935). Bombay-born and belonging to the Chandraseniya Kayastha Prabhu (CKP) community, Shankar was a curious boy, who once saw a statue whose eyes moved in sync with a clock that was placed over it. The movement of the clock's pendulum was synchronized with the statue's eyes. The six-year-old Shankar went on to dismantle it and study its mechanism. At the age of fourteen, he constructed a small apparatus at his home which produced coal gas. He decided to move to England or America to study science further when he was sixteen.

In Britain, between 1890 and 1895, he worked on optical illusions. His demonstrations in various cities there were regarded better than even those by Europeans. The first to recognize his talent was Alfred Webb, who chaired the tenth session of the Indian National Congress in Bombay in 1894. Bhise's works earned him a gold medal. One of his inventions, a machine that could mix sugar and flour to make bread and other products, was featured in London's *Inventors' Review and Scientific Record*, which created quite a sensation and was an instant hit. Another one of his inventions was a washing compound and, later, an indigenous type-caster machine, the 'Bhisotype', which had a speed of 1,200 characters a minute when other machines could only produce 150 characters per minute.

He wrote his name on over 200 inventions, of which forty were patented. It is quite astonishing that someone thought of patents at a time when India was not yet independent. Such was his story that, in 1910, Sir Ratan Tata, one of the two sons of Jamsetji Tata, the father of Indian industry, joined hands with him to set up an organization to support his inventions.

On one of his travels abroad, Bhise contracted malaria. He treated it with a compound made with a type of algae seaweed that saved his life. It helped him create the seaweed formula, a kind of liquid iodine preparation that was later recommended as a therapeutic measure for more than 600 ailments. The word 'Atomidine' comes from a company he founded in 1932.

Bhise wrote exclusively in Marathi to spread a scientific temper. He also began *Vividh Kala Prakash*, a science magazine in Marathi. The government's central science institute, the Council of Scientific and Industrial Research, rightfully describes him as 'Indian Edison'.

But like many of his fellow Marathi achievers, an accomplished scientist like him has also faded into oblivion. Giving him company in obscurity are Shridhar Sarvottam Joshi, another internationally acclaimed scientist of the famous Joshi Effect that studied the impact of light on various objects; Narasinh Narayan Godbole, a well-known chemist at Banaras Hindu University; Shankar Purushottam Agharkar, a renowned botanist; Vasant Ramji Khanolkar, a pathologist who headed the International Cancer Research Commission back in 1950; and many others. These were people who were pioneers in science, entertainment and a number of other fields. But there were two Maharashtrians who proved immensely successful in setting the agenda that defines India's polity even today on two important social fronts: Dalit as well as Hindu identity.

13

Many Poles, One Centre

Maharashtra has always been a fertile ground for philosophers and thinkers. Social and political ideas of all kinds – saffron on the right, the extreme red of the left, socialists following the middle path, the radical humanist approach, and most importantly the anti-caste Dalit movement – have all thrived in the region.

Take the issue of reservation for the oppressed classes, for instance. India continues to battle it to date. But Maharashtra's first brush with it came as early as 1902. An interesting fact is that of the over 500 princely states in pre-Independence India, only three were fair and just to the oppressed classes. Two of these were in the Marathi region and, interestingly, both were ruled by Marathas. (It is ironic that it is this very community that has been demanding reservations for itself in the twenty-first century.) The three that offered reservations to the underprivileged were Mysore, Baroda and Kolhapur.

The practice of reservation was first introduced in modern India by Rajarshi Chhatrapati Shahu Maharaj of Kolhapur in his state on 26 July 1902 – about forty-two years after Jyotirao Phule made such a demand in 1860. A progressive king, Shahu Maharaj offered 50 per cent reservation to all those who belonged to backward castes and left out only four communities: Brahmins, Parsis, Shenvis and Prabhus. A reformer at heart and a democrat by spirit, Shahu Maharaj soon became the face of the anti-Brahmin movement. Such was his commitment to reform that when Brahmin priests of the royal family refused to perform the rites of some non-Brahmins in accordance with Vedic hymns, he appointed a young Maratha as the religious teacher of the non-Brahmins. It was a step far ahead of its time. He then gave the non-Brahmin priest the title of 'Kshatra Jagadguru' (the world teacher of the Kshatriyas). In Maharashtra's social history, this is known as the Vedokta controversy that shocked society. Shahu is credited with bringing together the non-Brahmins in Maharashtra, who were later led by Keshavrao Jedhe and Bapurao Javalkar.

AROUND THE SAME TIME, some Marathi Brahmins were attempting to unite Hindus all across India. Post Tilak and after the rise of Gandhi, Maharashtra witnessed two contrasting crusades taking birth on its soil: the Hindutva and the Dalit movements. And both continue to determine India's politics even today, though their base later shifted to north India and they took a regressive turn. The call for a 'Congress-*mukt* Bharat' (Congress-free India), that has now been popularized by the Bharatiya Janata Party (BJP), was first given in Maharashtra at the beginning of the twentieth century. It is quite extraordinary for Maharashtra to have been the land of so many different political beliefs.

Another interesting fact is that some of Tilak's acolytes, like Narasimha Chintaman Kelkar, Balakrishna Shivram Munje and others, became the torchbearers of the Hindutva movement after his death. Most of them were not comfortable with Gandhi's views and his style of politics. Another section of Tilak's followers, such as Shripad Amrit Dange, Pandurang Sadashiv Khankhoje and others, veered towards communism and became the leading lights of the leftist movement. Dange, popularly known as Bhai Dange, was a founder member of the Communist Party of India, while Khankhoje was one of the early leaders of the Manabendra Nath Roy-led leftist movement.

It wasn't just them. In fact, it was Narayan Meghaji Lokhande (1848–97) who had formed India's first labour union in Bombay way back in the nineteenth century. The Bombay Mill Hands Association was the first Indian workers' organization and the brainchild of Lokhande, who worked for the welfare of Bombay's mill workers. Facilities such as the Sunday weekly off, lunch breaks, fixed working hours and so on which may appear normal now were the result of Lokhande's efforts. Around the same time, another Maharashtrian, Narayan Malhar Joshi (1879–1955), formed the All India Trade Union Congress (AITUC) to deal with labour issues. N.M. Joshi is considered a pioneer in modern Indian social work. In 1909, he set up the Social Service League to impart training to volunteers who could be deployed in natural calamities and help with welfare programmes.

This shows how Maharashtra was the birthplace or the centre stage of every important political thought. First, let's discuss the pro-Hindu or the Hindutvawadi movement.

Two Maharashtrians and two organizations played extremely important roles in organizing Hindus all over India. They were Vinayak Damodar Savarkar (1883–1966) and Dr Keshav Baliram Hedgewar (1889–1940). The two organizations were the Akhil Bharatiya Hindu Mahasabha and the Rashtriya Swayamsevak Sangh (RSS).

The Hindu Mahasabha was founded in 1915 as a direct reaction to the All-India Muslim League. Under British rule, the Partition of Bengal of 1905 was a landmark development that triggered the division of Indian society on religious lines. A year later, the Muslim League came into being. The newly carved province of Bengal had a Hindu majority while that of Eastern Bengal and Assam was mostly Muslim-dominated. Viceroy Lord Curzon justified the move citing administrative reasons. But many saw it as an attempt by the British government to divide Hindus and Muslims, thereby splitting the Indian freedom movement. This fear was justified when the British brought in the Morley–Minto Reforms in 1909, which floated the idea of creating a separate constituency for Muslims. Such developments only hastened the creation of an organization to protect Hindu interests.

A section of people in the Congress came up with the idea of setting up a separate body for Hindus. First was created the Punjab Hindu Sabha by Lala Lajpat Rai, Lal Chand and others in the same year as the Morley–Minto Reforms. Soon they were joined by Madan Mohan Malaviya for its maiden session in October 1909. The session resolved to protect the interests of all Hindus and criticized the Congress for its failure to do so. In a year's time, a number of Hindu Sabhas were formed – in Bihar, Bengal, Bombay Presidency, and so on. Eventually, the need was felt for an umbrella organization to protect and further the interests of Hindus. Initial attempts to create one, however, didn't succeed for various reasons. Finally, all the regional Hindu organizations came together on the auspicious occasion of the Kumbh Mela that was held in Haridwar in 1915.

The Haridwar conference not only witnessed a large congregation of all the regional Hindu outfits but also saw the presence of Gandhi, who had just returned from South Africa, along with Swami Shraddhanand of the Arya Samaj. Led by the likes of Malaviya and Lajpat Rai, it took another six years for the organization to adopt the name Akhil Bharatiya Hindu Mahasabha and also to amend its constitution to demand a 'self-governing Indian state'; the constitution had initially expressed loyalty to the British. The Mahasabha gained momentum after Munje and Savarkar joined it.

Munje was a strong Tilak acolyte who dissociated from the Congress after his mentor's demise. He had serious differences with Gandhi. However, Savarkar's story wasn't the same. A political revolutionary and religious rebel, he had a pro-Hindu inclination from his college days, in India and later in England. He set up Abhinav Bharat, an organization that espoused the cause of Indian freedom by revolutionary means. He wrote extensively, eulogizing the Indian uprising of 1857. His works attracted the wrath of the British government, which banned his books. He soon faced arrest for his activities at India House, London. Led by advocate Shyamji Krishna Varma, India House, a student residence in London, was a hub for like-minded Indians. One of them was Savarkar. He hoped for a guerrilla war against the British, quite like the one in 1857. He wrote about it in his work *The Indian War of Independence*, the first book that refers to the developments of 1857 as a war of Indian independence – as opposed to a mutiny, which the British were trying to project it as then.

The book brought Savarkar to the attention of the British government, which banned it across its colonies. Around this time, efforts were being made to bring Hindus under a single organization. Back home in India, Ganesh, Savarkar's brother, had organized an armed revolt to protest against the Morley–Minto Reforms. Soon enough, the British arrested him for it. This alerted Savarkar, who fled to the home of Bhikaji Cama, or Madame Cama, a prominent figure of the independence movement, in Paris in order to evade arrest. He, however, couldn't dodge them for long; the British caught him on 13 March 1910. As he was being taken to India on board the SS *Morea*, he escaped from his cell while the ship was docked at Marseille on 8 July. The daring act backfired as Savarkar was caught again. Finally, he was brought to India and, following a trial, was convicted and sentenced to fifty years' imprisonment. On 4 July 1911, he was moved to the infamous Cellular Jail in Andaman.

Savarkar was just twenty-eight when he was sentenced. He filed a series of mercy petitions, which were all initially rejected by the British. His supporters characterize his pleas as a tactical retreat, although many historians refuse to take such a charitable view. According to the latter, the petitions were nothing but a complete surrender before the empirical powers. In 1920, Gandhi, along with some other Congress leaders, too demanded his unconditional release despite the fact that Savarkar had always been extremely critical of Gandhi and his politics. Ultimately, the British did relent after he endorsed his trial, verdict and British law and renounced violence – all to gain freedom. He was then moved to a jail in Ratnagiri before being released in 1924, although he remained confined to the district till 1937. According to some historians critical of Savarkar, he ceased to be an anti-British fighter once he accepted the embarrassing conditions to end his jail term.

This was a tumultuous period of the Indian freedom movement. Tilak passed away in 1920 and Gandhi's leadership was yet to be established. Once he was out of prison and under confinement in Ratnagiri, Savarkar, along with Munje, started devoting more and more time to the Hindu Mahasabha. Both were against the Congress's secular politics and extremely critical of its pro-Muslim stance. They were staunch Hindus and their politics was clearly majoritarian. But Gandhi was soon all over the political space and Hindutvawadi leaders started getting rapidly marginalized. The Hindu Mahasabha failed to emerge as an organization leading the majority. Savarkar became increasingly bitter about the Congress over time; in response, the latter began alienating him more and more. He wanted to take Hinduism towards a modern path and rid it of its curse of casteism. According to him, the cow was just an animal with enormous utility; he refused to acknowledge it as 'Gau Mata' the way devout Hindus do. This may be one of the reasons why the Hindu Mahasabha failed to widen its base. Also, it was never regarded as an anti-British organization even when the struggle for freedom was gaining momentum. Already weakened by its limits, the Mahasabha was soon to receive a major jolt.

DR KESHAV BALIRAM HEDGEWAR walked out of the organization to set up another one for Hindus – the Rashtriya Swayamsevak Sangh (RSS). Unlike many leaders and reformers of the day who were predominantly Chitpavan Brahmins from Poona, Nashik or the Konkan, Hedgewar was a Deshastha Brahmin from Nagpur and was greatly influenced by Munje, who was also from the same city. It was Munje who encouraged a young Hedgewar to go to Calcutta, and not Poona, to study medicine. Medical degree in hand, Hedgewar returned to Nagpur in 1915. Always interested in social work and hugely influenced by Tilak and Savarkar, he soon followed in their footsteps and joined the Congress. But like Munje and Savarkar, he too was disillusioned by its secular ('pro-Muslim') politics. Hedgewar believed that the cultural and religious heritage of Hinduism was the only rubric which could bring Indians together, and that armed revolution alone would not free the nation. On the one hand he felt that the Congress did not have an Hindu-only view. The Hindu Mahasabha, on the other hand, had its own limitations in achieving the goal he had in mind. Upset with the situation around, he increasingly felt a need to set up a cultural organization to unite Hindus.

On Dussehra in 1925, the RSS was formed in Nagpur with the aim of character-building among Hindus. Hedgewar planned to enrol Hindu children and youth, who could be trained in military style to become foot soldiers and ambassadors of the RSS. Initially, all members wore a uniform that consisted of a black cap, a khaki shirt (which was later changed to white) and khaki shorts, and carried a *dand*, a bamboo stick used as a kind of weapon. The RSS shakhas, or branches, had a distinct identity – the *bhagwa dhwaj*, or saffron flag, and all the recruits were routinely exposed to the glorious past of Hinduism.

Initially, Hedgewar used to conduct the regular *baudhiks*, or discourses on Hinduism. But the RSS soon had thousands of *pracharaks* trained for the job. The organization was born to further the Hindu agenda and, right from its inception, it has always claimed to be a social and cultural body that has no connection with any political outfit. It was, however, against the Gandhi-led Congress, which it perceived as pro-Muslim and anti-Hindu. The most striking aspect of the RSS is its cold approach towards the freedom movement. Even as all of India was completely charged by the independence movement, Hedgewar didn't involve the RSS in any activity that would have pitted it against the British. However, he did participate once in an agitation launched by Gandhi in April 1930. Four years later, though, the Congress asked its members not to join the RSS because of its Hindu-centric approach. The list of 'prohibited' bodies included the Hindu Mahasabha and the Muslim League too.

The RSS pushed itself even further right on the ideological spectrum during the Second World War when it openly embraced Adolf Hitler and his racial views. It may sound contradictory, but the RSS was equally enamoured of Jews and their effort to create Israel. Madhav Sadashiv Golwalkar (1906–73), popularly known as Guruji, who succeeded Hedgewar as the RSS chief, praised Jews for their steadfastness in maintaining religious purity. This past continues to draw criticism even as the RSS is set to celebrate its centenary in 2025.

What helped the Hindu Mahasabha and the RSS become popular in their initial years was the support they received from the former supporters of Tilak, prominent among whom was N.C. Kelkar (1872–1947). He was the editor of *Kesari* and *The Mahratta* for forty-one years, along with being a member of the Kesari trust. After Tilak's death in 1920, he became one of the foremost leaders of the Tilakites in the Congress and was also a member of the Viceroy's Council from 1924 to 1929. However, like many of his associates, he too started drifting away from the Congress as it came under Gandhi's influence. Later, he went on to head the Hindu Mahasabha and became its president twice, in 1928 and 1932. Another prominent Tilak follower who became a staunch Hindu ideologue after the emergence of Gandhi was Gajanan Vishwanath Ketkar, Tilak's grandson. He edited *Kesari* and *The Mahratta* for a while but joined the Hindu Mahasabha after his grandfather's death. Later, he raised funds to defend Savarkar when the latter was implicated in Gandhi's assassination. He was also a mediator in the 1948 talks between the Nehru government and the RSS, which came under a ban after Gandhi's assassination.

Once again, it is interesting to note how Maharashtra accommodated completely divergent political thoughts. If Gokhale, Gandhi's guru, was Maharashtrian, so was Nathuram Godse, a product of the Hindu Mahasabha, Gandhi's antithesis,

Stamps showing the great social reformers of the nineteenth century, Jyotirao and Savitribai Phule, whose work extended to many fields, including the fight for the eradication of untouchability and the caste system. They were also the pioneers of women's education in India.

A portrait of Pandita Ramabai, a champion of the education and emancipation of women in India and a social reformer.

Rukhmabai Arjun, whose refusal to consummate her marriage as a child bride led to a landmark legal case that stirred public debate in India and England and contributed to the passage of the Age of Consent Act of 1891.

Uddhav Thackeray and Narendra Modi, the incumbent leaders in the state and at the Centre. Thackeray assumed office after a dramatic election in 2019, when the Shiv Sena, Congress and the Nationalist Congress Party formed an unlikely alliance to keep the BJP out of power.

Sharad Pawar remains the only leader from Maharashtra to have made an unabashed bid for the PM's post – in 1991, losing to P.V. Narasimha Rao – even as he has kept up a tradition of standing up to the power centres in Delhi, be it Sonia Gandhi earlier or Narendra Modi now.

and his assassin. Incidentally, both mentor and murderer were Chitpavan Brahmins.

Godse (1910–49), a staunch Hindu Mahasabha activist, started the newspaper *Agrani* (Leader), which was subsequently rechristened as *Hindu Rashtra*. Like many other staunch Hindu leaders, he never subscribed to Gandhi's philosophy and his politics. According to him, Gandhi compromised Hindu interests by fasting unto death on many issues. Such was his hatred towards Gandhian thought that he viewed Gandhi as anti-national and eventually eliminated him.

MUCH HAS BEEN WRITTEN about Godse, Gandhi and the role of the Hindu outfits in the latter's assassination. And just as much is known about Tilak's followers' embracing of the Hindutva ideology after deserting the Congress. But there is much that remains unknown about another equally important faction of Tilak's supporters that went on to lay the foundation of the leftist movement in India. One can only imagine the expanse of Tilak's persona that he spawned totally contrasting political thoughts and movements.

The two most important of the followers of this grouping – though relatively ignored at the state and national levels – are Khankhoje (1884–1967) and Bhai Dange (1899–1991). Of the two, the former is a relatively unsung hero. Born and brought up in Wardha in the Vidarbha region of Maharashtra, Khankhoje left for the US for his higher education. But even before he graduated from Washington State University, Khankhoje and some others, inspired by Tilak, founded the Indian Independence League in Oregon in 1908. His work there brought him close to many Indian nationalists residing in the US then. He was also instrumental in setting up the Pacific Coast Hindustan Association, and later went on to join hands with Sikh, Muslim and Hindu leaders to reincarnate it as the Ghadar Party, a mutli-ethnic political outfit with its headquarters in San Francisco.

When the First World War erupted, he was one of the most influential members of the party. Khankhoje also joined a West Coast military academy to get trained in warfare. This led him to join the Hindu–German conspiracy that planned a kind of mutiny against British rule in India. As part of this, he frequented Europe and played an active role in bringing together a group of Indian students there to launch an anti-British campaign. In the middle of the world war he travelled through Iraq, Turkey, Baluchistan and other countries, disguised as a Muslim, to launch a military campaign to oust the British.

After the war, members of the Ghadar Party divided into pro- and anti-communist groups. Khankhoje joined the former. As an active communist member, he travelled to the Soviet Union in 1921 with M.N. Roy to meet Vladimir Lenin. Needless to say, his revolutionary past and leftist ideology made him a persona non grata in India. Around this time, he earned the distinction of being labelled as 'dangerous' by the British.

Then came the third and equally important stage in Khankhoje's life. He shifted base from the US to Mexico to join as professor of botany and crop breeding at the National School of Agriculture in that country. He is credited with the South American nation's success in corn breeding. A grateful Mexican government appointed him as the director of its agriculture department. After India became independent, Khankhoje returned and settled in Nagpur and remained a leading proponent of the Royist movement.

Roy, an internationally active revolutionary who founded the Communist Party of Mexico, although originally from Bengal, preferred Poona to set up his League of Radical Congressmen. It propagated radical humanism, an alternative to communism. Roy had many prominent followers in Maharashtra – from politician Yashwantrao Chavan to scholar 'Tarkateertha' Lakshman Shastri Joshi and jurist Vithal Mahadeo Tarkunde. Imprints of the Royist movement can be found in the intellectual sphere of Maharashtra even today.

Maharashtra also happens to be home to the India-centric – unlike the otherwise Russia-centric – communist movement in India. One of its founding pillars was Shripad Amrit Dange. Born in Nashik, he was the son of a government officer who was also a landlord in the region. He was sent to Poona for his studies. The centre of the nationalist movement then, Poona encouraged the rebel in Dange, who was extremely influenced by Tilak. Having left college, Dange started working for the cause of the textile mill workers in Bombay as a first step before plunging into active politics. After being exposed to the miserable conditions of the mill workers, he resolved to live for their upliftment. Soon he joined the independence movement in response to Gandhi's call. Internationally, the dust raised by the Bolshevik Revolution in Russia was settling down and youth from all over the world were being drawn to communism. Dange was one such young man from India. Having grown doubtful about the efficacy of the Gandhian way, especially his economic thoughts, Dange switched over to Marxism.

In 1921, when Dange was in his early twenties, he published a pamphlet titled *Gandhi Vs Lenin* showing the politics and policies of the latter in better light vis-à-vis Gandhi's. The study turned out to be decisive in setting the course of his political life as it found two important readers: M.N. Roy, who came calling all the way to Bombay to meet the young Dange, and Ranchoddas Lotvala, a small businessman in Bombay who sponsored Dange's study of Marxism for several years. It is ironic that it was a capitalist who supported one of India's foremost leftist ideologues. Not just that, Lotvala even helped Dange raise a collection of Marxist literature besides his own works. He also played a role in the 1922 launch of Dange's *Socialist*, India's first Marxist journal, writings in which impressed even Lenin.

The following years were of industrial unrest all over the world, especially in England. It was also a period when the freedom movement in India was expanding. As Gandhi's politics was spreading its wings, also rising was the leftist movement. It was a honeymoon period for communism globally, and India too was in its grip. Dange was one of the early proponents of Marxism in India, and his handling of labour issues in Bombay's textile sector showed its influence. Roy, on his return from Russia, where he was invited once again by Lenin to discuss the setting up of a communist party in India, came to meet him. Even when he was in Russia, Roy had kept in touch with him through letters that were screened by the British, who saw the spread of leftist thinking as a major threat to their rule. Growing in stature as a Marxist, Dange too came under the lens of the British government. They eventually arrested him for his role in the Kanpur Bolshevik conspiracy case along with Roy and others. The British couldn't nab Roy as he was overseas at the time, but the rest of the group that included Muzaffar Ahmad, Nalini Gupta, Shaukat Usmani and Dange were imprisoned and sentenced. The case drew wide publicity, catapulting Dange to the national stage, besides helping popularize communism in India. A year later, in 1925, Dange was released.

In December of the same year the foundation of the Communist Party of India was laid at a conference organized by Dange and his former co-prisoners. Incidentally, it was the same year when the RSS came into being too. It all happened within five years of Tilak's demise in 1920. Even as the left and the right of the political spectrum were finding their feet, there appeared a young man on the horizon who gave a completely new dimension to India's politics. He was Dr Bhimrao Ramji Ambedkar.

14

Theatre of Thoughts

At a time when the Hindu Mahasabha and the RSS were busy uniting and mobilizing Hindus, there came along in Maharashtra a young, brilliant scholar who challenged the very tenets of Hinduism, the religion of India's majority, like never before and went so far as to proclaim that 'inequality is the soul of Hinduism'. He was Bhimrao Ramji Ambedkar, a man of unparalleled intellect.

Unlike many other social reformers of the time, Bhimrao was not the product of an upper-class Brahmin family. In fact, he was born as an 'untouchable' in the Mahar community to Bhimabai and Ramji on 14 April 1891 in Mhow Army Cantonment, Central Provinces (present-day Madhya Pradesh), and had a very difficult childhood. His father was a subedar in the British Indian army, but the family had to shift base to Satara after his retirement in 1894. It was there that Bhimrao lost his mother. Shortly after, the family moved again, this time to Bombay. As was the norm back then, his father got him married at the early age of fifteen to Ramabai, six years younger than him, in 1906.

There was no end to Bhimrao's quest for knowledge, even though he had to face discrimination and humiliation to achieve it. As a child, he and the other untouchable students at his school were made to sit outside the classroom by the authorities. Sitting inside was a privilege reserved for upper-caste students. This was Bhimrao's bitter social reality at the military school at Mhow and later at the local school in Satara. Life, however, was a little better for him in Bombay.

After completing his matriculation in 1908 from Elphinstone High School, he enrolled himself at Elphinstone College, graduating in 1912 with a degree in economics and political science from Bombay University. One of the brightest students at the university, he wanted to go abroad for further studies. His financial situation didn't allow it but he earned a Baroda State scholarship of £11.5 per month for three years under a scheme established by Maharaja Sayajirao Gaekwad III. This helped him study economics at Columbia University in the US, where he presented a thesis on the topic 'Ancient Indian Commerce' and earned his master's degree in June 1915. His dissertation there was on state–centre financial equations and helping him with it was his professor and renowned economist Edwin Seligman. It presented how the mobilization of resources can be decentralized with an efficient administrative system, which continues to be our dream even in the twenty-first century.

A master's from Columbia University was not to be the end of his education. The very next year he moved to the hallowed London School of Economics. His doctoral thesis in London was later published as the book *The Problem of the Rupee: Its Origin and Its Solution*. It came at a time when there was a debate raging amongst economists on the relative merits of the gold standard vis-à-vis the gold exchange standard. While arguing for the gold standard, Ambedkar questioned the eminent economist John Maynard Keynes's suggestion that India should embrace a gold exchange standard. The debate, and Ambedkar's contribution to it, led to the setting up of a committee by the British government to fix the rate of the rupee, which eventually led to the creation of the RBI. This role that Ambedkar played in establishing the RBI remains relatively less known than his numerous other contributions.

Later, Ambedkar became a professor of political economy at the Sydenham College of Commerce and Economics in Bombay with the active support of then Bombay governor Lord Sydenham. In 1920, he returned to England to earn his DSc degree from London University. On his way back, Ambedkar spent a few months at the University of Bonn, Germany, to study economics. He received his PhD in economics in 1927. He was also awarded a doctorate by Columbia University in the same year.

But before any of that, in 1918, came his masterly essay on farming, farm income and types of landholding. In it he put forward a seemingly contradictory argument, which explained how rapid industrialization can help the farming community. One of his arguments was:

> The cumulative effects of industrialization, namely, a lessening pressure (on land) and an increasing amount of capital and capital goods will forcibly create the economic necessity of enlarging the holding. Not only this, industrialization by destroying the premium on land will give rise to few occasions for its sub-division and fragmentation.

It is remarkable that he wrote on issues which became the backbone of development economics some thirty years later. It is often forgotten that Dr Ambedkar was an accomplished economist, who was overshadowed by the politician in him.

IN TIME, DR AMBEDKAR took up the issue of caste discrimination that had left a deep impact on him since childhood. In his honest and bold testimony before the Southborough Committee in preparation for the Government of India Act in 1919, he suggested that there should be a separate electoral system for untouchables and other marginalized communities. This was the first time he articulated the concept of reservations for Dalits and other religious outcasts. He wanted to reach out to them to make them understand the disadvantages of the prevailing social system. In order to further his cause, he launched the newspaper *Mooknayak* (Leader of the Silent) in 1920 and helping him in this endeavour was Shahu, the Maharaja of Kolhapur.

Alongside, he started his legal career as well. Initially, it was very tough for him to establish himself as a lawyer since there were no cases coming to him. His knowledge of the law was never the issue, his caste was. But there were also many who spotted talent in Dr Ambedkar and were willing to help him. One of his earliest and most genuine supporters was Sridharpant Tilak, son of Lokmanya Tilak. Even though Ambedkar was a staunch critic of Lokmanya Tilak's Brahminical bent, Sridharpant respected his talent. In fact, he even dared to defy the trustees of *Kesari* to invite Ambedkar to Tilak's Gaekwad Wada home in Poona for a music recital. Dhananjay Keer, scholar and biographer of Dr Ambedkar, has described this incident in his book *Dr Babasaheb Ambedkar: Life and Mission*.

Sridharpant, however, was an exception. Most of the litigants in those days preferred British lawyers to the 'backward' Dr Ambedkar. He had set up his office in Bombay's Parel with the help of a Parsi lawyer, who had lent him Rs 5,000, but he had no work. And yet, even this penurious situation couldn't stop the scholar in him from buying books. It made his wife Ramabai's task of running the house even more onerous. But things changed for the better soon enough. Ambedkar handled three cases that made history and also changed the course of his life.

The first case was regarding Dinkarrao Javalkar's book *Deshache Dushman* (Enemies of the Country), and the second was to do with Philip Spratt's book *India and China*. Javalkar in his book had described Lokmanya Tilak and Vishnushastri Chiplunkar as 'enemies of the country' because of their alleged Brahminism. He had also compared them to Gandhi and written that the latter was a much better leader than the other two. The book was aimed at answering the critics of Mahatma Jyotirao Phule. It sparked a controversy and Javalkar was slapped with a case of defamation. The first verdict went against him. When Dr Ambedkar entered the fray, he argued that the judge who had given the judgment was prejudiced in believing that Phule was a Christian. In October 1926, Ambedkar won the case, which was probably the first major battle between Brahminical and non-Brahminical forces. This victory raised Ambedkar's stature. By then, Tilak was gone and his son Sridharpant had become Ambedkar's acolyte. Sridharpant also became a member of the organization set up by Ambedkar to spread equality. It is difficult to imagine a young Brahmin man – the son of Lokmanya Tilak at that – becoming a torchbearer for Dr Ambedkar in the extremely conservative Poona of those days. It led to Sridharpant being cut off from his family, which eventually put a tragic end to his life. He is believed to have committed suicide.

Soon he also won Philip Spratt's case. Spratt was a British writer and communist who was believed to have been sent to India by the Moscow-based British arm of the Communist International (Comintern) with a mission to spread communism. In 1927, he was charged with sedition for writing *India and China* on the instructions of the leadership of the Communist Party of Great Britain. Dr Ambedkar took on the case and won, arguing that no disaffection had been shown to the Government of India.

The third case he fought was a landmark one and had international ramifications. It was to defend Raghunath Dhondo Karve, son of Dhondo Keshav Karve and the editor of *Samajswasthya*, a magazine founded by him to spread sexual awareness. Quite an audacious act in a predominantly conservative society, the magazine – that even distributed condoms – was possibly the first such initiative in India. It is no wonder, then, that Karve was charged with spreading vulgarity. The support for him to face the court and society came from Dr Ambedkar, who brilliantly argued that 'vulgarity is not in the content but in the expression'. The arguments put forward by him were quite extensive and stunning and make interesting reading even today. Although he lost the case, the issue nevertheless projected him as an independent thinker and someone willing to support progressive ideas irrespective of religion and caste.

Dr Ambedkar soon became so popular that people would flock to courts just to see him argue. He was always willing to extend legal support to poor labourers, workers, small shop owners and even sex workers. Justice John Newmont, a judge at the Bombay High Court, who was initially hostile to Dr Ambedkar, soon became his ardent admirer. He was later invited by B.G. Kher and others to become a member of the editorial board of the prestigious *Bombay Law Journal*, which he accepted. But the legal profession was just one of the weapons in Dr Ambedkar's hands to pursue a bigger goal – that of transforming society.

With that aim in mind, on 20 July 1924, he had set up the Bahishkrit Hitakarini Sabha in Bombay, with three principles: 'educate, agitate and organize'. It was preceded by a meeting at Damodar Hall, Parel, where he had his office, to discuss the possibility of setting up a national body to help untouchables address their issues. The sabha was a result of the deliberations of the meeting. Another important development that took place in Dr Ambedkar's life around this time was that he was appointed to the Bombay Presidency Committee that was tasked to work with the Simon Commission. The commission was to look into constitutional reforms for India but became hugely unpopular and attracted protests across the country for refusing representation to Indians. Not much credit is due to the Commission except that Dr Ambedkar's recommendations for it became the foundation for the future Constitution of India.

The legal profession, as Dr Ambedkar must have realized by then, could not do full justice to his aspirations. Unfortunately, he was also not earning enough. And so he started looking for a parallel activity – like teaching – that could allow him to earn a little more. From June 1925 to 1929, he worked as a part-time lecturer at the Batliboi Accountancy Training Institute and later, from June 1928, he taught at the Government Law College, Bombay. A job as an examiner at Bombay University also helped him make some money.

AROUND THIS TIME, DR Ambedkar launched a major movement with protests and rallies to establish the rights of the untouchables. The biggest and most momentous of them was the Mahad Satyagraha in the Konkan to allow the untouchables to draw water from the town's central water reservoir. The date on which it was launched, 20 March 1927, is now observed as Social Empowerment Day, for it changed the course of Indian history. Then came his attack on the ancient Hindu text *Manusmrti*. According to him, the *Manusmrti* was at the root of all social evil in Hindu society because it justified the caste system and untouchability. His public criticism of the *Manusmrti* sent shockwaves across the nation and was followed by the burning of its copies by him and thousands of his supporters on 25 December 1927.

In 1930, he launched the Kalaram temple movement, leading a gathering of over 15,000 volunteers demanding the right to enter the temple in Nashik. When they reached there, its gates were closed by the Brahmin authorities. Before this, Dr Ambedkar had launched two similar agitations. One had been in Amravati in the Vidarbha region to gain access to the Ambabai temple in 1928, and the second at the Parvati temple in Poona. Both had been unsuccessful. All eyes were now on Dr Ambedkar, who was leading a very large gathering demanding equal rights for Dalits. As expected, he met with strong opposition from the Hindu priests and other upper-caste members of the local community. Pertinent to note is that efforts to find a solution were undertaken by veteran Congressman B.G. Kher, a Brahmin, though they proved futile.

One of the reasons behind the stalemate was an appeal from Gandhi, who had launched the nationwide civil disobedience movement around the same time. He appealed to Dr Ambedkar through his newspaper *Young India*, requesting him to halt the agitation in the larger interest. Dr Ambedkar conceded, only to relaunch it the next year. Once again, it met with opposition from orthodox Hindus and the government supporting them. Processions were banned and stringent legal provisions were used to disperse crowds. Soon, some parts of Maharashtra witnessed riots between upper-caste Hindus and members of the Depressed Classes. The Congress tried to intervene but its local arm, the Nashik Congress Committee, was divided. The impasse continued until the next year. Eventually, Dr Ambedkar asked his followers to halt the movement. There was a larger cause demanding his attention.

It was time for him to plunge into national politics. The British provided him the right reasons for doing so and the person responsible for it was Prime Minister Ramsay MacDonald. On 16 August 1932, MacDonald announced the Communal Award, which granted separate electorates for the Forward Castes, Muslims, Buddhists, Sikhs, Indian Christians, Depressed Classes (now known as the Scheduled Castes), and so on for the election of members of the provincial legislative assemblies. The electorates were created keeping in mind the size of the population of each community and accordingly the principle of weightage was applied.

If MacDonald had hoped that this would help resolve social issues, he was wrong. The first one to revolt against the Communal Award was Mahatma Gandhi. He saw in it a clear ploy to segregate people along communal lines across India. However, many – including Dr Ambedkar and some from the minority communities – came forward to support it. The idea of separate electorates created quite a furore in political circles, especially as it pitted Dr Ambedkar against Gandhi, who undertook a fast unto death at Poona's Yerawada Central Jail. The Congress was in a fix. There was a flurry of activities to bring about a rapprochement between the two leaders. Finally, on 25 September 1932, the Poona Pact was signed between the two. Dr Ambedkar signed on behalf of the Depressed Classes, while Madan Mohan Malaviya represented the other Hindus, mainly the upper castes. It gave a total of 148 reserved electoral seats to the Depressed Classes in the legislatures within the overall electorate. The Communal Award had offered 71.

This was a huge development that bolstered his standing at the national level. From then onwards, Dr Ambedkar the politician played a dominant role in Indian politics. In 1936, he set up the Independent Labour Party. In the 1937 elections to the Central

Legislative Assembly, his party won fifteen seats. Subsequently, it transformed into the All India Scheduled Castes Federation. Throughout, he remained one of the very few who refused to be overwhelmed by Mahatma Gandhi's stature. He consistently objected to the Congress's views regarding the Depressed Classes and opposed Gandhi's decision to call the untouchables 'Harijans'. According to him, dubbing them as Harijans was like secluding them from other members of society, which was, in a way, true. In this period, he also published his magnum opus, *Annihilation of Caste,* on 15 May 1936. The book is rightly considered the strongest criticism of Hindu orthodoxy and its caste system. It was also seen as – and again rightly so – a rebuke of Gandhi.

Dr Ambedkar also openly supported the idea of Pakistan. It was in 1940 in Lahore that the Muslim League made the demand for an independent Pakistan. Dr Ambedkar wrote *Thoughts on Pakistan,* a 400-page book that thoroughly analysed the concept of Pakistan. He went on to argue that Hindus should concede Pakistan to Muslims, and demanded that the provincial boundaries of the Punjab and Bengal be redrawn to separate the Muslim and non-Muslims of the regions. His thoughts shook the political establishment while reshaping the discourse and relationship between the Muslim League and the Indian National Congress.

DR AMBEDKAR WAS TRULY multifaceted and could deal with various issues adroitly. His knowledge of economics brought him on the Defence Advisory Committee and the Viceroy's Executive Council as minister for labour. Later, India's Independence earned him even bigger responsibilities: independent India's first law minister and the chairman of the committee formed on 29 August 1947 to draft the Constitution. It was without a doubt the most important role Dr Ambedkar played in his life.

In that role, he sought to mend the divisions in Indian society. He sincerely felt that the nation's unity would be in jeopardy if the divides and differences between its various classes remained unbridged. He was one of the first to underline the importance of social, religious and gender equality in the newly independent nation. His consistent emphasis on it helped him receive support in creating a system that ensured reservations for members of the Scheduled Castes and Scheduled Tribes in education and government jobs.

Here was a Marathi boy from an extremely underprivileged background, who was denied even the most basic courtesies in his conservative society, and yet he went on to become not only the champion of the oppressed but also helmed the drafting of the Constitution of India. Dr Ambedkar studied the constitutions of as many as sixty nations to understand the best provisions in them. All law-loving Indians should be grateful to Dr Ambedkar, for it is thanks to his vision of a free and equal society that the Constitution of India provides a slew of civil liberties and prevents all forms of discrimination. He was the foremost champion for the economic and social rights of women as well. Reading his speeches and debates from the time when the Constitution was being put together gives a glimpse of the glorious intellect the man possessed. The adoption of the Constitution on 26 November 1949 by the Constituent Assembly was the result of his labour and rightfully earned him the title of the 'Father of the Indian Constitution'.

THEN CAME DR AMBEDKAR'S next mission – that of studying Buddhism. In 1950, he travelled to Ceylon, now Sri Lanka, to participate in the World Fellowship of Buddhists. Having studied and debunked the theory of Aryan invasion, which resulted in him writing the book *Who Were the Shudras?*, he was drawn to Buddhism. He is also believed to have toyed with the idea of converting to Sikhism or to Islam, although not much evidence is available on what prevented him from doing so. But there is one person who is believed to have played a key role in Dr Ambedkar firming up his decision to convert to Buddhism. He was Keshav Sitaram Thackeray (1885–1973) popularly known as 'Prabodhankar', one of the sharpest critics of orthodox Hindus, a radical social reformer and the father of Bal Thackeray, the founder of the Shiv Sena. Unfortunately, not much information is available in this regard that can throw light on this important part of history.

At a grand ceremony held in Nagpur on 14 October 1956, Dr Ambedkar and his wife, Savita, converted to Buddhism. Then followed the conversion of over 5,00,000 of his supporters. To express solidarity with him, many upper-caste Hindus also converted. He then travelled to Kathmandu to attend the Fourth World Buddhist Conference and organized Nepali Dalits as well. Later, he also worked on his final manuscript, *Buddha or Karl Marx*.

Dr Ambedkar had been diagnosed with diabetes back in 1948. It became a severe problem in the later part of his life and affected his eyesight too. His health weakened further, and being on constant medication didn't help matters much. Success on the social front while losing political battles may have had its impact on his health too, which deteriorated after 1955. On 6 December 1956, just three days after he completed his book *The Buddha and His Dhamma*, one of Maharashtra's most illustrious sons passed away peacefully in his sleep. Dr Ambedkar's enduring legacy is that he first put social reforms on the agenda of the freedom struggle in a significant way, and also led a movement against untouchability and the caste order that Hinduism is identified with. On this point, he stood far to the left of Gandhi. However, far to the right of Gandhi were the Hindu Mahasabha and the RSS. Interestingly, both were extremely hostile to Gandhi but not so towards the British. Even though of late many Hindutvawadis eagerly display their fondness for Dr Ambedkar, he, all his life, was at loggerheads with Hindus. 'Though I was born Hindu, I shall not die Hindu,' he used to say.

This might not be the place to get into the details of Dr Ambedkar's pro- and/or anti-Hindu positions, but it is well within the scope of this book to show how Maharashtra was the theatre where all – even contrasting – political thoughts unfolded and shaped the nation. Independent India witnessed Maharashtra underlining its pre-eminence.

THE POLITICALLY FERTILE LAND of Maharashtra had given birth to the Dalit movement, but it soon flourished and spread in north India. Even as the Republican Party of India (RPI), formed by Dr Ambedkar himself, floundered and could not go much further, Dalit politics branched out in other ways and directions. And although the man who carved a space for the movement in mainstream politics was born in Punjab, he was, incidentally, groomed in Maharashtra.

Enter Kanshi Ram (1934–2006), the leader of the next generation of the Dalit movement. He was born in Punjab's Ropar district in a family that belonged to the Chamar (cobbler) caste. The state, as compared to some of its neighbouring ones, wasn't exactly conservative or caste-conscious. His first brush with caste discrimination took place in Poona while working in the government's Explosive Research and Development Laboratory. This social realization brought him to Dr Ambedkar's *Annihilation of Caste*, which awakened the activist in him. By then, Dr Ambedkar, the founder of the RPI, was no longer around. Kanshi Ram initially joined the RPI but was disillusioned due to its hobnobbing with the Congress. He wanted the party to be an independent force dedicated only to the Dalit cause. He, however, was a novice and could not influence the established leadership. The situation left only one option for him – that of setting up his own organization.

In 1971, Kanshi Ram founded the All India SC, ST, OBC and Minority Employees Association, which later came to be known as BAMCEF (the All India Backward and Minority Communities Employees Federation). It aimed to create a Dalit/OBC-sensitive bureaucracy by training students from the backward classes. At first it was more of a social body, which was to soon set a political agenda. BAMCEF believed, contrary to the prevailing point of view, that

Dalits, OBCs, and SC/ST members were the 'Mul Nivasi' (original Indians), and Brahmins, Kshatriyas and Vaishyas, considered as Aryans, were the invaders who took over the country. This caused quite a stir in those days because Kanshi Ram propagated a completely unheard-of theory that dubbed the socially strong upper castes as outsiders. BAMCEF members were often found leading agitations and attacks against upper castes.

Kanshi Ram, at this juncture, seems to have realized the need to build a political force as, in 1981, just three years after BAMCEF, he set up another body: the Dalit Shoshit Samaj Sangharsh Samiti (DSSSS), which popularly came to be known as DS4. He struck the right chord, thanks to catchy and creative slogans like '*Brahmin, Thakur, Bania chor, baki sab DS4*' (the Brahmins, Thakurs and Banias are crooks, the rest are DS4). This was his first attempt at consolidating the Dalit vote and its success led him to launch the Bahujan Samaj Party (BSP) in 1984 on Dr Ambedkar's birth anniversary.

Founded in Maharashtra, the BSP resonated in Uttar Pradesh. 'We will fight the first election to lose, the second to get noticed and the third to win,' Kanshi Ram would say. He was extremely pugnacious when it came to dealing with other established Dalit leaders such as Jagjivan Ram and Ram Vilas Paswan. According to him, they were stooges of the Brahmin leaders of other parties and hence had no understanding of Dalits' needs. He impressively, though unsuccessfully, fought elections against stalwarts such as Rajiv Gandhi and V.P. Singh, but the successor he named, Mayawati, went on to serve four terms as the chief minister of Uttar Pradesh.

In 2006, on 14 October, the fiftieth anniversary of Dr Ambedkar's conversion to Buddhism, Kanshi Ram wanted to follow in his footsteps too. But he died a week before that. In his condolence message, Prime Minister Manmohan Singh described him as 'one of the greatest social reformers of our time ... He had a larger understanding of social change and was able to unite various underprivileged sections of our society and provide a political platform where their voices would be heard.'

Kanshi Ram wasn't Maharashtrian but Maharashtra features in his legacy in some measure as his early thoughts and work were shaped in the state and he was influenced by Dr Ambedkar. At the same time, one can only wonder if he would have had the same impact on Dalit polity had he not shifted base to the Hindi heartland of Uttar Pradesh – a move that proved instrumental in transforming him into a national icon. The answer would reveal a lot about Maharashtra's diminished role in India's political and social order.

15

Post-Independence Turmoil

Independent India's first cabinet, comprising fifteen members and sworn in on the dawn of 15 August 1947 under the leadership of Prime Minister Jawaharlal Nehru, had two Maharashtrian ministers: Dr Babasaheb Ambedkar (Minister of Law) and Narhar Vishnu alias Kakasaheb Gadgil (Minister of Works, Mines and Power). A third, Sir Chintaman Dwarakanath Deshmukh, joined in 1950 as the Minister of Finance.

Kakasaheb Gadgil (1896–1966) was one of the many freedom fighters from Poona who had joined the Independence movement thanks to Tilak and his politics, facing imprisonment as many as eight times after earning a degree in law. In his ministerial role, Gadgil is credited with undertaking an important road in Jammu and Kashmir that connected Pathankot in Punjab to Srinagar via Jammu, which played a crucial role in the subsequent Indo-Pak wars. He also played a significant role in India's mega dam projects such as Bhakra in Punjab and Koyna in Maharashtra. An erudite intellectual, Gadgil was also an author of eminence, writing books on topics ranging from the government to the history of the Sikhs, and was associated with various social and cultural institutes in Maharashtra. Later in his career, he also served as the governor of Punjab and vice chancellor of Poona University.

Sir C.D. Deshmukh (1896–1982), hailing from the CKP community in Raigad in the Konkan, was a scholar, economist, the first Indian governor of the RBI, a Sanskrit pandit, and the first Marathi ICS officer. After finishing his schooling in his native village, a young Chintaman moved to Bombay for his higher education. A brilliant student, he was awarded the Jugonnath Sunkersett Sanskrit scholarship for his extraordinary success in the matriculation exam. Later, he went to England for further studies. He won many an accolade there as well. In 1918, he took the ICS exam, which was held only in London then. Considered to be one of the toughest examinations then and open only to the British until the early years of the twentieth century, Chintaman not only cleared it in his very first attempt but also stood first.

A year later, he returned to India to work as undersecretary in the Central Provinces and Berar, which was part of Hyderabad State. He went on to take up various other responsibilities in British India, among which was a secretarial role in the 1931 Second Round Table Conference, one of the three organized by the British government and Indian leaders to discuss constitutional reforms. It saw the participation of then British Prime Minister Ramsay MacDonald, Mahatma Gandhi and M.A. Jinnah, among several other luminaries. Of all his bureaucratic roles, C.D. Deshmukh is best remembered for his stint with the RBI.

He was appointed on the RBI's board in 1939 and made its governor in August 1943, remaining in that role until 1949. As its first Indian governor, there are many things in the institution to his credit, including the setting up of the Industrial Finance Corporation and giving a major thrust to rural credit. Under his leadership, the RBI launched a Research and Statistics Department and also laid down the structure to regulate India's banking sector. After Independence, on 1 January 1949, the institution was nationalized under the RBI Act of 1948. Interestingly, Deshmukh opposed the move, which was considered as an encroachment on the RBI board's freedom. 'The Government of India's desire to nationalize the Reserve Bank is not shared by the Board of the Bank,' he noted in a speech then. His stand can be considered as the first assertion of the RBI's autonomy, a debate which continues to date. While addressing the audience at the Founder's Day celebration of the Gokhale Institute of Politics and Economics in Poona, he said, 'Such a step is both premature and logically unnecessary in the present stage of the economic development of the country.' He, however, assured the government that should it decide to go ahead with nationalization, 'all authorities [of RBI] would cooperate with the government in evolving a scheme of nationalization'. According to him, 'more than the theoretical constitution of the bank', the need of the hour then was the 'close cooperation between bank and the Government of India'.

He didn't come in the way of the RBI's nationalization and accepted the government's request for him to continue as the chairman of the board of directors presiding over the transition. He led the institution until July 1949, when Benegal Rama Rau succeeded him. Deshmukh was to become the finance minister in Nehru's cabinet.

But before that, he had the privilege of representing India at the 1944 Bretton Woods Conference, which played a key role in shaping the world after the Second World War. It was at this conference that two premier institutes came into being: the World Bank and the International Monetary Fund (IMF). He was not a mute witness to deliberations at the conference. As one of the five members of the Indian delegation, he was the first among those present to oppose the quota system related to foreign exchange reserves, which would have denied India its legitimate right. It was on his insistence that the International Bank for Reconstruction and Development (IBRD), one of the offshoots of the conference, was forced to take up the issue of poverty in underdeveloped nations. His performance at Bretton Woods was exemplary, and his masterly arguments caught the attention of many. One of those enamoured by him was the legendary British economist John Maynard Keynes; in fact, he was keen on having Deshmukh as the first head of the IMF. The US, however, vetoed the idea. Deshmukh continued as a member of the board of governors of both the IMF and the IBRD from 1946 to 1956, along with being the chairman of the joint annual meeting of the boards of governors of these institutions at its Paris Conference in 1950.

Sir Deshmukh also happens to be one of the founding members of India's Planning Commission, which witnessed his power tussle with John Mathai, then finance minister, who eventually resigned and was replaced by Deshmukh. It was Deshmukh who conceived India's First Five Year Plan. Revenue generation was a major concern for the Indian government, which forced him to propose high taxes in his first budget presented in 1951-52. As finance minister, there are many firsts to his credit, such as setting up the Indian Institute of Public Administration in New Delhi, converting the erstwhile Imperial Bank into the State Bank of India and establishing the Life Insurance Corporation. He presented six budgets and an interim one in 1952-53 ahead of the general elections, and his vision helped India mitigate the economic impact of the post-Second World War situation. His term in the Union cabinet, however, ended on a sour note with Nehru.

India was in the throes of the reorganization of states on the basis of language. And Deshmukh, a staunch Maharashtrian, objected to the idea of dividing Bombay State between Gujarat and Maharashtra and designating the city of Bombay as a Union Territory. The move angered Maharashtrians, who resolved to challenge the Centre's plan by setting up the Samyukta Maharashtra Samiti. Deshmukh threw his weight behind the cause and resigned from the cabinet. Considering his stature, his decision was seen as heroic.

But before that, India was to witness a major catastrophe, with a group of Maharashtrians at the centre of one of the darkest and most shameful chapters in Indian history. It was the assassination of Mahatma Gandhi.

WHEN INDIA'S FREEDOM WAS still just a few weeks old, Calcutta witnessed massive communal riots between Hindus and Muslims. Mahatma Gandhi tried to douse the fire, which was rapidly spreading to other parts of the country. Having failed in controlling the spread of communal hatred, a heartbroken Gandhi returned to Delhi on 9 September 1947 from Calcutta. Independence had brought immense pain with it, which was showing no signs of receding. The following month witnessed Pakistan's infiltration bid in Jammu and Kashmir. Finally, on 26 October 1947, Maharaja Hari Singh of Kashmir signed the Instrument of Accession, which saved the entire region from falling into the hands of Pakistani invaders. As if that wasn't enough, Pakistani finance minister Ghulam Muhammad raised the issue of the Rs 55 crore that India had agreed to pay the new nation as part of the agreement of Partition. Home Minister Sardar Vallabhbhai Patel had halted the payment till the tensions between the two countries eased. Gandhi, on the other hand, was keen that India give Pakistan its due. All of this infuriated right-wing Hindus – they were upset with Gandhi for his perceived pro-Muslim stance.

At the same time, Hindu–Muslim relations in the country were worsening. In such a situation, Mahatma Gandhi undertook another fast for communal harmony on 13 January 1948, which angered right-wing Hindus even more. They saw it as yet another attempt to pressure the Nehru government to give Pakistan the money. Five days later, on 18 January, he ended the fast after a large number of important politicians and leaders of communal bodies agreed to a joint plan for the restoration of normal life. It caused further indignation to the Hindu fanatics, and a bunch of them decided to eliminate the Mahatma.

The first attempt on Gandhi's life took place on 20 January. Most of those involved were Maharashtrians: Nathuram Godse, Gopal Godse, Narayan Apte and Digambar Badge along with a few others, including Madanlal Pahwa, a Punjabi refugee. As per the plan, Godse and the others followed Gandhi to a park where he was to address a gathering. Pahwa threw a grenade towards the crowd and it exploded about 75 feet away from the dais where Gandhi was speaking. The loud explosion scared the audience but Gandhi was unmoved. He asked the people to stay calm as they ran for cover. Gandhi was left alone on the stage, at which point, according to the plan, a second grenade was to be hurled at him. Badge was tasked with that job but lost his nerve. Instead, he ran away. Joining him were the Godse brothers and Apte. Meanwhile, a nearby woman spotted Pahwa and alerted the security men. He was caught and Gandhi was unhurt.

The next attempt took place on 30 January, which, unfortunately, proved successful. Mahatma Gandhi was assassinated at the hands of Nathuram Godse, a Hindu hardliner who had earlier been Savarkar's follower but had fallen out with him over the question of who would lead the Hindu Mahasabha. Savarkar wanted Syama Prasad Mukherjee to head the organization but, according to Godse, he wasn't the right choice. In that sense, Godse considered himself more Hindutvawadi than Savarkar. That apart, both of them were on the same page on one point: Gandhi. After his assassination, both were arrested along with Narayan Apte, Gopal Godse, Shankar Kistaiya, Vishnu Karkare, Dattaram Parchure, Madanlal Pahwa and Digambar Badge, who had helped in arranging the weapon. Of the nine arrested, eight were Maharashtrians, of whom six were Chitpavan Brahmins.

It resulted in Brahmins facing the wrath of common people all over Maharashtra. Members of the community were attacked and stoned, and their homes torched. This went on for nearly four days. The situation was especially bad in western Maharashtra, where Marathas, who were seen leading the attacks against Brahmins, had a strong presence. The antipathy between the two communities is palpable even today.

In a letter to his wife, Dr Ambedkar wrote that it was unfortunate that a Maharashtrian was responsible for Mahatma Gandhi's death. Dr Ambedkar, his serious political differences with Gandhi notwithstanding, was emotionally shattered by the mindless violence that took his life. And he was particularly pained by the fact that the assassins were Maharashtrians.

Further, the RSS was banned on 4 February, four days after Mahatma Gandhi's assassination. M.S. Golwalkar, who had taken over the reins of the organization following the death of its founder, Dr Hedgewar, was also arrested. The police suspected that he and the RSS had also played an active role in the killing. They, however, could never prove it conclusively. Even so, the RSS was always considered a co-conspirator. Golwalkar was released from prison on 6 August, following which he met Home Minister Sardar Patel to lobby for lifting the ban on the RSS. But Sardar Patel did not relent. The ban continued as the RSS refused to accept the terms laid down by Patel. Golwalkar asked the RSS swayamsevaks to restart the organization's activities from 13 November even as the ban remained in force. This angered Patel, who ordered Golwalkar's arrest the very next day. From 9 December onwards, RSS volunteers launched a satyagraha to protest against the Centre's act. Sardar Patel remained unmoved. Finally, Golwalkar blinked and gave a written commitment that the organization would respect the Constitution of India and conduct its activities within the constitutional framework. On 14 January 1949, the RSS called off its satyagraha and six months later, on 12 July 1949, the ban was lifted.

COMING BACK TO 'SAMYUKTA Maharashtra', or Unified Maharashtra, it was the agitation which eventually gave Maharashtra its present shape in 1960. But its seeds were sown way back in 1920. It was the year when a decision for the linguistic reorganization of Indian states was passed in the Congress's meeting held in Nagpur. Proposed by Gandhi, the bill suggested a process to restructure state boundaries based on their languages. But the British administration ignored it and formed regions irrespective of regional languages.

The bill was resurrected after India became independent. Many regions witnessed demands for statehood based on their respective languages. The Congress leadership, especially Nehru and Patel, vehemently opposed the linguistic structure because they felt it was a threat to national integration. Maharashtrians wanted their state to comprise all the Marathi-speaking regions of Bombay, Goa, Belgaum, Karwar, Parbhani, Nipani and Varhad. The rejection of this demand by the government triggered the campaign for Samyukta Maharashtra, which later turned violent, killing dozens.

The Maharashtrians had reason to be angry. The death of Potti Sriramulu, who was on hunger strike demanding the state of Andhra Pradesh, in 1952 had forced the government to concede the demand for a Telugu-speaking region. It also formed the States Reorganization Commission in 1953. But it was decided that Bombay would be kept separate from Maharashtra on the absurd grounds that Marathi-speaking people would be in a minority there. The local sentiment notwithstanding, the Congress Working Committee introduced a tri-region scheme, which recommended the creation of the state of Gujarat comprising the entire Gujarati-speaking region and 100 square miles of Bombay, and the state of Maharashtra consisting of Marathwada but excluding Belgaum and Karwar. It further recommended the creation of a separate Vidarbha state along with the Marathi-speaking areas of the erstwhile Hyderabad State and regions from the Central Provinces and the former state of Berar. The Nehru government entrusted the responsibility of implementing this decision to the chief minister of Bombay State, Morarji Desai.

The proposed composition of Maharashtra ignited a wave of protests. Widespread demonstrations were held in November 1955 to oppose the Centre's scheme. The biggest of them was in Bombay, which witnessed a huge turnout. Desai was adamant and did not believe in discussions and deliberations. He deployed a large number of security personnel, with barricades to prevent demonstrators from reaching central Bombay. His government ordered a lathicharge and the firing of tear gas to disperse the crowd.

A strike was declared in Bombay and over four lakh workers joined the protests on the road. The police tried blocking all the roads to the city's Fort area and along Bombay University but were unsuccessful. Desai responded by ordering the arrest of all leaders. They picked up Prabodhankar Thackeray, Nana Patil, Lalji Pendse and many other prominent figures, taking the total number of arrests to 350. Bombay turned into a fortress. Even as the leaders were behind bars, common people kept the protests going. On 21 November 1955, the Left parties took out a morcha to the state legislature, which the police tried to stop. Fifteen people died and 200 were injured as they opened fire on the demonstration at Flora Fountain. On 15 January 1956, Nehru declared Bombay as a Union Territory. Immediately protesters came out on the streets. From 16 to 22 January, a call for Bombay Bandh was issued by union leaders. The government once again issued orders for firing upon the protesters that then left ninety dead and over 400 injured. Thus, more than a hundred lives were lost in police atrocities since November. It led to immense resentment among Maharashtrians against the state and central leadership. Finally, Nehru was compelled to take note of it.

Around the same time, the Marathi cause got a major boost as C.D. Deshmukh, the finance minister in the Nehru government, resigned from his post in January 1956 in protest against the government's handling of the issue. Later that year, Morarji Desai, a Gujarati, was removed as chief minister and replaced by Yashwantrao Chavan, a Maratha from Karhad, a small town on the banks of the Krishna river near Kolhapur in western Maharashtra. Even though he had been a member of the Bombay legislative assembly since 1946, Chavan was a thorough Congressman and had stayed away from joining the pro-Marathi forces. He was loyal to Nehru, who according to him was 'bigger than Maharashtra'. His position was ridiculed and he was perceived to be anti-Maharashtrian. Leading the charge against him was writer and editor Prahlad Keshav Atre, whose strident criticism created quite a stir then.

A committee was formed under the leadership of veteran Congressman Keshavrao Jedhe – and included other leaders such as S.A. Dange, Prabodhankar Thackeray, Senapati Bapat, S.M. Joshi and P.K. Atre – to oppose the Centre's anti-Maharashtrian attitude. The committee was initially called the Samyukta Maharashtra Parishad but later became the Samyukta Maharashtra Samiti. It assumed huge significance as it was among the first anti-Congress political outfits in independent India. It was no easy task to take on the might of the Congress just after Independence. The RSS, too, was on the side of the government on the issue. Thus, the Samyukta Maharashtra Samiti consisted mainly of socialists and former Congressmen.

Maharashtra happens to be the birthplace of two movements that had anti-Congressism at their core. In the pre-Independence times, the Congress was more of a people's movement and not the political party it is today. It had leaders and workers of different political and social hues. Like Hedgewar, who walked out of the Congress to form the RSS in 1925, the socialists in it too were thinking of setting up an independent group. The first such suggestion came from Jayaprakash Narayan on 8 January 1948. He appealed to all socialists to walk out of the Congress and create an alternative. On 19 March, the socialists held their convention in Nashik and passed a resolution to position themselves as a strong anti-Congress force. Nearly a year before that, on 3 August 1947, when India was twelve days from embracing freedom, a section of Congress leaders gathered at Alandi near Poona to form a pressure group within the party to handle farmers' issues. The same group then walked out of the Congress on 26 April 1948 to set up what came to be known as the Peasants and Workers Party (PWP), known for its anti-Congress stance, which exists even today.

There was anti-Congressism in the air in Maharashtra. It was witnessed yet again when Nehru landed in Bombay to attend a Congress meeting. He was welcomed with black flags. That same evening he held a public meet, where demonstrations were held against him. Instead of trying to pacify the protesters, Nehru got angry and lashed out at the crowd. This infuriated them all the more and they went berserk, and the police had to fire tear gas to disperse them. The firing at the venue witnessed the death of one activist. The incident was followed by a mammoth meet organized by the Samyukta Maharashtra Samiti at the city's Shivaji Park, where the gathering pledged for 'Samyukta Maharashtra along with Mumbai'.

With public sentiment very strongly against it, in the middle of 1959 the Centre finally initiated the process to carve out the state of Maharashtra comprising the Marathi-speaking regions, including Bombay, and that of Gujarat for the Gujarati-speaking areas. Both states came into being on 1 May 1960. It was a big victory for the Marathi Manoos, although Goa, Karwar and Belgaum were not included in Maharashtra despite the demands to that effect. Jivraj Mehta was handed over the reins of Gujarat as its first chief minister. Yashwantrao Chavan, who became the first chief minister of Maharashtra, was to lay the foundation of a modern state.

16

The Best Prime Minister India Never Had

Yashwantrao Chavan can easily be described as the best chief minister Maharashtra has ever had. A staunch rationalist and an erudite, visionary, progressive and pragmatic leader, he effectively created the architecture that made Maharashtra as we know it today possible. From moulding the state's cooperative movement to pushing for industrial growth and forming a special body to promote art, literature and culture – Yashwantrao Chavan did everything that helped Maharashtra stand head and shoulders taller than many other states in India.

Chavan was, intellectually and politically, influenced by Nehru. For a while he had been under the influence of Gandhi – he was fined for his participation in the Non-Cooperation Movement in 1930 and was later sentenced to eighteen months in prison for hoisting the Indian flag in Satara in 1932 – but he never became a Gandhian perhaps because he realized the limitations of Gandhian thought, especially in the field of economics. Once out of jail, he read the recently published autobiography of Nehru. From then onwards for the rest of his life, he aligned himself with Nehruvian thought. To build an independent India, he felt the country needed a leader like Nehru. A mentor to Chavan, Nehru handed over the responsibility of the newly carved Maharashtra to his trusted follower.

It is safe to say that Yashwantrao Chavan did not disappoint Nehru or Maharashtrians. It is thanks to his visionary leadership that the western state continues to be ahead of most others in economic, social and industrial development. A few weeks into his chief ministership, Chavan drew up a comprehensive industrial policy and created an independent body, the Board of Industrial Development, that took over barren lands across the state to set up industrial estates. The move helped avoid the kind of friction between farmers and industrialists looking for land to set up plants that often turns ugly. Some of his decisions and plans, such as the Employment Guarantee Scheme, served as templates for several other states and also for the Centre to emulate later. It was he who initiated the three-tier Panchayati Raj system. The visionary leader that he was, Chavan set up two important universities in the state – Shivaji University in Kolhapur and Marathwada University in Aurangabad – along with agricultural universities.

With his keen interest in literature and culture, he founded a body to put together an encyclopaedia in Marathi. The Marathi Vishwakosh Mandal, led by the towering scholar Tarkatirth Lakshmanshastri Joshi, was his creation. An Indian classical music aficionado, a writer and a voracious reader, Chavan was among the Congress's most important leaders with a capacity and vision to lead the nation. Political leaders from Maharashtra are often seen as lacking a national image or outlook but Chavan was an honourable exception to this parochial attitude. As mentioned before, he had also stood by Nehru on the question of the composition and formation of Maharashtra, antagonizing many Marathi leaders. Chavan's loyalty and other attributes in governance were probably what Prime Minister Nehru had in mind when he sought his services in New Delhi barely two years after making him the chief minister of Maharashtra.

CHINA'S INVASION IN 1962 and Defence Minister V.K. Krishna Menon's failure in handling the situation opened the road to Delhi for Chavan. An intellectual and a left-leaning Menon was a controversial leader who evoked mixed reactions nationally as well as internationally. To the West, he was a 'menace', while his followers in India eulogized him as truly great. For his knowledge of and experience in handling international issues, Nehru made him the defence minister in 1957. But his high-handed handling of the forces angered those in uniform – so much so that the then Chief of Army Staff, General K.S. Thimayya, quit in protest in 1959, although Nehru managed to persuade him to withdraw his resignation.

China's invasion exposed India's unpreparedness, as also Menon's inept handling of the forces. He was accused of ignoring intelligence reports that had warned of China's moves. The situation turned so bad that even his ardent supporter, the prime minister, could not save him. Having come under a scathing direct attack from the opposition, Nehru finally forced Menon's resignation on 31 October 1962.

Enter Yashwantrao Chavan in his place on 14 November, in the middle of India's war with China. Conditions were not ideal for a rookie to take on an extremely important portfolio on the national stage. But Chavan's inexperience at the Centre did not prevent Nehru from handing over the responsibility of defending India to him. R.D. Pradhan, private secretary to the defence minister during those crucial years, wrote extensively in his book *Debacle to Resurgence: Y.B. Chavan, Defence Minister (1962–66)* about Chavan's baby steps in national politics. Chavan was a novice in New Delhi and also relatively inexperienced in front of a battery of high-profile Congressmen. But he was sincere, a non-confrontationist and, more importantly, a quick learner. His maiden speech in the Lok Sabha on 8 April 1963 also gives a glimpse of his global vision:

> The year 1962 seems to be a year of significance. That year produced two very significant events – one was in Cuba and the other was the Chinese aggression on India. I think the world has

started appearing rather different, in very clear terms; not that it has started changing from that moment onwards. But it started making a little different turn from the time of those two events. After these two events one can very clearly say that despite the conflict of ideologies, despite the historical enmities, many countries are coming together to save the world from war.

Two other contenders for the defence portfolio at the time were T.T. Krishnamachari, the finance minister in Nehru's cabinet, and Biju Patnaik, a pilot-turned-politician from Orissa whom Nehru liked chiefly because of his role in the Indonesian freedom struggle. His daring act of rescuing key Indonesian politicians during that country's war with the Dutch in July 1947, and later his role in Kashmir, where he flew many sorties to save injured Indian soldiers in October that year in India's first confrontation with Pakistan, had earned him Nehru's praise, perhaps making him hopeful of leading independent India's defence ministry. The prime minister, however, preferred Chavan to the other two.

Krishnamachari made peace with Nehru's decision, but that was apparently not the case with Patnaik. One episode that made his displeasure evident involved the Nehru government's decision to set up a manufacturing facility for the air force. Patnaik was keen to have it in Orissa, which according to some defence experts was not an ideal location. They suggested a site in central India instead. With Patnaik unwilling to concede, it was a tricky situation for a newly appointed defence minister. But Chavan wriggled out of it by setting up an expert committee under the chairmanship of the widely respected J.R.D. Tata, who had founded Air India back in the 1930s and was known as an ace aviator himself. Given the socialist nature of Nehru's government, it was quite a remarkable move to appoint a committee headed by an industrialist. The panel recommended Nashik, a decision that was accepted by all, putting an end to the dissenting voices.

Chavan was also the defence minister when India fought its second war with Pakistan in 1965 under Prime Minister Lal Bahadur

Shastri, who succeeded Nehru after his death in 1964, bypassing the more senior Morarji Desai. The conservative and right-wing Desai was kept in check by Congress president K. Kamaraj, who put his weight behind Shastri. As compared to the war with China, India fared much better this time around – but the outcome was a stalemate. India gained some territories while losing some to Pakistan. The war was finally settled at the negotiating table in Tashkent in January 1966 under controversial Soviet mediation. The following day Shastri died of a heart attack in Tashkent itself. Indira Gandhi then stepped into the prime minister's shoes with Desai as her deputy. This was the first instance when the Nehru loyalist Chavan was ignored for Desai.

THERE WAS A GENERAL election the next year. By then, several states had non-Congress governments, which made the party's position a little weak. Moreover, Indira Gandhi was yet to prove her leadership skills. At this crucial time, it was Yashwantrao Chavan who judiciously handled the Centre–states balance as home minister in her cabinet. His speeches in those days set a high benchmark and helped him raise his stature even higher. Although he was a staunch Nehru loyalist who had also carved out a place for himself, Chavan's relationship with Mrs Gandhi started developing some strain around this time.

The first episode where it became evident was the split within the Congress in 1969 following Mrs Gandhi's decision to support V.V. Giri in the election for President of India against the Congress's official candidate, Neelam Sanjiva Reddy. Before the selection of candidates, Chavan was constantly in touch with Mrs Gandhi to find out her choice for the position. But she held her cards close to her chest. At this point, Chavan was neither in the Congress's anti-Indira camp nor was he considered to be on her side. As she was reluctant to make her choice known despite repeated attempts, he extended his support to Reddy. And then Mrs Gandhi brought Giri forward as the candidate of her choice.

It created quite a stir as party president S. Nijalingappa expelled Mrs Gandhi for indiscipline. She then formed her own group – Indian National Congress (Requisitionists) – and retained power with the support of regional parties. It was at this point that Chavan faltered in managing his relationship with the Congress's first family. As a strict disciplinarian who always had the party in mind over its personalities, he had committed his support to Reddy. But once he realized that the Indira Gandhi-led faction would emerge as the real Congress, he changed his mind and supported Giri. It was this miscalculation that robbed Chavan of the goodwill he had earned until then.

In terms of ideology, Chavan was in no way close to the likes of K. Kamaraj, Morarji Desai and others – all conservatives, who were in the opposite camp. He had more in common with the left-of-centre Indira. But his flip-flop created doubts about his intentions in Mrs Gandhi's mind – which, unfortunately, he failed to clear until the end of his life. But at least on paper, his rapprochement with her worked as she appointed him as her finance minister in 1970.

Compared to his performance as defence minister, his stint in the finance ministry was nothing to boast about. Under him, the Indian economy went into recession and saw a fall in GDP growth. Then came the election of 1971, which Indira Gandhi fought with her popular slogan 'Garibi Hatao' (Eradicate Poverty) and won with a clear majority. The year also saw the India–Pakistan war and the creation of Bangladesh. But unlike during the previous two wars, Chavan was not the defence minister this time around. Mrs Gandhi had elevated the more loyal Jagjivan Ram to the defence ministry. Chavan was shifted to external affairs in 1974.

Even as his national role kept shifting with mixed results, Chavan continued to have immense clout in Maharashtra and remained the tallest leader of the Congress there. But Mrs Gandhi started sidelining him slowly there as well. It was around this time that Chavan too began doubting his relevance to the leadership as he haplessly watched Mrs Gandhi impose the Emergency. He saw a crisis looming but missed the opportunity to be a mediator between Jayaprakash Narayan and Mrs Gandhi. His letters in those days to his wife, Venutai, reflect his helplessness and exasperation. In one written to her from Jamaica on 4 May 1975, he wrote:

> Of late I am facing a question about the relevance of my existence in power ... Srimatiji [Mrs Gandhi] continues to consult me on important issues, but I can see her efforts to keep me away from the inner core. I feel hurt. It makes me think whether it is an insult to those who voted for me. But I console myself with the thought that personal emotions should take a backseat while deciding on issues of national importance.

Although Yashwantrao remained in Mrs Gandhi's cabinet, many believe he failed to make something bigger out of his political capital. Unlike many leaders surrounding Mrs Gandhi, he was the only one with a state as large as Maharashtra backing him completely. Even then he failed to seize the opportunity and challenge Mrs Gandhi. From then on began his downward journey.

In the 1977 general election that followed after the Emergency was lifted, the Congress faced a complete rout, with Mrs Gandhi failing to save her seat. Chavan was elected as the leader of the Congress Parliamentary Party and the leader of the opposition. The Janata Party government started floundering soon. At this point, yet another calculation of Chavan's went awry.

AS 1978 WAS COMING to an end, the Congress was seen heading for yet another split. And the driver was again Indira Gandhi. A national convention of Mrs Gandhi's loyalists unanimously passed a resolution to elect her as the party president – K. Brahmananda Reddy had been in that position since the previous year. The resolution was so wide-ranging that it authorized her to take appropriate steps 'to organize the Congress at all levels'. Helping her in that task were leaders such as Shankar Dayal Sharma, C. Subramaniam, Kamruddin Ali Ahmad, Umashankar Dikshit, A.R. Antulay and the relatively lightweight Gulabrao Patil. All of them resigned from the party to be with Mrs Gandhi as the Congress (Indira) was coming into being.

The notable absentee on her side were Yashwantrao Chavan and his protégé Sharad Pawar. They preferred to stay away from her to be with D. Devaraj Urs of Karnataka. The faction led by him became the Congress (Urs). Giving company to Chavan, Pawar and Urs were the likes of Dev Kant Barooah, A.K. Antony, S.C. Sinha, Priyaranjan Das Munshi and K. Brahmananda Reddy. Except for Chavan and to some extent Urs, none in this camp had any mass base. It was little surprise, then, that the Congress (Urs) disintegrated soon, with Urs himself choosing to join the Janata Party. The Congress (Urs) became the Congress (Socialist).

On the other hand, various sections of Congress (I) were eager to topple the Morarji Desai-led Janata Party government and their patience was running out. On 11 July 1979, a no-confidence motion was moved against Prime Minister Desai, who put up a brave face for the duration of a ten-hour debate spread over two days. But his fate was sealed. Sensing the mood, he resigned. President Neelam Sanjiva Reddy then invited Chavan to form the government. Aware of his tenuous position, Chavan met the President only to convey his inability to form the government but was given more time to explore other options. Congress (I) leaders then held back-channel talks with Chaudhary Charan Singh, who had openly revolted against Morarji Desai. Charan Singh's Bharatiya Lok Dal was a prominent constituent of the Desai government. He could not get along with Desai and wanted to be the prime minister himself. Congress (I) nurtured his ambitions and promised to extend him support if he formed the government after the fall of the Desai government. But Chavan was reluctant for various reasons. Firstly, he was aware of the RSS's machinations and Indira Gandhi's ability to bounce back. Caught in a fix, Chavan finally gave in and extended Congress (S) support to Charan Singh. With just sixty-four members on his side, Charan Singh was sworn in as the seventh

Prime Minister of India on 28 July 1979. In return, he made Chavan the deputy prime minister.

This was the closest Chavan came to the top post, though in a rather unfortunate way. His time in office was so short that even before the newly cobbled government could face Parliament, Congress (I) withdrew its support to Charan Singh. The ill-fated government collapsed on 20 August. With no possibility in sight of anyone forming the government, the President dissolved the Lok Sabha and ordered fresh elections.

The year 1980 began with the general election that was held in January. By then the Janata Party had split into various factions, with leaders who had egos that were larger than their political might. By then the people of the country were fed up with all the internal bickering. They decided to put the Emergency excesses and agonies behind them and vote Indira Gandhi back to power with an overwhelming mandate. The Congress and its alliance partners won 374 seats out of 531 in the Lok Sabha, with the Congress alone bagging 353 as against 153 in 1977. On the other hand, the Janata Party and its allies were reduced to double digits. With a clear majority, Indira Gandhi was once again sworn in as the prime minister on 14 January 1980.

Even as the Indira wave was sweeping the nation, there was one exception in Maharashtra. Yashwantrao Chavan held on to his Congress (S) candidature and still won. But there was no way forward for the veteran Congressman. He was slowly fading into oblivion. Some of his well-wishers advised him to stay away from electoral politics as politicians and politics had undergone a substantial change over the years. Money and muscle power had become more important than values and political ideologies. The country had also witnessed en masse defections and the culture of 'Aaya Ram, Gaya Ram' (here today gone tomorrow) had become the norm instead of being the exception. And encouraging these trends was the Congress, which had always been dear to Chavan. He was in a fix because neither could he identify with the Congress any more nor could he stay away from it. Notwithstanding the complete transformation the party had undergone, Chavan had his old Congress in mind. With no other place to go, he finally knocked at Indira Gandhi's door to seek re-entry into the party.

It was the moment when all of Maharashtra felt let down. Once applauded by everyone from Nehru downwards, and described as 'the Sahyadri who had rushed to the Himalayas' call for help' during the 1962 war, Chavan was now a pale shadow of his glorious past. Rubbing salt into his – and Maharashtra's – wound was Mrs Gandhi's act of ignoring his plea to readmit him into the Congress fold. She kept him waiting for as many as six months before the party's gates were reopened for him. He was admitted to Congress (I) in 1981. Almost a year later, Mrs Gandhi appointed him as the chairman of the Finance Commission.

Yashwantrao Chavan thereafter lived out his life in political wilderness. The number of visitors to his doors had shrunk drastically since Indira Gandhi had deliberately kept him away from state politics. His voice was no longer heard, nor was his opinion sought. Except an occasional advice to Mrs Gandhi on the growing Sikh militancy, Chavan lived a kind of solitary life. It became all the lonelier for him when in June 1983 he lost Venutai, his closest companion and wife of over four decades. A day before their wedding anniversary, Venutai's health took a turn for the worse after she had already been unwell for a week or so. Chavan wanted to admit her to a hospital but, frail and weak, she was not willing in spite of the doctor's advice. She asked Chavan to sit next to her and, with the image of him in her eyes, left this world. Yashwantrao Chavan was shattered. He did not live much longer after that. The following year, just after witnessing the assassination of his leader Indira Gandhi on 31 October, Chavan too passed away on 25 November.

A highly rated administrator, a visionary leader and a genuine secular, Yashwantrao Chavan can easily be described as the best prime minister India never had. The irony is that Chavan's close disciple was also to meet the same fate a decade and a half later.

17

So Near, Yet So Far…

If Yashwantrao Chavan was diffident about making a bid for the premiership, his disciple Sharad Pawar was assertive and ambitious. And he had every reason to be. There had been quite a few stalwarts from Maharashtra in various Union cabinets over the years who would have been deserving of the top job but remained coy about it. Besides Chavan, another leader with wide appeal was S.K. Patil, who served in Lal Bahadur Shastri's and then Indira Gandhi's first cabinet. After the Emergency, however, the situation changed, with Mrs Gandhi successfully clipping the wings of all leaders who had a mass base. That saw the rise of durbari leaders such as Vasant Sathe, Vitthalrao Gadgil, Shankarrao Chavan and others, who got key ministries in Delhi. It is not that they were not able politicians and leaders. Indeed, they were. But none of them had any popular base worth taking note of. Indira Gandhi – and later Rajiv Gandhi – successfully used them as counterweights to only one Maratha leader worth his salt: Sharad Pawar.

Pawar was barely thirty-seven years old when he became the chief minister of Maharashtra in 1978. That in itself was an unparalleled achievement in Indian politics. Unlike his mentor, Pawar had the amazing ability to take risks. He first entered the Maharashtra assembly from Baramati in 1967, when he was in his late twenties. That was a time when Maharashtra's political arena was crowded with heavyweights such as Chavan himself, Vasantdada Patil, Vasantrao Naik, S. Nijalingappa, S.K. Patil and many others. Amidst these veterans, Pawar carved a place for himself with his ingenuity and Chavan's blessings. He was considered Chavan's true successor, and he proved his mettle soon enough.

Chavan had him inducted him into the system as Maharashtra's agriculture minister in 1975. The portfolio is not something politicians vie for in India. But then Pawar was not an ordinary politician. Considering Maharashtra's large agricultural sector, he made the best of it. On the one hand, he gave a big boost to Maharashtra's agro-economy by undertaking various initiatives to encourage horticulture, floriculture, and so on in the state, while on the other he slowly brought the lucrative sugar cooperative industry in his clutches. The former helped Maharashtra take a major lead in agriculture, while the latter helped Pawar take a giant leap in politics. His contribution to agriculture had farmers expressing their gratitude by naming a variety of grape after him: 'Sharad Seedless'. The steps he took to free the sugar industry from bureaucratic hurdles resulted in a big boom for the sector, making him the richest sugar baron in the process. At one point, he single-handedly controlled over a hundred sugar mills in Maharashtra – more than two-thirds of the total number. On this front, he was one step ahead of his guru, Chavan, who too had roots in the state's cooperative sector but failed to encash and exploit it the way Pawar did.

He remained a Congress minister through the Emergency. Later, when the party split, he became part of the Congress (U). Essentially Congressmen at heart, members of this group made Vasantdada Patil the chief minister with the support of Congress (I), led in the state by N.R. Tirpude, who was made the deputy chief minister. The relationship between the two factions, however, was far from smooth, with both trying to undermine each other. The situation offered Pawar a near-perfect opportunity to bring out his backroom political skills. Chief Minister Patil was a little laid-back and believed that the Congress (U), his own party, would never let him down. Pawar shook him from his slumber. He negotiated a deal with the Janata Party, toppled the government and grabbed the post for himself. Patil denounced Pawar for what he alleged was backstabbing. Pawar of course saw it as a daring act that proved his skill for having the cake and eating it too.

THE POLITICAL COUP LANDED him the first of his four chief ministerships. During his first stint, he made an important contribution to Maharashtra's Dalit movement. The state had witnessed a demand to rename Marathwada University after Dr Ambedkar in 1974. It was, however, in 1978, under the Pawar-led Progressive Democratic Front's government, that a resolution was moved in both houses of the legislature to make the modification despite its political fallout as the decision divided society and Marathwada was on fire.

However, Pawar's first term in office was short-lived. He, as it turned out, had underestimated Indira Gandhi. Such was the Congress (I) resurgence in the 1980 national election that the Congress group he led lost all but one seat in Maharashtra. The only saving grace was Satara, where Yashwantrao Chavan managed to hold on. Mrs Gandhi returned as the prime minister in January 1980 and didn't waste the opportunity to punish Pawar. She dismissed his government the very next month. Fresh elections were held to the Maharashtra assembly, and the Congress faction led by her swept the polls by winning as many as 186 seats out of 288. Congress (U) did not manage to cross even 50.

Enter Abdul Rahman Antulay, a Konkani Muslim, as the chief minister, while Pawar was left to lead the Congress (S). Antulay was the first chief minister of the state who was outside the sugar barons' influence. But his high-handedness soon gave an opportunity to the state's mighty sugar barons (Pawar and others) to get back at him. He found himself engulfed in a corruption controversy that ended his chief ministership. The state then witnessed four other chief ministers – Babasaheb Bhosale, Vasantdada Patil, Shivajirao Nilangekar and Shankarrao Chavan – in as many years.

A weakened Congress, however, did not help Pawar raise his stature even though he led the combined opposition in the 1985 state assembly election. Congress (I), riding the sympathy wave after Indira Gandhi's assassination, pocketed 161 of the 288 seats. Pawar's Congress (S) managed just 54. The man who was eyeing the chief ministership became the leader of the opposition.

However, similar to what he had done to Vasantdada Patil, this time Pawar deceived the opposition and left them in the lurch by lobbying for his re-entry into the Congress. Rajiv Gandhi, just like his mother, was wary of Pawar's machinations and kept him waiting for over a year. But Pawar offers a different story about his homecoming in his autobiography *On My Terms*. According to him, it was Rajiv Gandhi who hinted at the possibility of them working together when Pawar went to offer his condolences on Mrs Gandhi's death. Pawar writes that it was at that point he thought a new leadership had emerged within the Congress and he should consider returning to it. Whatever be the truth, the fact remains that it took Rajiv Gandhi well over a year to admit Pawar into the Congress fold. Some say his friend-turned-foe Suresh Kalmadi lobbied with Rajiv Gandhi on Pawar's behalf for his return.

Pawar was now back in the Congress but without any post and made to wait, with his bête noire Shankarrao Chavan leading the state. Once back in the Congress, many accused him of stoking factionalism, which eventually ended when Rajiv made him chief minister in 1988. Shankarrao Chavan was moved to the Centre as the finance minister in Rajiv's cabinet, paving the way for Pawar in the state.

Back in the saddle, Pawar used his second term to initiate some landmark decisions. The most notable of them was the introduction of a 33 per cent quota for women in local bodies. Maharashtra was the first state to take such a progressive step and for that the credit goes to Pawar, who, despite strong opposition from within and outside his party, stood by his commitment. He also gave a big thrust to industrial policies along with the agricultural economy. It was his vision and efforts that brought major global engineering and automobile brands to Maharashtra. This gave the state a clear edge over others during the IT boom that followed after the liberalization of the Indian economy in 1991.

AROUND THE SAME TIME, Vasantrao Bhagwat, another Marathi Manoos, played a key role in shaping the nation's politics. The Jana Sangh, which had been part of the Janata Party, had become the Bharatiya Janata Party in 1980. Bhagwat, a senior RSS man, was an organizing secretary in the BJP. He put forth a strategy to expand the party's social base in Maharashtra to counter the Congress's pro-Maratha and pro-minority politics. Organizing secretaries, necessarily functionaries lent to the BJP by the RSS, play a crucial role in shaping the party's policy besides being a bridge between the parent organization and its political arm. A low-profile Bhagwat was the epitome of a backroom planner.

He was the first to realize the importance of OBCs (Other Backward Classes) as a counterweight to the politically strong, pro-Congress communities. He devised a strategy christened as 'MADHAV', which entailed a coalition of prominent OBC castes such as the Malis, Dhangars and Vanjaris. Over the years, the party has consistently worked upon this strategy, which led to the BJP's rise all over India. It was this vision that propelled leaders such as Narendra Modi, Uma Bharati, Kalyan Singh, Gopinath Munde and others to the national stage. But before it became a major success nationally, it was tested in the RSS's home turf of Maharashtra, which had seen a series of powerful Maratha chief ministers ever since the state came into being. Pawar was to face the brunt of the strategy in the 1990 assembly election. The Congress, though still the single largest party, fell short of an absolute majority by four seats, winning 141 out of 288. The BJP, which saw a rapid rise in the

1980s, bagged 42, with alliance partner Shiv Sena taking 52. Pawar was sworn in as chief minister yet again on 4 March 1990, but with the support of 12 independents. He was to face a major turmoil soon.

A little more than a year later, Rajiv Gandhi was brutally assassinated when a suicide bomber blew herself up while greeting him during a poll event in Tamil Nadu's Sriperumbudur on 21 May 1991. His death – and his wife Sonia's unwillingness to enter politics despite the Congress emerging as the winner of the general election held that year – opened an internal race for the top job. There were three or four serious contenders. One of them was Narain Dutt Tiwari, a former finance minister under Rajiv who had also been Chief Minister of Uttar Pradesh. Another was the erudite and scholarly P.V. Narasimha Rao, who had worked under Indira and Rajiv Gandhi in various capacities. And the third candidate in the ring was the powerful Chief Minister of Mahrashtra, Sharad Pawar.

In his fifties then, Pawar was said to have the backing of various corporate honchos along with the sugar lobby in Maharashtra. The situation, with no Gandhi dynast on the scene, threw up the first major opportunity for a Marathi leader to take a shot at the top post. But he was outwitted by the wilier Marathi-speaking Telugu leader Narasimha Rao. Pawar's campaign for the prime ministership was loud, lavish and not Congress-like, while Rao worked a discreet backroom strategy. Assisting Pawar was the raucous and flamboyant Suresh Kalmadi, while Rao was aided by the low-profile K. Karunakaran, who quietly conducted the exercise of finding out the Congressmen's choice. The whole drama was typical of the party: opaque and unostentatious. Congressmen would enter a room, Karunakaran would ask them briefly about their choice and note down what he thought they wanted. In this game of thrones, Pawar lost. Rao, in a truly political display of generosity, pardoned Pawar's misadventure and appointed him as the defence minister.

Sonia Gandhi was also the reason behind Pawar missing the bus then. Though she had refused to join active politics, a section of the Congress convinced her to throw her weight behind Rao instead of Pawar, who was always considered a challenger to the Congress's first family. Pawar was the only leader in the party with a significant base. But it was no longer considered a virtue in the Congress and, like his mentor Yashwantrao Chavan, he too lost the battle for Delhi. On 26 June 1991, Pawar took over the defence ministry. However, the demolition of the Babri Masjid and its aftermath cut short his stay in the national capital. Shrewd politician that he was, Rao sent Pawar back to Bombay, which was engulfed in post-Babri communal riots.

The Maratha strongman became Maharashtra's chief minister for the fourth and last time on 6 March 1993. Within a week, on 12 March, Bombay was rocked by serial bomb blasts. In just one day the city witnessed as many as twelve blasts that killed 257 people and injured twice that number. Sensing the danger of a communal backlash in the wake of Islamic terror striking the city, Pawar made a statement about a thirteenth blast – which never took place – in the city's Muslim-dominated Masjid Bunder. This statement about a fictitious blast prevented the situation from taking a communal turn. In the chief minister's saddle, Pawar displayed exemplary courage and statesmanship in bringing the city back to normal in just twenty-four hours. He won many accolades for his administrative skills. His time in office, however, was later marred by a series of corruption allegations. Though none of it was ever proved, it resulted in eroding his considerable clout.

As a result, the Congress lost to the resurgent BJP–Shiv Sena combine in the 1995 state assembly election. The following year, Narasimha Rao lost the general election, which triggered a string of coalition governments at the Centre. The situation presented yet another opportunity for Pawar to take a shot at the PM's post. He offered himself for the party's presidency but lost to Sitaram Kesri, who eventually lost the post to Sonia Gandhi. With no place in the Congress, and the BJP on the rise, Pawar chose to leave the party in 1999 to launch his own outfit, the Nationalist Congress Party (NCP).

This was Pawar's third major miscalculation as he believed Sonia Gandhi's foreign origin would become a national issue with the rise of the BJP. It, however, didn't. And the situation thereafter compelled him to mend fences with the Sonia-led Congress first in Maharashtra and later in Delhi. In 1999, the BJP–Shiv Sena combine lost to the Congress–NCP partnership in Maharashtra, and the Congress later also defeated the BJP's Atal Bihari Vajpayee-led alliance at the Centre in 2004. Pawar thereafter was a key member of the Manmohan Singh government.

WOULD PAWAR HAVE HAD a better chance of becoming prime minister in 2004 had he not quit the Congress in 1999? Pawar disagrees. With his nonchalant attitude, he once told me, 'Not really. They (the Congress leadership) always had some kind of reservations about me as I always had a mass base.' He believes that it was Sonia Gandhi who played a decisive role in selecting P.V. Narasimha Rao as the prime minister in 1991 even though the majority of Congressmen were behind him. For, Pawar was the only top Congressman who never needed to draw his political strength from the Gandhi family.

Though he claimed his relations with Sonia became cordial later, his autobiography *On My Terms* suggests otherwise. 'Sonia did not say much but the "distrust" was evident,' he writes. 'It also found reflections in her actions. When she and I decided something, she would do the exact opposite. If I selected P.C. Chacko to open a debate on the party's behalf, she would replace him just because he was supposed to be close to me.' He doesn't hide his discomfort about an amendment to the Congress Parliamentary Party (CPP) rules, brought solely to suit Sonia Gandhi. 'Though she was the Congress president, Sonia Gandhi was not an MP while I was a Lok Sabha member and a CPP leader,' he writes. The memoir also shows Pawar's disillusionment with the Congress as it failed to adopt a new culture with the rise of Sonia Gandhi. His autobiography also tells a lot about his personal tenacity – his battles with cancer, a tough regime of chemotherapy sessions, heart trouble and pelvic fracture, all the while negotiating the punishing rough and tumble of Indian politics.

Pawar may have been a loser in his battles to win Delhi, but he will go down in history as the first strongman from Maharashtra who did not hide his aspirations for national power. Unlike Yashwantrao Chavan, Pawar unabashedly tried to reach the top post. And, as in the case of his mentor, qualities such as being an able administrator and a socially progressive, pragmatic libertarian were not enough for him to fulfil his dream. Delhi remains so near yet so far for the Marathi Manoos.

IF SHARAD PAWAR MADE significant contributions to India's farm sector, there is another Maharashtrian who shares that legacy in a different way – and, incidentally, his name – though he is not nearly as well known. He was Sharad Joshi (1935–2015), who took up the cause of farmers and made them aware of their right to the market and profitable pricing.

Joshi, a trained economist, set up the Shetkari Sanghatana in 1979 to press for higher prices for agricultural commodities along with free access to markets. He coined the phrase 'India vs Bharat', which summed up the country's urban–rural and rich–poor divide. It encapsulated how India's industry-fed cities do better while agriculture-dependent rural areas continue to live in impoverished conditions. It was Joshi who highlighted the farmers' plight in a language familiar to the urban middle class. 'Foodgrain is the only product whose price is decided by consumers, and producers have no say in it,' he would say.

Born into a Brahmin family in Satara, western Maharashtra, Joshi had no connection to agriculture. He studied commerce at Bombay's Sydenham College and went on to serve in the Indian Postal Service, and later did an eight-year-long stint with the United Nations in Switzerland. His interest in poverty eradication brought him back to India. He quit his UN job and returned to undertake experiments in farming. He wanted to experience the agonies of a farmer's life before he could find a remedy to them.

And to live up to his philosophy of being a 'kriyashil vidvan (an active intellectual)', Joshi used his savings to buy a 25-acre plot in Ambethan near Pune in 1977 to learn the challenges of rain-fed farmers. With his very methodical and scientific approach to farming, he soon experienced how impossible it is for a farming family to make ends meet even with state support. Using his hands-on approach and analytical mind, he demonstrated how farmers spent around Rs 180 to earn a meagre Rs 100. He pointed out that the state's support to farmers is nothing but an illusion and it's a case of net negative subsidy – the farmers' contribution to the government and society is much greater than what the two offer them in return.

Our industry-centric development is skewed against farming, Joshi argued time and again. According to him, this results in the prices of foodgrains remaining artificially low and in turn the farming community being paid a low remuneration. Successive governments in India have believed that what they do to keep the input cost low for farmers – various subsidies for things such as fertilizers, electricity and so on, along with the minimum support price (MSP) – is the best service to Indian agriculture. The model remains popular as it allows governments to tweak it at times by offering some more freebies or by raising the MSP. It was Joshi who first exposed and later opposed and demanded the complete dismantling of the statist system that exploits farmers to the hilt.

He explained how the MSP system benefits big farmers with marketable surpluses and ignores the small and marginal ones. He advocated doing away with the Essential Commodities Act along with the provision of mandatory procurement. He supported contract farming to establish a direct link between buyers and sellers. He, in a way, wanted to do what P.V. Narasimha Rao and Manmohan Singh did in 1991 to the Indian economy: complete liberalization of the agricultural sector. He brought a fresh approach to farming issues by openly demanding high remunerative prices while exposing the governments of the day for keeping prices artificially low. In his massive rallies, he would demand that farmers be considered as entrepreneurs and that the government should unshackle them.

It was not as though there were no farmers' leaders then. There were many – such as Chaudhary Charan Singh, Devi Lal and Mahendra Singh Tikait from the northern parts of the country or M.D. Nanjundaswamy of the Karnataka Rajya Raitha Sangha – who were active in the 1980s. But their views were almost always focused on caste and subsidy. However, Joshi, intellectually the most competent and articulate of them, completely changed the way agrarian issues were seen. The Shetkari Sanghatana espoused higher output prices and also complete access to markets and technology for farmers. Joshi wasn't simply a thinker who could speak out but also someone who was able to galvanize lakhs of farmers irrespective of their caste, language and religion. Ahead of his time, he shot to prominence in 1980 when he led an agitation of the onion farmers of Nashik district in Maharashtra against crashing onion prices. It witnessed over a million farmers taking to the state highways. Incidentally, this was the time the Green Revolution had begun to show diminishing returns and farmer discontent was rising. The situation demanded complete restructuring and reframing of agrarian issues. And Joshi did exactly that. Soon, he spread his wings in other states as well in the form of kisan sabhas.

He was probably the first agro-economist who believed in a free-market approach. He also called for commodity derivatives and demanded the regulation of moneylenders instead of an outright ban. His agri-vision was not limited just to farm produce and its price; he even advocated that farmers should own joint stock companies so that they handle supply chain management on their own. The reformer in Joshi could be seen in his demand for equal property rights for women in farmlands. He had the impressive ability to break complex concepts down to simple statements for lay people and farmers, which helped him provide intellectual vigour to the farmers' movement.

This was the time when the World Trade Organization (WTO) was setting the economic agendas for various nations. Many were confused about and unaware of the issues the WTO had unleashed. But Joshi weighed in complete support, which rattled the traditional leadership – political and otherwise. A farmers' leader airing his views on such complex matters was unheard of then. Time and again he argued for global access to Indian farmers to make them profitable. Some of the issues he raised transcended agriculture and fell in the political arena. So, it was inevitable for him to enter politics. He tried joining hands with various political forces but, unfortunately for India's farming community, he met with little success, which eventually led to his Sanghatana splitting into several factions. His political overtures to various parties also resulted in alienating his associates, who accused him of making compromises to secure a seat in the Rajya Sabha.

In later years, Joshi was an isolated figure and out of the public eye. He died in December 2015, leaving behind a great intellectual legacy and a void that will be difficult to fill. As India continues to grapple with farm distress and struggles to find solutions to date, the absence of this jeans-clad farmer is palpable to those familiar with his legacy. Unfortunately, he is now almost forgotten – a fate he shares with many others from Maharashtra who made significant contributions to the nation but for whom a greater glory remained out of reach.

18

Renaissance Once More

The year 2019 began on a tumultuous note for India. An overall lacklustre performance and a floundering economy had the Narendra Modi government worried ahead of the general elections. In February, however, Pakistan-backed militants' misadventure in Pulwama, Jammu and Kashmir, and the subsequent response by India's defence forces sealed the second term for the BJP leader from Gujarat.

To go back in time a little, even before Modi's meteoric rise, the BJP had a leader from Maharashtra who aspired for the top job and was moving slowly but surely in that direction. Like Sharad Pawar, he too built connections across all political parties, was extremely good at pulling corporate strings and had mastered the art of managing the media: electronic and print. Another thing made this leader stand apart from Yashwantrao Chavan and Sharad Pawar. He was an impeccable orator in Hindi, the speech craft that Marathi leaders inevitably fail to acquire. So much so that north India's Hindi-speaking class considered him as one of their own. Of course, his second name, Mahajan, also allowed him to downplay his Marathi origin. Atal Bihari Vajpayee had virtually set out a succession plan when he declared Lal Krishna Advani and Pramod Mahajan as the party's 'Ram–Lakshman' duo at a rally in Mumbai's historic Shivaji Park in 2005 while declaring his retirement from electoral politics. So Advani was to step into Vajpayee's shoes and Mahajan into Advani's as his trusted lieutenant. But, as fate would have it, he was removed from this world when his brother Pravin fatally shot him over a family dispute in April 2006. In his death, Maharashtra lost yet another prime ministerial candidate – a popular, charismatic leader with appeal across the political spectrum.

His assassination threw the game of thrones wide open in the BJP. It helped the relatively junior Narendra Modi look at the national theatre. With Mahajan's death, Vajpayee's failing health and the ageing Advani's failure to lead the party to power in the 2009 general election, there was no one in the BJP to rein in or challenge Modi. After his back-to-back victories in 2014 and 2019, and with the party looking invincible, the discussion soon shifted to the question: Who after Modi?

A COMMON NAME EMERGED in all such discussions: Devendra Fadnavis, the young chief minister of Maharashtra, who had made a name for himself as an able administrator from the time he took office in 2014. Everything was going very well for the dynamic, suave and soft-spoken leader from Nagpur, the headquarters of the RSS. Considered the blue-eyed boy of Prime Minister Modi and their party's parent organization, the cautious and calculative Fadnavis played every card well. Except, probably inadvertently, one slogan that his followers popularized ahead of the Maharashtra state assembly elections in October 2019: 'Narendra nantar Devendra' (Devendra after Narendra). It turned out to be his nemesis and cost him a chance in Delhi.

The election outcome produced a political potboiler like no other. The BJP fell short of a clear majority as it bagged just 105 seats in the 288-member assembly. It was nonetheless the single largest party and initially it seemed like a foregone conclusion that it would form the government again with alliance partner Shiv Sena, which won 56 seats. But the Sena eyed the CM's post, which the partner wasn't willing to concede, and, following drama that lasted over a month with several twists and turns, formed the government with the NCP (54 seats) and the Congress (44 seats). Fadnavis, who made a misguided attempt in the interim to form a government with the NCP that lasted barely three days, lost face and, eventually, political relevance.

Once the dust of government formation had settled, the real shocker was not that the Sena, NCP and Congress had cobbled together an alliance to deny the BJP a second chance. Politics, after all, is known to throw up stranger bedfellows. The real shocker was the BJP's unwillingness to negotiate with the Sena and allowing a significant state like Maharashtra to slip out of its hands. It was all the more mind-boggling because of the swiftness with which the party grabbed power in Haryana, which went to the polls along with Maharashtra. The BJP had displayed similar aggression and resorted to back-door methods to win states like Goa, Arunachal Pradesh and many others. But it adopted a different approach in Maharashtra, a state that sends as many as 48 MPs to the Lok Sabha. What could be the reason behind the BJP's inexplicable reluctance in Maharashtra?

The political grapevine indicates one. It was Fadnavis's – or his supporters' – overzealous act of projecting himself as Modi's successor. If party insiders are to be believed, this misstep cost him dearly. Party bosses did not take a generous view of it and clipped his wings even before he could take flight for Delhi from Mumbai.

Hardly a surprise. When it comes to making it all the way to South Block – from where the Prime Minister of India leads the nation – the Marathi Manoos has invariably missed a step or two.

The other interesting angle to analyse is of course the coming together of the Shiv Sena, NCP and Congress. It underlined how Delhi underestimates or miscalculates Maharashtra. After the 2019 general election, there was no stopping the BJP juggernaut. It seemed that other political parties had given up and the BJP would easily steamroll state after state. After all, it was the BJP's aim to paint the entire nation, from Kashmir to Kanyakumari, saffron.

But the jolt came from Maharashtra after two state satraps showed amazing creativity in forging an alliance with the sole aim of challenging Delhi's hegemony. Sharad Pawar and Uddhav Thackeray's near-impossible feat of forming a front and dragging the Congress along with them not only deprived the apparently invincible BJP of an important state but also sent out the message that the BJP in Delhi could be reined in, no matter who was ruling.

Interestingly, the wheel was coming full circle for the Shiv Sena – and, in a way, for Sharad Pawar too.

FIRST ABOUT THE SHIV Sena. Though it came into being in 1966 to espouse the cause of the Marathi Manoos, the truth is that it failed miserably to present itself as a real regional force to reckon with. Bal Thackeray, a brilliant cartoonist-turned-politician, fiery orator, excellent organizer and an extremely unpredictable leader, always underperformed electorally as compared to, say, M.G. Ramachandran of the All India Anna Dravida Munnetra Kazhagam in Tamil Nadu, N.T. Rama Rao of the Telugu Desam Party in Andhra Pradesh or even Mamata Banerjee of the Trinamool Congress in West Bengal. Even at the peak of his career and charisma, Thackeray and his party could never come to power single-handedly.

Not that the voter – the Marathi Manoos – was not parochial-minded. The reason was that the Shiv Sena was far from being honest about the Marathi cause. In its early days, Thackeray allowed his political muscle to be used by Marathi leaders in the Congress in their tussle with non-Marathi ones. The last Marathi leader the Congress had from the state capital was S.K. Patil (1898–1981). Since then the city unit has been controlled by non-Marathi people such as Barrister Rajni Patel, Bhanushankar Yagnik, Murli Deora and so on. As such, the Congress faced a unique challenge. It was running the state but had very little social or political connect in

Mumbai. The Marathi Manoos also hardly had any control over the financial capital's money-spinning industries and businesses. Adding to the complications were Left parties, which led workers' unions in the city's once-famous mills and other companies run mostly by Marwaris and Gujaratis.

And here the Shiv Sena allowed its muscle power to be used to break into industries run by non-Marathi businessmen but with a large Marathi workforce. The regional party became a two-pronged tool for the Congress. It was used to neutralize the Left-led workers' unions and also to scare non-Marathi industrialists. In those days, the Sena was considered the B-team of the Congress and had earned the moniker of Vasant Sena, hinting at its nexus with Vasantrao Naik, a Congress veteran who was Maharashtra chief minister for twelve years from 1963 to 1975. This, incidentally, was also the period when the Sena registered an impressive growth, although not much outside Mumbai. Content with Mumbai, the party was unable to understand the ramifications of its political short-sightedness. It effectively reduced the Sena to a Mumbai-only party.

This was why the Sena could not scale heights the way other regional parties did and so never had a chance to run the state on its own. This failure also robbed the party of its main plank: the Marathi Manoos. Having realized this, it was then compelled to don saffron robes and proclaim itself Hindutvawadi when Advani and the BJP were seen gaining major ground. It was win-win for the BJP and the Sena, the former looking for regional, like-minded partners and the latter in search of a new agenda. The alliance paved the way for the first BJP–Sena government in the state in 1995. The arrangement was perfect: the BJP was to concentrate on Delhi while managing Mumbai was to be left to the Shiv Sena.

It worked well till the rise of Narendra Modi. Until his ascent, the saffron camp had only one Hindu Hriday Samrat: Bal Thackeray. With the BJP having its own Hindu heartthrob in Modi, it no longer needed the Thackerays. Also, the BJP of Modi and his lieutenant Amit Shah lacked the benignity of the Vajpayee–Advani era. As such, there was hardly any warmth between the new leadership of the two parties. Unwilling to respect old understandings, the new BJP rubbed the Sena the wrong way on every possible front. Having experienced this treatment for five years from 2014 to 2019, the Sena increasingly realized that riding pillion on the saffron juggernaut was not going to take it any further. It had two options: dump the BJP or get dumped.

It found solace in Sharad Pawar, who himself had a long axe to grind. Originally a Congressman, Pawar had always been at the receiving end of the party – from the time when Indira Gandhi had dismissed his government in 1980 to when Sushilkumar Shinde and Vilasrao Deshmukh rebelled against him a decade later with the tacit support of Rajiv Gandhi and when Narasimha Rao was selected to be the prime minister instead of him after Rajiv's assassination. In all this, a feeling had gained ground in Maharashtra that Delhi always trampled upon regional sentiments and ignored or even humiliated regional leaders. For the Congress, it served as a template for handling various state satraps – be it N.T. Rama Rao of Andhra Pradesh, Ramakrishna Hegde of Karnataka, Devi Lal of Haryana or Yashwantrao Chavan of Maharashtra. In fact, it was this insensitive, big brother attitude of the party that gave rise to many regional parties all over India. And so it was poetic justice for Pawar as the Congress now had to play second fiddle to a leader it had once humiliated. It became the ignominious third partner in the Shiv Sena–NCP power game.

Two leaders beaten and battered by Delhi – Pawar and Uddhav Thackeray – thus joined hands. Interestingly, the BJP, that has replaced the Congress at the political centre stage, appears no different. Its behaviour after coming to power at the Centre in 2014 has been the same as that of the Congress of the 1980s and '90s. Its approach in handling both parties, first the Shiv Sena and then the NCP, was no different from that of the Congress. It didn't realize that being dismissive of these outfits, in fact, limited its elbow room, which is crucial in a overstrung political atmosphere. Indications are that soon many states will replicate the 'Maharashtra model' in an effort to keep the BJP at bay.

'Now I plan to look beyond Maharashtra,' Sharad Pawar told me soon after his eightieth birthday bash in December 2020. The inimitable Maharashtrian, who wears his never-say-die attitude on his sleeve, wants to bring all secular forces together ahead of the 2024 elections.

HOW SUCCESSFUL PAWAR WILL be one will get to see. But till then an interesting question to ask is: What could be the reason for the failure of the Marathi Manoos in winning Delhi?

In my book, the answer lies – as I have tried to show in the course of the story of the making of this great land – in Maharashtra's history, which is divided into two phases: pre- and post-Panipat.

In the pre-Panipat era, the Marathi Manoos led from the front and ventured out of the state. He sought to be the master of himself and aspired to conquer Delhi. Things, however, began to change post-Panipat. The defeat in the war of 1761 left him devastated. The lingering burden of history, it seems, shattered his confidence and shrank his ambitions. He confined himself to regional borders and preferred to stay in the company of his own ilk. '*Gadya, aapula gaon bara*' (It's better to be home) became the guiding principle of Marathi ethos. As a result, unlike his counterparts from several other states, the Marathi Manoos hardly ventured on journeys, both literal and figurative, that broke new ground. He would rather serve than lead. He might be the power behind the throne, a kingmaker, but not the king.

However, considering Maharashtra's magnificent past and its ability to produce many powerful, intelligent and visionary men and women, it may only be a matter of time before a reawakening of political aspirations takes place in this Renaissance State. And while the Marathi Manoos may not have conquered Delhi just yet, he keeps alive, in the meantime, Maharashtra's old tradition of never bowing before it either.

Bibliography

1. Agarkar, Gopal Ganesh. *Sampurna Agarkar, Vol. 1 and 2*. Varda Prakashan.
2. Chousalkar, Ashok. *Mahatma Phule Aani Shetkari Chalval*. Lokwangmay Gruha, 2009.
3. Deshmukh, Durgabai and Kusum Kulkarni. *Aamchi Katha*. Continental Prakashan, 1987.
4. Deshpande, Prachi. *Creative Pasts: Historical Memory and Identity in Western India, 1700–1960*. Columbia University Press, 2007.
5. Golwalkar, M.S. *Vichar Navneet*. Gyan Ganga Prakashan, 2018.
6. ——. *Bunch of Thoughts*. Sahitya Sindhu Prakashan, 2017.
7. Hasan, Zoya. *Politics of Inclusion: Castes, Minorities and Affirmative Action*. Oxford University Press, 2011.
8. Inamdar, N.R., ed. *Political Thought and Leadership of Lokmanya Tilak*. Concept Publishing Company, 1983.
9. Keer, Dhananjay. *Dr Babasaheb Ambedkar*. Popular Prakashan, 2011.
10. Kulkarni, A.R., ed., et al. *Marathyancha Itihas: Sadhan Parichay*. Diamond Book Depot.

11. Palshikar, Suhas, ed. *Satyagrahi Samajwad (Acharya Javdekar Articles)*. Maharashtra Sahitya and Sanskruti Mandal.
12. Phadke, Y.D. *Agarkar*. Mouj Prakashan, 2006.
13. ——, ed. *Mahatma Phule Samagra Vangmay*. Maharashtra Rajya Sahitya ani Sanskruti Mandal, 2006.
14. ——. *Ambedkari Chalval*. Shrividya Prakashan.
15. ——. *Visavya Shatakatil Maharashtra: Vol. 1 to 4*.
16. Rajwade, V.K. *Rajwade Lekhsangraha*. Varda Prakashan.
17. Ranganathan, Murali, ed. *The Collected Works of J.V. Naik: Reform and Renaissance in Nineteenth Century Maharashtra*. Asiatic Society of Mumbai, 2016.
18. Rege, M.P. *Acharya S.D. Javdekar: Vyakti Aani Vihar*. Pradnya Pathshala Mandal.
19. Salgaokar, Jayraj. *Ajinkya Yoddha Bajirao*. Param Mitra Publication, 2016.
20. Salunkhe, A.H. *Mahatma Phule Aani Dharma*. Lokwangmay Gruha, 2015.
21. Sarkar, Jadunath. *Shivaji and His Times*. Orient Black Swan, 2010.
22. Savarkar, Vinayak Damodar. *Vidnyannishtha Nibandh, Parts 1 and 2*. Swantantryaveer Savarkar Rashtriya Smarak Prakashan.
23. Singh, Hulas. *Rise of Reason: Intellectual History of 19th Century Maharashtra*. Routledge India, 2015.
24. Srinivas, M.N. *Social Change in Modern India*. Orient Black Swan, 1995.
25. Vaidya, Chintaman Vinayak. *History of Mediaeval Hindu India*. Alpha Edition, 2019.
26. Vhora, Rajendra, ed. *Adhunikata Aani Parampara: Ekonisavya ShatakatilMaharashtra*. Pratima Prakashan, 2000.
27. NA. *Madhyayugin Kalkhand: Rajkiya va Samajit Itihas*. Maharashtra State Gazetteer.
28. NA. *Shejvalkaranche Lekh: Vol. 2*. Mauj Printing Bureau.
29. NA. *Unsung Heroes: A Tribute, Vol. 2*. Indus Source Books, 2012.
30. NA. *Sources of Maratha History*. Archives of Mumbai University.

Index

About the Author

Girish Kuber is the Editor of *Loksatta* and writes frequently in the *Indian Express*. He is the author of *The Tatas: How a Family Built a Business and a Nation,* which won the inaugural Gaja Capital Business Book Prize in 2019. He has also written six books in Marathi. He lives in Mumbai.

ALSO BY GIRISH KUBER

The Tatas: How a Family Built a Business and a Nation
Translated from the Marathi by Vikrant Pande

The story of India's leading business family

The nineteenth century was an exciting time of initiative and enterprise around the world. If John D. Rockefeller was creating unimagined wealth in the United States that he would put to the service of the nation, a Parsi family with humble roots was doing the same in India.

In 1822, a boy was born in a priestly household in Gujarat's Navsari. Young Nusserwanji knew early on that his destiny lay beyond his village and decided to head for Bombay to start a business. He had neither higher education nor knowledge of trade matters, just a burning passion to carve his own path.

What Nusserwanji started as a cotton trading venture, his son Jamsetji—born in the same year as Rockefeller—grew into a multifaceted business, turning around sick textile mills, setting up an iron and steel company, and building a world-class hotel. Stewarded ably over the decades by Jamsetji's sons Dorabji and Ratanji, the charismatic and larger-than-life JRD, and thereafter the more business-like Ratan, the Tata group today is a 110-billion-dollar empire.

The Tatas is their story. But it is more than just a history of the industrial house; it is an inspiring account of India in the making. It chronicles how each generation of the family invested not only in the expansion of its own business interests but also in nation building. Few know, for instance, that the first hydel power project in the world was conceived of and built by the Tatas. The Indian Institute of Science, the Tata Institute of Fundamental Research, as also the national carrier Air India—the family has a long, rich and unrivalled legacy.

A tribute to a line of visionaries who have a special place in the hearts of ordinary Indians, this is the only book that tells the complete Tata story spanning almost two hundred years.

Available in hardback, paperback
and also as an e-book and audio book

30 Years *of*

HarperCollins *Publishers* India

At HarperCollins, we believe in telling the best stories and finding the widest possible readership for our books in every format possible. We started publishing 30 years ago; a great deal has changed since then, but what has remained constant is the passion with which our authors write their books, the love with which readers receive them, and the sheer joy and excitement that we as publishers feel in being a part of the publishing process.

Over the years, we've had the pleasure of publishing some of the finest writing from the subcontinent and around the world, and some of the biggest bestsellers in India's publishing history. Our books and authors have won a phenomenal range of awards, and we ourselves have been named Publisher of the Year the greatest number of times. But nothing has meant more to us than the fact that millions of people have read the books we published, and somewhere, a book of ours might have made a difference.

As we step into our fourth decade, we go back to that one word – a word which has been a driving force for us all these years.

Read.